OM VEI

CW01506639

BE HAPPY AND M

MA

SI

NA

VA

YA

SEVAL SEER

OM VEL Way

Copyright © 2023 by OM VEL Way Pty Ltd ATF OM VEL Way Trust

All rights reserved. No part of this publication may be reproduced, distributed, or transmitted in any form or by any means, including photocopying, recording, or other electronic or mechanical methods, without the prior written permission of the author, except in the case of brief quotations embodied in critical reviews and certain other non-commercial uses permitted by copyright law.

Tellwell Talent
www.tellwell.ca

ISBN
978-1-77941-064-1 (Hardcover)
978-1-77941-065-8 (Paperback)
978-1-77941-063-4 (eBook)

MY HEARTFELT DEDICATION

To my father, who set me on the path
of self-actualization as my guru.

To my mother, who made our house into
a living and disciplined home.

To my siblings, my best friends, and wonderful
companions throughout my life.

To my sons, for the opportunity and privilege of
learning to be a nurturer of two wonderful souls.

To my sons, nieces, and nephews, here is my
gift on behalf of our generation to yours.

To two others who joined my life and parted ways
but were part of two crossroads of my life.

To Gaylon Ferguson and Mary Lang and those at
Shambhala Meditation Centre, for providing another
arena to play with ideas that I have learned.

To all the practitioners of self-actualization, here
is my small contribution amongst the mountain
of gifts from many others before me

TABLE OF CONTENTS

PERSONAL SEARCH AND RESEARCH

PERSONAL SEARCH

When we succeed, we develop confidence. The harder the challenge, the sweeter the success, and the more resilient our confidence. With time, what initially evolved as confidence in a given area soon becomes part of our personality—for example: "Give me any challenge. If I put my heart and mind to it, I can overcome any setback." This confidence becomes part of who we are. It's not sheer arrogance but confidence that was experientially etched into the depths of who we are. There's some truth in it. Human effort is a key factor in achieving target outcomes. When our heart, mind, and spirit are focused on something, we can go a long way. Having faith and confidence in what we can do is essential for realizing our goals.

The early part of my life until the age of 14 was like a fairy tale. I was born into an upper-middle-class family with everything a child needs without any uncertainty. My father was a very charismatic and successful man and, above all, a very dedicated and loving father. He was well complemented by my mother—a very silent but devoted parent. She excelled in instilling discipline in us and making our house a home. I was blessed with wonderful siblings. To date, they are my best friends.

My life took a big turn between the ages of 14 and 24. Political turmoil in Sri Lanka, with ethnic riots and the start of a civil war, brought uncertainty to my life. We moved from place to place—within three years, I had studied at four schools. In my first move, I missed three months of school and instead stayed at home due to safety concerns and a government-imposed curfew. I had to catch up on what I'd missed at a new school in a new city. During the second move, we moved from Sri Lanka to India, where the language of instruction changed from Tamil to English. This was a steep change, having to learn the subjects in a different language in a new curriculum while living in an unfamiliar country and preparing for a public exam. The final change was a shift to an international school back in Sri Lanka. The British system of education was quite different from the Indian system. I had experienced continuous challenges in multiple dimensions—academic, social, and my place of residence. However, it brought out the best in me, academically and personally. I became a top-scoring student at all my schools and during my university days in the UK. I evolved on multiple fronts, sharpening my mind and instilling a high degree of discipline. Above all, I built up a great degree of confidence that I could overcome any challenge.

Life is a great teacher. When we think we have it all under control and are at the top of our game, something happens that awakens us to some foundational weakness we have overlooked in ourselves. I got married early at the age of 24; my wife was 21. It was quite a mismatch regarding who we were and what we wanted to pursue. After two years of a difficult relationship for both of us, we decided to part ways. When you face failures in new areas, the mind tends to cling to what it's familiar with and good at; it's a self-preservation mode when we slip into unchartered territory. Thus, following my divorce, I began to focus more on career growth. I moved from the UK to the US and had a few years of great success.

However, there was an underlying emptiness building within me. Initially, I did not pay attention to it, but over time, it became suffocating. Ironically, the "silent emptiness" within me progressively became unbearably loud, overwhelming all the worldly music around me. Looking at my life from the outside, everything was great. I'd experienced explosive career growth—working for a Tier 1 company and doing well. With the challenging experience of my marriage, I was more than happy to be single for a while. Yet, there was still a void. It was not a void in terms of not having what I wanted; it was more of not *knowing* what I wanted. Some deeper questions began to bubble up: Who am I? in a deeper sense (spiritually/psychologically). What is my life's purpose?, providing an overall context for my actions and achievements. Without having answers to these questions, it looked like I was just drowning in a busy life. The more I ignored it, the more suffocating it became.

It occurred to me that all my life, I had only been focusing on the ways of the world and what is expected or considered to be the right thing to do. However, I was not a victim in the sense that something was forced upon me. I enjoyed my journey and succeeded in realizing my goals. I was brimming with confidence and was on a joy ride, so I had no qualms there. The issue was that in succeeding in the ways of the world, I had not paid attention to something more fundamental—my spiritual needs and clarity of my purpose at a more fundamental level. So, when there was a setback, I began to see the inherent weakness in my approach to that point. It felt like I was a mighty tree that had not grown its roots deep enough to weather the storms. The issue was not with the height of the tree but the depth and grip of the roots.

This was the beginning of my spiritual search. Before this, I had only been focused on gathering educational and work-related knowledge and skills, and any wider knowledge was a passive process of assimilation—what my parents taught, discussions with friends, TV, etc. But gathering knowledge is not the same as a spiritual search. Spiritual seeking is not about learning more about what others have said; rather, it's an intrinsic search and a journey of self-discovery. The subject of inquiry is not about other things but one's true nature.

During this time, my relationship with my father transformed from "father–son" to "spiritual guru-apprentice." He had also walked a hard path in his youth and had searched for and formed a spiritual seal/outlook. What I had learned directly from my father proved to be my spiritual foundation, but by foundation, I don't mean initial studies. In spirituality, Hinduism (esp. Siththandha tradition), and Buddhism (including Zen Tradition), what the guru offers to his students is a lot more than an introduction to established knowledge. The primary transfer is that of a mental seal—an archetype or pattern of the spirit that leads to an outlook and way of responding to life. In my late twenties, I only subconsciously felt that my inner nature was changing in a very subconscious and subtle way. But only after 20 years since then, I have a better appreciation of it.

The interactions I had with my father were through long-distance and monthly calls, each lasting two to three hours, or when we would meet once a year for two weeks. It used to be four to six hours. During our interactions, all I did was receive what he had to say. Rarely was there a debate or discussion, as it was not meant to be a study or acceptance. I just allowed him to share whatever he thought was relevant. He never interfered or even enquired how or if I was applying what he had shared with me in my life. Our interactions were not time-bound or external goal-driven; they were simply a transfer of a spiritual seal. It is hard to explain in words. Frankly, I only felt good after each session. I must admit that at times, I had to drag myself mentally to these sessions, which was not a natural thing to do for someone in his late twenties. But deep within, I was thirsting, and he was quenching. Even now, I am not sure if I deserved his generosity and patience. Like most fathers and sons, our relationship was not always smooth outside these sessions. But this session was not about the father-son relationship but rather the apprentice-spiritual guru.

Once he was satisfied with what he had bestowed upon me in our long sessions, he gave me a long list of books to read, not as a task for gathering knowledge or with a timetable, but as avenues for exploration, where I could find nuances and breadth in spirituality. These texts ranged from Hinduism, Buddhism, and Christianity and ranged from ancient and relatively modern. I then began to explore psychological and philosophical ideas to broaden my search.

This time, however, I was not reading for knowledge. I was looking for clues or insights that might help me in my search. The focus was not so much on reading from the first to the last page; it was more on scanning through various books and taking selective deep dives based on what helped me in my search. It also strengthened my faith in my understanding that some of the core aspects of life seem more universal across time, space, and culture.

I then began to explore various spiritual centers—Hindu Meditation Centers, Zen Centers, and so on. My work as a consultant at a Tier 1 company required a lot of travel. Monday to Friday, I was in various cities on the East Coast of the US—New York, Boston, Philadelphia, and Washington DC. Sometimes, I traveled across Europe, particularly in the UK and Germany. During office hours, I was fully focused on my work. I was very successful and well respected. But after hours, I was obsessively and relentlessly pursuing self-discovery. It was like living a dual life. I was staying in five-star hotels, and my peers were out there in bars and socializing. From time to time, I did this, too, to be part of the workgroup. But my primary focus was elsewhere. Looking back, it was amusing. It was as though I was Bruce Wane during the day and Batman at night, except that it was not about saving the world; it was about saving myself from drowning in a busy life and losing the sense of who I am.

It was an intense three to five years of searching. I began to get to know myself as a spirit, going beyond the awareness of body-mind experience. I began to look at my body and mind as an instrument. They are available for me to experience the world—physically, physiologically, emotionally, and intellectually. But I am not my instrument. I experience the world, but I am not what I experience either. I am aware of the experience.

I began to find my answers. The more I became aware, the more I found inner stability and peace in my life. But to be intuitively aware is only the first step. To live according to that awareness is a greater challenge altogether. However, living a dual life is also suffocating. I had to find ways to integrate my awareness into my day-to-day living, not just as passing intuition or a topic that I only focused on after hours. How does one invoke and practice deep insights and maintain awareness in their day-to-day routine? Not just by reading or meditating as hobbies.

After trying various things, I began to systematically study Tibetan meditation at the Shambhala Meditation Center for some years. It suited my traveling lifestyle, as there are Shambhala Meditation Centers in most of the major cities in the US. They also have a good spiritual and meditation program that suits all practitioners, from beginners to those who are more advanced. I vividly remember my first formal lesson. It was about "basic goodness" and "spiritual warriors. "Discovery of basic goodness is the realization that we can directly experience and work with the reality of the real world that we are in." "The essence of warriorship or the essence of human bravery is refusing to give up on anyone or anything." I was very lucky. One of the senior teachers, Gaylon Ferguson, was visiting the Boston Centre and was very kind to take that lesson, which was for beginners. His words and, more importantly, the way he spoke just pierced through my heart. Subsequently, I was also lucky that some later lessons were taken by a great lady called Mary Lang. She saw something in me instinctively, among 15-30 students, that not many others (other than my immediate family) had detected. She encouraged me to nurture that. The way she looked at me when I spoke and encouraged me made me look at me deep within again. Tibetan Buddhism, like the Tamil tradition of Hinduism, is full of symbolism and great emphasis on the discovery and application of the higher truth of the Self in the "here and now" moment. Less on academic knowledge gathering as a primary means of spiritual evolution. The notion of "Drala," the art of invoking magic, felt so familiar to me. It was "connecting the wisdom of your being with the power of things as they are. If you can connect those two, out of that, you can discover magic in everything." The vision of the great eastern sun as a way of celebrating life with great appreciation of sacredness within us and the world around us. The core idea of applying the most sophisticated spiritual ideas to the very moment before us, "here and now," and the practical tools that go with it, revived interest and renewed confidence in the universal nature of what I already learned before. Evolved ones are called siddhas in both Tibetan Buddhism and Tamil practice of Hinduism. There was something so familiar and homely about what I learned at Shambhala. As I continued with my training there, I picked a few more very useful visualization and meditation techniques that are valuable as a practitioner to nurture and cultivate oneself and others as applicable.

Alongside this, I began to use what I became aware of in my day-to-day life. Experience obtained through the body and mind ceased to be the end in itself and instead became a subject of meditation. This allowed me to reflect and become aware of higher truths, which in turn evolved my awareness of who I am and what I wanted in life more directly and consciously. I was then able to engage with the tangible world as a slightly more evolved person. This was an iterative journey. The emphasis was on the journey itself rather than an external destination (, i.e., worldly outcomes). This soon became a lifestyle that allowed me to maintain greater inner stability and a progressively happier life, regardless of what happened in the external world around me. It was not an escape into fantasy land, living in denial or deprivation, nor was it about identifying myself with what I have, what I do, who I relate to, or how I am recognized; rather, it was a result of anchoring onto deeper truths about who I am. While what we have and what we do are important for physical and mental well-being, they are not the anchoring truths of who we are. They provide us with occasions to engage and evolve, but they are not the underlying and ultimate journey.

The real journey is that of evolving awareness—a process of self-actualization, evolving toward who we truly are, ultimately. Every encounter provides an opportunity to engage, meditate, and evolve our awareness. Once there is enough clarity in us and progress in our practice (conscious living), we can help others to evolve in their own lives. The measure of progress is based on the progressive increase in happiness in our lives that is around us. In short, to be happy and contribute toward the lives of others is the primary journey. However, this cannot happen in a vacuum. Physical (words, deeds) and psychological (emotions, thoughts) expressions and engagement offer an arena in which we can evolve.

I am now approaching my mid-fifties. Through a journey of trial and error and self-discovery, I have formed a spiritual seal for living, a way of looking at life and living. As one gets older, the challenges we encounter become deeper and broader. It is also because we become more mindful about even small and subtle aspects and see them in a more boarder and deeper context. Many events have happened since early 2000. My father passed away. After being diagnosed with cancer and going through initial treatment, he found peace with it. During his last two years, he and I had three crucial email exchanges. It was as if his final contribution to my spiritual journey with him. The topics included: (A) Symbolic Representation of Thatchina Murthy (see Chapter 2); (B) Song on Senthanar and its interpretation (see Chapter 6); (C) the crucial and nuanced concept called "Kaivalyam" (see Chapter 7). He was determined to be useful till the very end. Such was the person my father and Guru. The generosity and dignity with which he passed away was a very deep teaching for me. The years rolled on. Then, my mother passed away. She went peacefully after the age of 80. She was a silent and subtle contributor. God bless her soul. I separated from my second wife, which was followed by a few years of financial struggle—a new experience. With all the worldly challenges, I stayed calm and focused. Being there for my sons became my highest priority.

Guiding my two sons through the separation of their parents was a new chapter in my life. In my eyes, they were like diamonds in the making and were at the most vulnerable age. In nature, diamonds are made after facing intense heat and pressure over a prolonged time. My sons were going through a challenging experience, and I was keen to ensure it didn't harm their lives. Instead, I hoped they would evolve with this challenge and come out of it stronger. Nothing else mattered more to me than being there for them. I changed my career priorities, regardless of the short-term worldly impact (financial, etc.). Everything I did revolved around them directly or indirectly, not just to deal with disruptions across personal, social, and academic dimensions of their lives but to find a way to make the best use of the challenge to evolve. Trying to be the best father could have also made me the best person that I could be. Everything I learned over the years was put to the test; it was a baptism by fire. A fire of awareness inspired me to consume the best of what I learned to help two kids in a vulnerable stage. It has been nearly ten years since then. It was one of the most intense yet deeply satisfying periods of my life to date. It changed me as a person and brought out the best in me. It has transformed the way I look at myself, the world, and life. The journey of a parent goes on, but my sons have evolved out of their most vulnerable stage.

Taking a step back, life has thrown me a few challenges over the years, but what I learned during my early twenties and throughout my evolution has significantly helped me to maintain inner stability and peace and, more importantly, to look at these challenges as opportunities for further spiritual evolution. Yes, some of these events were difficult and, at times, incredibly stressful. However, beneath the surface-level tremors, I was able to retain inner stability and bliss for the most part.

For the last few years, I have been interested in sharing what I have learned and experienced. To evolve and then contribute to the evolution of others is a natural progression of needs. Initially, however, I was reluctant. I did not know which format would be best for sharing these insights. I was particularly interested in writing a book, but I did not want to write one just to transfer knowledge; it would not be enough to simply explain what I've learned from various sources. Instead, I also wanted to share some techniques that help with practicing them.

My father always wanted me to write a book about what I had learned. However, he was very careful not to say this was his "wish" as he was not keen to leave this as a burden or obligation. But twenty years after his death anniversary, I thought I should do it, not so much as his message to the world but sharing my understanding of what I have learned and used in my journey, which he guided as a guru.

Secondly, a drive arose from the need to want to share my thoughts with my sons, nieces, and nephews. But looking back and reflecting on my life, I was not sure whether sermonizing to young adults as a parent or uncle was the best way. I was desperate for a spiritual seal, but my sons, nieces, and nephews are in quite different circumstances. So, sharing knowledge was not going to help. I was keen to make this available if and when they needed it. On the other hand, I was not sure if I would be willing and able to, or even around if they ever needed it. So, I decided to write the book and leave it for whom it may be of use.

I am also curious to know whether what I learned and practiced will have universal receptivity and applicability—across geography, time, and culture. So, writing this book was also a way of putting my ideas out there and seeing what happens. Whether this book will be successful or not, it will not add or take away from the value of this book to me, as I have tested and tasted the ideas in this book in my own life, and at this stage, I am not seeking vindication from the world. What I am curious about is its applicability in other people's lives. So, I wrote this book with no expectations, only curiosity about its consequences.

While I am keen to put something out there and leave it to its destiny, at this stage, I am not keen to use my name for personal reasons. So, I am writing this under the name "Seval Seer." "Seval" in Tamil means rooster. "Seer" has many meanings, including song, discipline (in this case, spiritual discipline or seal), and sacred meaning. The significance of "Rooster" will be known to the reader at the end of Chapters 1 and 2.

UNDERSTANDING AND PRACTICE

There are two key aspects. One is to understand key ideas, outlooks, and truths. The second is to be able to live by the best of our understanding in daily occasions, "here and now." Understanding makes up the core of the effort, and there is no easy way. Each of us goes through a process of learning. In a book, learning is achieved through written words and the synthesis of ideas that are coherently developed to present a way of life. Although this learning is necessary, it is not sufficient on its own to be able to apply it in life; it requires genuine and relentless practice. To practice, we need additional tools and techniques.

Thus, in this book, I attempt to do two things:

1. First, to provide an overview of what I've learned from various fields of study (psychology, philosophy, religion, and spirituality) and practice (meditation and life itself).

2. Then, to provide details on how we embed this information into practice, a way to summon a state of being at the point of engagement (moment of truth).

Of these steps, the first is the foundation. However, if we stop there, this information remains background knowledge that can only be applied subconsciously. The second step allows us to practice consciously and live mindfully. Both steps are important.

In this book, I hope to share what I have become aware of through stories and discussions and leave the reader with insights on how to invoke this awareness and develop their practice. This includes some of the following techniques I collectively call **Invokable Representations.**

1. **Mantras**: Sounds or compressed words that represent a set of key ideas or outlooks. They don't have much of a meaning in terms of common worldly usage. But for the person who is aware of what they represent, it is a powerful technique.

2. **Tantras**: A series of mental and physical activities that simulate a key concept. They can be in the form of statements or songs. However, their effectiveness is based on how the application of a series of activities or mental orientation brings about a state of being.

1. **Visualization**: Visual representations of deep understanding

   a. Life-like representations (statues, paintings, etc.)

   b. Geometric symbols and representations (Yantras)

The following forms a bridge between a purely rational process that is detailed and voluminous and Invokable Representation, which is a highly compressed form of intuitions.

1. **Sutras:** These are well-crafted verses or songs that carry deep insights and are outlined intuitively, like an abstract painting. It is a simple but powerful way to invoke a sophisticated idea or a state of being with few meaningful words.

2. **Spiritual/Devotional Songs** Invoking a heartful spiritual experience.

3. **Parables/Stories:** while they are not necessarily in compressed form, they engage the reader/listener in a more intuitive way than pure rational/theoretical discussions.

The use of these invokable representations is useless without understanding what they represent. Otherwise, they are just empty procedures, leaving us worse off than an ordinary man living a life based on common sense. Without understanding the underlying truths and outlooks, performing these rites is like the performance of trained circus animals. However, only concerning ourselves with rational thinking or prose limits us to behaving like academic students, gathering knowledge but not applying what we've learned to day-to-day life. If primary ideas are like water, the invokable techniques are like the pipe system. We cannot go to the river or pond each time we need a glass of water. However, without water sources, empty pipe systems are useless.

MY RESEARCH AND KEY SOURCES

Before writing this book, I decided to revisit the ideas and messages I have gathered from various sources. However, this book is not an interpretation for academic purposes; it is about sharing my thoughts on what I found useful in my life. But some masterpieces have outlined some core ideas and provided invokable representations. Therefore, it is more effective for me to use them to convey my understanding, like riding on the shoulders of giants while the journey is a personal one.

So, I use them in this book in the way I understand them. Whether my understanding is consistent with traditional interpretations is irrelevant; however, I ensured my interpretations are supported by both the literal meanings of the words and the spirit of the sources and their messages.

Primary Sources

These are some of the masterpieces from the Tamil Community. Some of them are part of what is collectively called "Siththantham," and others were widely revered. The primary ones I have used in the book are:

1. **Thirukural:** I have used the Thirukural to strengthen the skeletal framework of this book. I have also used it to communicate and capture the soul (or essence) of each chapter. Thirukural belongs to the Sutra category. It is defined as a series of couplets called "Kural" to describe an insight. The first ten Kurals (of 1330), in my view, describe the core of self-actualization. I have used them at the beginning of each chapter to create a state of mind that helps the reader gain a better understanding of the chapter. Where I have used them, I have pre-fixed them as "TK-#", where the # refers to the number of the Kural (TK stands for the Thirukural)

2. **Thirumandhiram:** It is used both as Tantra as well as Devotional songs to help expand and illustrate the subtle, condensed, and compact ideas expressed in the Thirukural. I have used selected verses of Thirumandhiram throughout the book. It has been used to provide flesh bones to subtle ideas expressed in Thirukural, in a soul-stirring way. I have used a similar convention to refer to them, i.e., "TM-#"

(where TM stands for Thirumandhiram). There are 3,000 of them in the original scriptures. I have only picked the ones that were needed for this book.

3. **Sivajnana Podham:** Used in Chapter 3 as a core of the self-actualization process. There are 12 Sutras, and I have outlined them in Chapter 3. It is like the heart of this book.

4. **Thiruvasaham:** To outline a heartful journey of a soul (Chapter 9). This is one of the greatest spiritual works and very eloquently outlines the spiritual journey of a soul. I have used the whole song. These verses are like the blood flow that takes life energy to all the parts of the body - it is a way of putting together key elements of self-actualization in an experiential and heartful way.

All the above are some of the most treasured masterpieces on par with Upanishads, Bhagavat Gita, and Buddhist Classics. They are available in many languages. But they are not as widely known as Bhagavad Gita except for the Thirukural.

The Thirukural is one of a kind. Early sections focus on spirituality. Its clarity and sophistication are on par with any of the spiritual or religious classics or holy books. But the Thirukural is one of the few (if not the only one) that speaks about spirituality without being aligned to a religion. As the state religions of Tamil Kingdoms have changed from time to time from Hinduism, Buddhism, and Jainism, Tamil spirituality has acquired a shade of all of them. I am not familiar with Jainism, but I certainly can see shades of Hinduism and Buddhism in the Thirukural. But the Thirukural does not stop there. It goes on to other aspects of life, including Leadership, Conflict Resolution, and otherworldly focus. In that, too, it excels in its depth. Anyone comparing Art of War (by Sun Tsu) with relevant chapters of the Thirukural will also find that they are on par with each other. The final section of the Thirukural is dedicated to the experiential perspective of spiritual life. One is a romantic attraction, and the last is a wedded commitment. In short, in my view, the Thirukural is the only work that serves as a life framework – across spirituality, character building, competence building, and experiential view of life.

In this book, I have only used the first 10 Kural (of 1330). I am using this book as Series 1, focusing on self-actualization. I hope to add three more books, God willing. One each of Faith, Eminence, and Relentlessness in Practice (of self-actualization). That will complete the first 40 of the Thirukural, which forms the quintessence of the Thirukural (Payiram)

Others are also classics. They are part of Sithantham (Tamil tradition of Hinduism).

Interpretation and Challenge

In all these, I faced one challenge. These were written when the Tamil community was at its peak; the Chola, Pandya, and Cheran empires nurtured Tamil and spirituality. They are one of the longest empires in the world (ranging from 1400 to 2000 years). At its peak, the Chola Empire was bigger than modern-day India. Why is this relevant to spirituality? Longevity is important as a given spiritual tradition could evolve from generation to generation with continuity and consistency. The size of the empire was a proxy measure for the resources it had to attract the best minds. Through three Tamil Sangam (between 200 BC and 200 AD), Tamil literature and spirituality were nurtured. These books are part of this scrutiny or benefits of that knowledge.

Just out of curiosity, I plotted the Tamil empires along with some of the better-known empires on the graph. They are all plotted with longevity (duration of the empire) and size of the empire at their peak. This is not academic or formal research, just as a hobby.

But the modern translations date many years after the end of the last great Tamil empire. The authors were citizens of a colonized nation. As such, in my view, some of the depth of the idea has been lost, and most of them are literal translations. To understand these

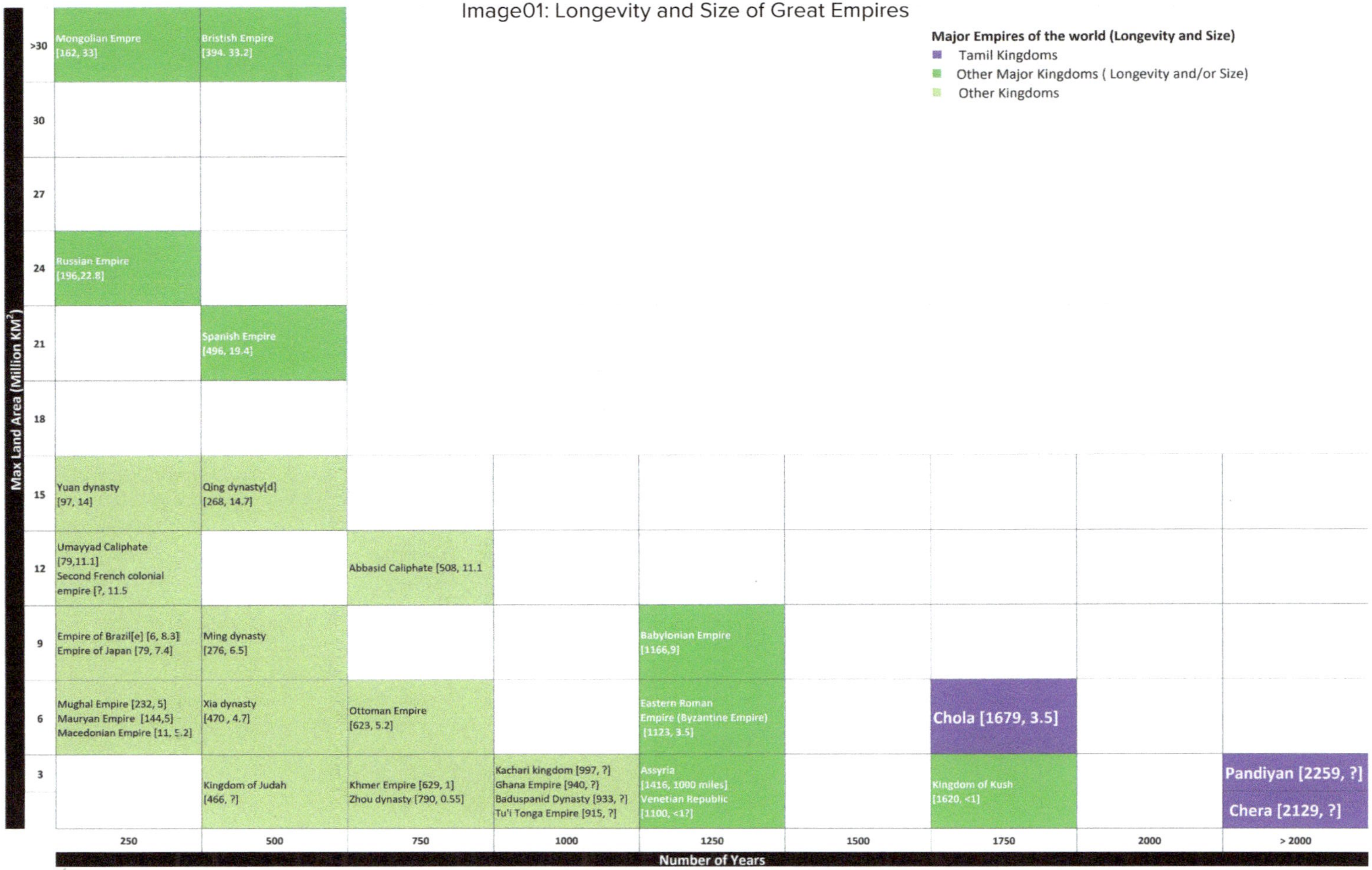

Image01: Longevity and Size of Great Empires

Major Empires of the world (Longevity and Size)

- ■ Tamil Kingdoms
- ■ Other Major Kingdoms (Longevity and/or Size)
- ■ Other Kingdoms

Chart: Max Land Area (Million KM²) versus Number of Years

Max Land Area (Million KM²)	Entries
>30	British Empire [394, 33.2]
	Mongolian Empire [162, 33]
30	
27	
24	Spanish Empire [496, 19.4]
	Russian Empire [196,22.8]
21	
18	
15	Qing dynasty[d] [268, 14.7]; Yuan dynasty [97, 14]; Abbasid Caliphate [508, 11.1]
12	Umayyad Caliphate [79,11.1]; Second French colonial empire [?, 11.5]
9	Ming dynasty [276, 6.5]; Empire of Brazil[e] [6, 8.3]; Empire of Japan [79, 7.4]
6	Xia dynasty [470, 4.7]; Ottoman Empire [623, 5.2]; Mughal Empire [232, 5]; Mauryan Empire [144,5]; Macedonian Empire [11, 5.2]
3	Kingdom of Judah [466, ?]; Khmer Empire [629, 1]; Zhou dynasty [790, 0.55]; Babylonian Empire [1166,9]; Eastern Roman Empire (Byzantine Empire) [1123, 3.5]; Kachari Kingdom [997, ?]; Ghana Empire [940, ?]; Baduspanid Dynasty [933, ?]; Tu'i Tonga Empire [915, ?]; Assyria [1416, 1000 miles]; Venetian Republic [1100, <1?]; Chola [1679, 3.5]; Pandiyan [2259, ?]; Kingdom of Kush [1620, <1]; Chera [2129, ?]

Number of Years axis: 250, 500, 750, 1000, 1250, 1500, 1750, 2000, > 2000 sources, one has to look at the use of language in contemporary or other classics.

The translation I have provided is, in most cases, different from a common modern translation. I took care that it was aligned with the dictionary meaning of the words, the spirit of the book, and that of contemporary works. In any case, the focus of the book is not academic. But as one practitioner sharing his understanding with other practitioners – those who want to be happy and make others happy.

Primary Stories

Stories play a critical role in communicating in simple ways otherwise sophisticated concepts. Spirituality is not about gathering knowledge but being aware and practicing it. For this purpose, stories are essential. In this book, I have used the following stories.

1. **Kantha Puranam:** It is a Hindu epic that illustrates many of the key concepts that I will be covering in this book. It is described in Chapter 2.

2. **Story of Siva as a Column of Fire:** A Hindu Epic that illustrates the supreme nature of the infinite in Chapter 6.

3. **Story of Bageerathan:** Describing the concept of intuition, emphasis on bringing a flash of intuition (sky-river) to the moment of truth "here and now" (earth), in the wider context of Ultimate Self (Siva) in Chapter 7.

4. Brief description of the **life of Jesus, Buddha, and Krishna** to illustrate 3 (of 4) paths in Chapter 8.

Complimentary

I have used many other sources across various fields of study developed across time and space. To bring about wider and richer nuances and emphasis. Also, it shows the universality of core ideas across time, place, and fields of study. Here are the key ones.

- **Philosophy, Spirituality, and Religion**

  - Upanishads, and Bhagavad Gita as additional masterpieces sources of Hinduism

  - Buddhism – including the ideas of Dependent Arising, Two-notions of Truth

  - Christianity (Bible, Kierkegaard – the idea of sickness unto death as a drive "To become the Self one Truly is" (the Ultimate Self)

  - Frederick Nietzsche (3 stages of Metamorphosis, Philosophy)

- **Science:** This includes works of

  - Kurt Goldstein (Neurology/Psychology) and leading Psychologist who first coined the term self-actualization in the scientific community

  - Abraham Maslow – Hierarchy of Needs and self-actualization

  - Carl Rogers – Self-Actualization, Fully Functioning Person and psychological concept of Good Life

  - Carl Jung – Individuation, Unconscious Mind, Intuition

INTRODUCTION

The primary theme of this book is to "**Be Happy and Make Happy**," and its title is **OM VEL Way.**

The purpose of this section is to

- provide an introduction outlining the primary theme.
- explain the meaning of the title.
- introduce "Invokable Representation" (which are aids that will help to both understand the ideas outlined in this book in an intuitive way and to apply/practice them in day to day living).
- provide an overview of the structure of the rest of the chapters of this book.

PRIMARY THEME: BE HAPPY AND MAKE HAPPY

This book is anchored on the theme "Be Happy and Make Happy."

Everything we do is to increase the quality and scale of happiness in our lives. Quality refers to the richness and intensity. Scale refers to the scope (across more situations, number of people, etc.) and longevity. To evolve, to increase happiness in our lives and that of others is a foundational and the ultimate theme of human life.

But what is happiness? Let's look at it from the perspective via 3 lenses – (1) external, (2) internal, and (3) synthesis or unified view.

Ease (External)

Ease is an experience based on the correlation between our needs related to the external world and our ability to meet those needs. If most of the world's needs can be met by what we have or what we can obtain, then our daily life is hassle-free and goes smoothly from the time we wake up to the time we go to bed. This experience can range from the reduction of struggle in the world (pain relief) to happiness in the world (pleasure).

Peace (Internal)

Peace, or internal joy, reflects the correlation between our expressions (words, thoughts, and deeds) and what we think of as internal measures (ethics, morals, our definition of success, etc.); for example, "I am a good parent, child, sibling, friend, etc." or "I am a good professional, member of a community.". In short I am good at doing my duties as I see it. It is more of whether my expressions (deeds, words, thoughts) align with my inner standards. The experience ranges from momentary peace to sustained peace for a longer period.

Bliss (Synthesis or Unified)

Bliss is a type of happiness based on how we are evolving compared to a notion of our Ultimate Self, i.e., the extent of self-actualization. It is about progress along the notion of our ultimate nature. The question of who we are and whether the life we are leading is meaningful in the context of who we are. It is about discovering who we are and leading a meaningful life in that context.

In the ultimate analysis, the most intrinsic and ultimate form of happiness results as we progress along the journey of self-actualization — to progressively be the Self we truly are. The highest gift we can give another, therefore, is to contribute toward their self-actualization process.

Ultimately, each of us needs to arrive at our truth through the experiences of our lives and the evolving awareness along with it. We will look at the above in detail throughout the book.

BOOK TITLE: OM VEL WAY.

"OM" is the Spirit. "VEL" is the Sport. "Way" is how the Spirit plays the Sport.

OM

OM refers to who we are intrinsically and ultimately. We are not our possessions, what we relate to, how we are recognized by others, or anything in terms of body-mind experience. We are an "evolving awareness", that which is aware of the body-mind experience and evolves with it. We are not a fixed profile — i.e. not a fixed physical, physiological or psychological profile with a notion of "I am This". Instead, we are that which is aware of all of them yet not defined by them. In short, we are an evolving awareness (spirit) with the notion of "I am that I am" and we evolve with each experience towards our ultimate nature (along the process called "self-actualization).

We will discuss this in more detail across four states of awareness in Chapter 6. Here is a quick summary. OM (aka AUM) looks at four states of awareness. A state is represented by "A," "U," and "M". The fourth state is represented by their synthesis, collectively called an OM (aka AUM).

1. A — Physical and physiological awareness: that which is aware of the external world.

2. U – Psychological awareness. Emotions, intellect: that which is aware of the mental/internal world.

3. M – Meditative or intuitive awareness, i.e., revelations: that which is aware of one's nature and that of life as a whole.

4. AUM (aka OM) – Wholesome or sacred awareness: This state is a synthesis of the above states applied to each moment, here and now, as a whole organism, not as an isolated capability, in other words, as a living awareness.

Symbolically – OM is represented by the Tamil letters ("O" and "M") as follows.

Image01: OM

VEL

VEL refers to our self-actualization tendency to drive our unfoldment.

- **V**erity: The power to be aware of our true selves - lead a progressively authentic life
- **E**volution: The power to evolve toward our ultimate – life is an evolving process toward its ultimate state
- **L**ove: the power to love that fuels our evolution toward our Ultimate Self - lead a progressively benevolent life

We will discuss more across the book but more so in Chapter 7. Symbolically – the spear represents "VEL" across OM

Image02: OM VEL

Way

Each occasion in life is a crossroads. We can take the path of self-preservation (clinging to the known and comfortable) or self-evolution (self-actualization). The former impedes self-actualization and leads to suffering. Progress along the journey of self-actualization leads to happiness that progressively increases in quality and scale.

Self-Preservation (Clinging):

What then holds us back? What leads to suffering? Our needs, occasions (opportunities, challenges), and experiences (positive and negative) are like waves in the sea of life. What leads to "sinking" in our journey across our lives?

The root of our suffering is ignorance of who we are. The world we experience is dependent on who we are. What happens to us is secondary. How we perceive, process, and choose to respond to them are the primary factors of our life. These are what make us who we are, not what happens to us. What happens to us creates an occasion to become who we truly are, i.e., self-actualization. According to Hinduism and Buddhism, what sustains this ignorance is craving and resentment.

Ignorance, forged by craving and resentment, leads to us clinging to three fetters.

The three key fetters are:

1. **Kanmam:** Clinging on to the relative truth (or body-mind experience) about dualities related to deeds and outcomes as an ultimate and independent reality. Good and bad deeds and outcomes are relative truths based on who you are and what circumstances you live in. They are used to perform day-to-day activities in life. But if we define who is based on customs and deeds of the past and cling to the notion of "I am This," it becomes an impediment to further evolution. This is called *"Kanmam."*

2. **Mayai:** Clinging to the experience of the body and mind as ultimate as a whole, as the ultimate and independent reality is the second fetter. What we experience is based on our physical, emotional, and intellectual capability. Memory gives a sense of continuity. Depending on our body-mind capability and memory is our experience of the past (recollection), present (how we respond to the arising moment), and future (anticipation). Clinging onto a set of body-mind experiences as ultimate truth freezes the Self in a fixed sense of reality and impedes further evolution. This is another form of a fixed notion of Self, i.e., "I am this," defining Self as the body-mind experience. This fetter is called *"Mayiai."*

3. **Anavam:** This is the result of clinging onto (1) and (2) as a composite fetter. It is the atomization or the "finitization" of the Self. The true nature of the Self is boundless. The core nature of the Self is truth and love, which are boundless. When an individual Self evolves toward the Ultimate Self, its nature becomes progressively infinite and eternal. Instead, if the Self is fettered by (1) and (2), Anavam completes the final step of taking a fixed notion of Self as "I am this.." It is a synthesis of (1) and (2) but gives it a total form as the last nail in the coffin of a living being. The Self has the nature to perpetuate, and augment based on what it identifies with. The three fetters make the Self cling and strengthen the grip of such clinging in everything we do. Anavam, for instance, distorts every event and experience to fit this mold of "I am this." As such, it is also called the "darkness" (Irul in Tamil) that impedes self-discovery, i.e., it blocks the ability to be aware of the true nature of the Self. Kanmam and Mayai help perpetuate this type of life based on ignorance (of who we truly are).

Clinging to the three fetters makes us a "fettered Self" and impedes further self-evolution.

Self-Actualization (Evolution)

What propels us forward? What leads to happiness? What enables us to "swim" in our journey across the sea of waves in life?

The way is to evolve from where we are toward our ultimate nature. There are five aspects to the path of self-actualization. They are each represented by a letter in a cardinal mantra in Hinduism called "Panchatcharam" (translates to "5-letter Mantra," and the five letters are "Si," "Va," "Ya," "Na," "Ma"). This is represented by the pentagon on the cover page. Chapter 2 provides more details illustrated with visualization.

- **Fettered Self:** When the Self clings to a fixed notion as "I am This," based on the three fetters, the Self increasingly experiences suffering [Ma].

- **Ultimate Self:** "The Self that one truly is" and forms the foundation, refuge and goal of self-actualization for the evolving Self. It provides the potential for the Self to evolve toward that which is eternal and infinite [Si].

- **Self as a Process of Evolving Awareness:** A sense of Self that evolves with each experience toward its ultimate nature ("I am That I am") [Ya].

- **Concealing Grace** – the flow of ignorance forced into craving and resentment. This, in the short term, may be useful as a protective shield when we confront an overwhelming occasion. It triggers a way of self-preservation. But in the long run, what may appear as a scaffolding may itself become a prison and impede further evolution [Na].

- **Revealing Grace** – the flow of intuition that reveals the higher truth of our ultimate nature. This is often a progressive revelation of who we are and the truth about our lives as we become receptive (meditative receptivity) [Va].

The way out is increasing awareness (as an antidote to ignorance) of who we are and actualizing that awareness in our day-to-day lives. In short, the way out is the way through. There is no escaping from the reality of the arising moment and running away to a fantasy land. We eventually need to return to reality, one way or another. To be open to each occasion, engage it fully, experience it fully, then meditate on it, discover more of your true nature, evolve, and then engage the next movement as a more evolving being. This is the fastest and most effective way. Everything else is to take a detour or slow down the process. The direct path requires clarity and courage of conviction. But each of us progresses toward it in one way or another. That is the universal direction for every being.

But we can do this passively as we are tossed around by life as a series of pain-relief reactions or consciously and proactively as a blissful journey.

Until we see us as separate from the Ultimate and what we experience via our body and mind are independent and ultimate reality, there will always be fear (of the other). As pivot our journey with the primary drive being self-actualization, realize that our body-mind experience is dependent on who we are (Buddhist notion of relative truths and dependent arising – see chapter 5) and as we experience increasing happiness. Our faith in the process self-actualization as the primary way of life, becomes more resilient and fears about worldly ramifications takes a secondary position. i.e. to continue the path of self-actualization, courage of conviction is vital.

In other words, an evolving Self, at every cross, has a choice to make. It continues with a fettered life based on ignorance or evolves based on awareness (of who one is and what one should do based on that). This is discussed in more detail in Chapter 5.

Four-Fold Path

There are four-fold paths to this way. Each is represented by a specific sequence of the five letters as a variation of a cardinal mantra (Panchatcharam). The details of the Four-Fold Path and the Mantra are described in detail in Chapter 9.

1. **The Way of Service:** Where we use every physical and physiological engagement as a steppingstone toward self-actualization, this is an "outside-in" process where we discover who we are in the experience and evolve [Na-Ma-Si-Va-Ya].

2. **The Way of Worship**: Where we use our psychological experience (Emotional, intellectual) as a steppingstone toward self-actualization. This is an "inside-out" process where we reform ourselves toward a notion of the Ultimate Self and engage the world with a reformed state of Self each time [Si-Va-Ya-Na-Ma].

3. **The Way of Witnessing:** Where we are primarily a witness of the unfolding of our life. Just meditating on our life helps us evolve. Worldly engagement and psychological evolution are byproducts. The unfolding of our ultimate nature is the primary phenomenon [Si-Va-Ya-Si-Va].

4. **The Way of Unity:** This is meditation in action where we are in continuous union with our ultimate nature and in harmony with life as a whole [Si-Va-Si-Va].

In short, each path is about using each moment to engage, become aware, and evolve to meet the next moment as an evolved being. The choice of the way is dependent on who we are at a given moment. One can choose to stick with one of the paths throughout one's life and progress along its journey. Or choose to evolve from one to another (from 1 to 4). The journey is one of self-actualization toward one's ultimate nature. The path is richer but more demanding as we look across paths (1) to (4). In other words, the destination is the same, but the experience along the journey and introspection needed is higher from paths (1) to (4).

The spiritual path does require conscious and mindful living. One cannot go on auto-pilot mode. It requires openness to experience, living fully in the moment, meditating, and evolving. So, it will demand us to get out of our comfort zone. It allows no comfort zone as each moment is pregnant with something new to explore and evolve. So we need to be willing to let go of the fettered notion of "I am this" (as a fixed thing) and be willing to evolve with each experience, i.e., align to the notion that "I am that I am" (as an evolving process of awareness).

We will look at an overview of the Way, in Chapter 8 and detail of each way in Chapter 9.

STRUCTURE OF THE BOOK

The following is a quick outline of the subsequent chapters of this book.

1. **Self-Actualization Epic:** Here, we start with a story that illustrates the self-actualization process and the various challenges that appear along the way. This is based on *Kantha Puranam*, an ancient Hindu Epic.

2. **Key Takeaways and Visualization:** In this section, we discuss the story's key takeaways and introduce the visualization of the key message. This allows us to "see" the ideas intuitively. This section will also introduce a mantra that can be invoked to understand the dynamics of self-actualization as an interplay of five aspects, which are represented by a visual called the "Dance of Bliss."

3. **Sink or Swim across the vast sea of life:** In this chapter, we look at life as a vast sea of waves of needs. This is illustrated by Abraham Maslow's hierarchy of needs and the corresponding Sheaths of Experience from the *Taittiriya Upanishad*. We discuss what it means to Sink in Life (using a key Buddhist concept called "Dependent Arising") or Swim Across (using the revered Hindu script, *Sivajnana Podham*).

4. **Self-Actualization—Multiple Perspectives:** In this section, we look at the notion of self-actualization as it appears in multiple fields of study:

   a. The Biological View: Self-actualization at a cellular level.

   b. The Neurological and Psychological View: The Self as an integrated organism.

c. The Psychoanalytical View: Individuation, the process of becoming an integrated being.

d. The Existential and Philosophical View: Three-staged Metamorphosis.

e. The Humanistic and Psychological View: The good life of a fully functioning person.

f. The Philosophical and Spiritual View: Motivation to be the Self one truly is.

5. **Mindful vs. Mechanical Living:** In this section, we contrast two types of living: going through the motions and conscious living. We look at the notion of self-actualization in a bit more detail and introduce a sutra (Sivajnana Podham) that represents the entire concept. Finally, we outline eight qualities that can be evolved in the process of self-actualization.

The next four chapters discuss the following qualities in detail:

6. **Q1: "I am" an Awareness [OM]:** In this chapter, we discuss the four states of awareness (OM) in more detail, as well as how our experience of life is dependent on who we are (re-visiting the Buddhist notion of Dependent Arising). This is to explore the first part of the title of this book, i.e., OM (of **OM** VEL Way).

7. **Q2: "I am" an Evolving Process [VEL]:** We will explore the notion of self-discovery as a critical part of self-actualization. This chapter explores the middle part of the title of the book, i.e., VEL (as in OM **VEL** Way).

8. **Q3: "I am" the Way:** This chapter provides an overview of the final part of the title of the book, i.e., "Way" (of OM VEL **Way**).

The next chapter uses the remaining five qualities (Q4 to Q8) to describe the Four-Fold Path: This chapter describes the four paths of the "Way" in more detail. It also outlines specific variations of the 5-letter Mantra that represent each of the Four-Fold Path.

9. **Q4–Q8: The Four-Fold Path Toward Self-Actualization:** The Four-Fold Path was described earlier in this chapter. It is provided repeated here for convenience with related Qualities (Q4 to Q8).

    a. **The Way or Service:**

    ○   **Q4: The Self transcends beyond the dualities of Outcomes.** To view the Self not as a fixed profile in terms of body-mind experience or outcomes, i.e., I am not what I process or receive.

    ○   **Q5: The Self transcends beyond the dualities of deeds.** – to view the Self not as a fixed profile in terms of what we do, i.e., I am not what I do. I am beyond that, and deeds arise from me but do not limit my future evolution.

    ○   Outlines the variation of the 5-letter Mantra (Panchatcharam) Na-Ma-Si-Va-Ya.

    b. **The Way of Worship:**

    ○   **Q6: The Self transcends beyond the outlook of the world** – to view of Self, not as a fixed profile in terms of our overall outlook of the world (external and internal) at a given point in time. Being open to experience to discover higher truth and evolve.

    ○   Illustrated with the story of Jesus.

    ○   Introduces an invokable representation – a variation of the "Panchatcharam" Mantra – Si-Va-Ya-Na-Ma.

c. **The Way of Witnessing:**

○ **Q7: The Self as the witness to the expressions of the Ultimate Self (the Divine Dance) –** To look at life as an evolution toward the Ultimate Self and individual Self as a witness.

○ Illustrated with the story of Buddha.

○ Introduces an invokable representation – a variation of the "Panchatcharam" Mantra – Si-Va-Ya-Si-Va.

d. **The Way of Unity:**

○ **Q8: The Self as that which is in union with the Ultimate Self (Verity and Love) –** to look at every occasion of life as a progressive union of individual Self and Ultimate Self, i.e., individual Self as a vehicle for the expression of the Ultimate Self.

○ Illustrated with the story of Krishna.

○ Introduces an invokable representation - a variation of the "Panchatcharam" Mantra - Si-Va-Si-Va.

The final chapter describes the journey of an Evolving Soul:

Conclusion – Journey of the Self:

• This section includes my translation of Thiruvasaham, a heartful journey of a soul along the path of self-actualization.

• Twilight Dance of Siva – an experiential view of "OM."

• Song and Dance of Self-Actualization – an experiential view of "VEL Way."

(1) SELF-ACTUALIZATION EPIC

ULTIMATE DRIVE IN LIFE

Each of us has many needs at different stages in life—these span physical, emotional, intellectual, and spiritual needs. In terms of physical needs, we want to be healthy, fit, strong, attractive, and resourceful (wealthy). In terms of emotional needs, we like to have rich relationships. In terms of intellectual needs, we like to be recognized for our achievements and contributions. In terms of spiritual needs, there is an innate desire to explore our identity (who am I?) and the significance of our life's path (self-actualization).

Ultimately, we want to be happy. Everything we do is to increase the quality and scale of our happiness. By quality, I mean the richness and intensity of being happy. We will look at the hierarchy of needs, outlined by psychologist Abraham Maslow, in a later chapter. By scale, I mean longevity and scope—lasting longer and having wider applicability. This includes making contributions that have a lasting impact beyond our time. In short, we want to be happy and make others happy.

Many works across various fields of study, such as biology, psychology, philosophy, religion, and spirituality, point toward the same thing. Despite the diversity of needs and ultimate goals, there is an intrinsic and ultimate drive for self-actualization that transcends them all: to be one's true Self. This spiritual need can be conscious or subconscious, while others are preliminary and lead to becoming aware of the ultimate need and are partial representations of the most intrinsic need.

There are two major approaches to life.

The first approach mistakes the relative truth of day-to-day needs (body and mind) as the ultimate needs. It confuses means with ends. We cling to the relative truth of Self, based on body-mind experience in day-to-day life as the ultimate truth of who we are. We cling to the body-mind and think these experiences define our identity ("I am this"). We cling to what was useful at a given point in time and make it a prison that traps us and prevents us from evolving with experience progressively. We build this perspective until reality bursts this bubble through a life-changing event. Then, we pivot to recognizing our spiritual need as the most intrinsic and ultimate need.

The second approach is to realize this from the beginning and use the pursuit of other needs as stepping-stones toward this most intrinsic and ultimate spiritual need—self-actualization. With this approach, we engage in the pursuit of body-mind needs, experience them fully, become more aware of who we are in the experience, and evolve beyond it. We then encounter the next moment as a more evolved person.

This goes to the heart of the question, "Who am I?" Am I the body and the experiences that go with it? Or the mind and the experiences that go with it? Or the spirit that is aware of the body-mind experience but transcends it? Am I the spirit, the indweller of body and mind? Are the body and mind instruments at the disposal of the spirit? Then what exactly is the spirit? It is a process of evolving awareness, not a fixed thing. The spirit is in a constant process of self-becoming. For this to be true, there must be a notion of the Ultimate Self and an evolving Self. Whether the Ultimate Self already exists but we are not conscious of it, or it exists as a potential that needs to be evolved is a question for the ages. Either way, one progressively discovers one's ultimate nature and evolves toward it.

These are very deep and very subtle topics that have been explored across time, geography, and various fields of study. This book is a synthesis of various works but with my interpretation and synthesis of them into a coherent view as I understood and experienced.

Let's begin with a story, a great Hindu epic called *Kandha Puranam*. The Tamil version was written by Kachiappar in Kanchipuram (Southern India) during the 8th century. This chapter is a summary of a story that helps to illustrate the message of this book. Again, I intend to use it as a means to share my views. It is not meant to be an academic knowledge transfer. Instead, it is meant to be a useful aid for the practice of living happily. Therefore, I have exercised creative freedom in selecting sections of the story and emphasizing these as I see fit.

The author of *Kandha Puranam* outlines the benefit or purpose of the book as follows:

> **To become heavenly beings on earth, being blissful, and pursuing the good**
>
> **Let that which arises in awareness find its fulfillment toward the State of Siva** (Ultimate Self)
>
> **Evolve with love by learning the story of wholesome Muruhan** (embodiment of Ultimate Self)
>
> **The one who ended the boundless strength of Asura's capabilities** (tendency to cling to body-mind).

Let's now dive into the story.

SIVA AND SAKTHI AS INTRINSIC AND ULTIMATE SELF

Siva is the ultimate God and the essence of all beings. The word "Siva" means auspicious or sacred. His nature is Verity (truth and authenticity) and Love. His consort is Sakthi, which means power. She represents the power to actualize Siva's essence in every being. She represents three types of powers: (1) the power to be aware, (2) the power to love, and (3) the power to evolve or execute. If Siva is the potential essence of all beings, Sakthi is the dynamic or kinetic essence as an actualizing tendency that helps realize Siva in every being. Siva-Sakthi is the most intrinsic and ultimate nature of all beings.

There is no Siva without Sakthi, and there is no Sakthi without Siva; they are inseparable. They create, evolve, and dissolve every being as well as the universe. They also initially conceal and later reveal the ultimate nature of the Self as one progresses along the process of self-realization (becoming one's ultimate nature is becoming one with Siva-Sakthi).

Every being born has the aspects of Siva-Sakthi in them. While beings are born with unique body-mind capabilities and evolve through different circumstances, in their essence (spirit), they all share Siva-Sakthi aspects. Looking from a body-mind perspective, every being is different and pursues diverse needs. But the essence of their spirit is Siva-Sakthi. They intrinsically and ultimately evolve toward becoming Siva-Sakthi consciously or unconsciously in their day-to-day lives.

TWO APPROACHES – THE DEVAS AND ASURAS

The universe is ruled by two major empires: Deva and Asura. They differ in the way they approach life.

The Deva clan are angelic who rule from the heavens. Their approach to life is evolutionary and is guided by the pursuit of truth (Verity) and fueled by love. They use every life experience (of body and mind) to meditate and evolve toward their ultimate nature of Siva-Sakthi. Along with their growth, they contribute to the welfare of all beings across the universe. They worship Siva-Sakthi and receive their blessings for their evolution and the evolution of others. They consider spiritual needs as the most intrinsic and ultimate needs, and they consider body-mind needs as subservient to spiritual needs.

The Asura clan is motivated by their body-mind experience, and their priority is to maximize their body-mind potentialities. Strength, wealth, power, domination, and pleasures are initial motivations. As they grow, they conquer other nations and dominate them. Their approach is a zero-sum game. They see others as a threat and wish to conquer and subjugate them. As they expand, others—Devas, humans, and other beings—suffer. They, too, pray to Siva and Sakthi. But the blessings they entreat are self-preservation. They use these blessings to conquer others to augment the Asura clan's welfare exclusively. They disregard spiritual needs and only focus on those of the body-mind.

The Devas and Asuras were in never-ending battles much of the time and were equally poised. At times, the Devas could completely defeat the Asuras and bring about universal evolution across all beings, while the Asuras could do the same to the Devas and dominate the universe.

ONCE UPON A TIME...

There was a time when the Devas ruled across the universe. Devendran, the king of the Devas, became emperor of the whole universe. His queen was Indrani, and Jayanthan was his son and heir. They were guided by Viyazhan, their Deva guru. They brought about peace and progress across the whole universe with the blessings of Siva-Sakthi.

The Asura king, Asurendran, was in exile. His wife, Mangalakesi, daughter (and heir), Surasi, and their guide, Sukran, along with a small community, refused to live under Deva's rule. They preferred to live in exile and had not given up hope of regaining their past glory completely.

As time passed, Asurendran was becoming old and losing his will to fight back. He was slowly becoming resigned to his fate. With no obvious threats over the years, the Devas became complacent and were slowly falling behind in their worship of Siva-Sakthi, the pursuit of self-evolution, and their contribution to the welfare of the universe.

The universe is an interconnected ecosystem. Change, in some respects, affects others. While the Devas indulged themselves in merry-making and empty rituals without being mindful of Siva-Sakthi in their lives, the Asura guru, Sukran, was coaching the princess in various Asura ways. These included becoming an expert in the art of illusions and having an unwavering mind driven by ambition and fueled by lust and resentment—lust for regaining their fame, fortune, and powers, and resentment toward Devas or anyone else in their way (including humans and animals). As she became an expert in these ways, she was given the name Mayai (or Maya).

Surasi had completed her training. Sukran felt that the time was right to outline his plan to defeat the Devas and win back the kingdom. Surasi had become a well-trained young adult, while the Devas had become complacent and vulnerable. This was the right time to execute the plan.

One day, Sukran summoned Surasi and assigned a mission to her. He told her about Kasiban, who was a highly learned human on Earth. He had received many boons from Siva-Sakthi. His skills and boons were extremely valuable for the Asuras' plan to defeat the Devas. He was young and had lived in a monastery since birth. As such, he was innocent and inexperienced in the ways of the world.

The first phase of the mission was for Surasi to seduce Kasiban and marry him. The second phase was to have children with him and train them in advanced techniques to attract Siva-Sakthi so that they could receive powerful boons. While the children should learn the techniques from their father, the directive was that they should align with their mother in terms of goals and values. They should identify as Asuras, not as humans with spiritual goals. The next phase was to receive boons from Siva. The final phase was to defeat the Devas and regain the lost kingdom.

Surasi was then given strict and detailed instructions, including that she should mate only in darkness when Asura tendencies reach their peak. Additional instructions were given in terms of conception and raising her children to maximize the success of the mission. In addition to this, she was to raise an army using her illusory power. To gain strength in number and variety, she should mate in various forms with Kasiban, including human, animal, etc. Detailed plans and guidelines were given to her.

Surasi listened attentively. She added her own goals. She wanted to not just win back the lost kingdom but take over the whole universe and send the Devas into exile or imprison them. Her hatred toward the Devas had been fueled by growing up in exile and witnessing her father become a broken man living in deprivation. Surasi was also very skilled and ambitious. She had a lust for power and wanted to dominate the universe. Fueled by lust and anger, Surasi not only accepted the mission but planned to augment it.

Surasi then met with her parents, Asurendran and Mangalakesi. She explained her mission and obtained their blessing. She then set out to Earth to meet Kasiban.

THE LEARNED IS WEAK, WITHOUT COURAGE OF CONVICTION, WHICH COMES WITH EXPERIENCE.

Surasi descended to Earth with a clear mission and steely determination. She found the monastery Kasiban was living in and established a place of residence for herself close to it. She used her magical powers to create lotus ponds, beautiful gardens, and other natural settings that were conducive to seducing Kasiban. Her tactic was to lure him into her trap rather than actively pursuing him. Surasi did not want Kasiban to be suspicious of her intent at any stage until it was too late. Occasionally, Surasi assumed an invisible form to observe Kasiban's routines, listen to his discussions, and make a full study of his physical and psychological profile and habits.

When the time arrived for Surasi to be noticed, she enhanced the environment In a way that was targeted to exploit his vulnerabilities. During one of his regular outings, Kasiban started to notice the changes in his neighborhood. He was a very young saint in the monastery, and years of strict yogic practice to receive many boons had made him tired of his monotonous routine. He felt deprived of the pleasures of the world. Looking at this attractive set-up made his young mind curious. At first, it was just a cursory glance, but as time passed, he became increasingly curious. Then he came across a stunningly beautiful lady in the form Surasi took.

He started making conversation. She came across as innocent and vulnerable and told him that she wanted to learn about the ways and experiences of a quiet life close to monasteries, away from the busyness of the major cities. Yet, she clarified from the beginning that she was not inclined to pursue a monastic life. Instead, she hoped to marry someone and lead a comfortable life. It was a passing phase to learn about other aspects of life.

When the mind does not (or wishes not to) see the truth, it can make up its version. Kasiban was swept away by Surasi's beauty and youthful energy. He began to feel that she was a gift from the Devas as a reward for his disciplined life thus far. All the mental discipline he practiced until that point took a back seat as the urges of his body and mind rose to the foreground. Surasi made sure that she never came across as romantically interested in Kasiban for fear of triggering suspicion and putting the whole plan at risk. She wanted to make sure that he felt it was he who was pursuing her and that he was in charge.

Visiting Surasi eventually became part of Kasiban's routine. The mind has a nature that dictates that if an experience is pleasant, it frequently wants more and more of it, and more often. It clings to it and craves it increasingly. Their meetings evolved from daily catch-ups to becoming the focus around which all other events had to fit. Kasiban began to crave Surasi's company, leading him to abandon his routines related to meditation, yoga, spiritual studies, and other activities. Being with her went from occasional visits to part of his routine to obsession and then addiction.

Surasi carefully played her part. She initially played the part of an innocent and naive lady curious about the lives of people in the monastery, listening to Kasiban's words and achievements with wide eyes and respect, then progressively making subtle and inviting gestures. She worked on them becoming comfortable being in close physical proximity, with the occasional and seemingly unintentional touch. The clothes she wore were not outwardly revealing but highlighted her physical beauty. The conversation was engaging and exciting to him, with Surasi meeting him at his intellectual level. All the while, she kept up the appearance that she looked up to him and admired him.

She did not take any overt steps, just lured him subtly. One day, she told him she was going away for a few weeks to be with her relatives. He was distraught. He tried to persuade her otherwise, then eventually accepted it. Every day felt as long as a year. As they say, absence makes the heart grow fonder. In his case, his lust and desperation escalated. He began to feel that he must have her at all costs.

Suarasi returned after a few weeks. This time, Kasiban decided to go for it. He proposed to her, explaining that after years in a monastery, yogis can still pursue their spiritual life as part of a married couple if they find a like-minded partner. He was certain she was a gift from the gods for his life thus far. Living with her was the way to heaven, and he needed her support.

Surasi smiled sheepishly. She said that she was just a naive young girl with worldly ambitions. Her father was an old leader of a small community and led a very humble life. Her primary focus was to help her aging parents and evolve the community. Her aspirations included having lots of children who would make their own lifestyle choices rather than a pre-determined ascetic life. Kasiban had led an effective ascetic life and obtained lots of boons, so she told him he should continue his journey to reach the peak in his path. Surasi felt she might not be suitable as the wife of an evolved and powerful person like him, who was looking for a liberated and ascetic life. She might disrupt his life by being an impediment that distracts his energy toward worldly things. On the other hand, she was not ready to abandon her wishes and lead an ascetic life. She went on to say that he had made a big impact on her life, and she was very appreciative of that, but she was not worthy of being his wife. They should not evolve their relationship to the next stage as husband and wife.

Kasiban, impelled by lust, had only one goal, which was to marry her. With all the boons he had, agreeing to what Sursai wanted was such a trivial concession, he thought. Every human needs to follow their destiny. If she wanted a bit of worldly comfort, and their children chose the same path, then so be it. After all, spiritual life was the most powerful in terms of reaching the ultimate. Therefore, those who take detours via other routes will still end up on their path. After all, Kasiban, with all his knowledge, had been swept away by this young girl. After quenching some of the thirsts of his body and mind, he intended to get back to spiritual ways through married life with Surasi, who he believed was needed for his evolution.

Kasiban told her, "I have enough power to give you the life of an empress while living in the neighborhood of the monastery. You can have any number of children. Each person needs to pursue the life they wish. But the spiritual path gives the greatest joy. One day, you, too, will realize this. Until then, you are free to pursue any worldly needs, and so can our children. With all the boons that I receive from Siva-Sakthi, it is a trivial effort for me to ensure that you get what you need. I, on the other hand, need your support for my evolution. I am certain that you are a gift from the gods to help me to evolve into my destiny. Do not hesitate any further. This is mutually beneficial and the highest blessing for both of us."

She showed nervousness and reluctance and asked for a few days to think it over. He agreed to give her some space to think. Now, every hour felt like years to him. His everyday walk was around the path that allowed him to spend more time near her residence. After a week, it was all too much for him, so he visited her. She came close to him and said that she did not want to be the person who impeded his evolution. Also, she had great worldly ambitions that she was not willing to compromise. She enjoyed his company as a friend and always would. However, she was not sure if it would be a good idea to get any closer.

She looked extremely stunning. Everything was set up to push him over the edge emotionally, and it worked. He began to plead with her. He promised her everything she wanted. She just needed to show mercy on him and his plight. She stared at him with a piercing look.

She pretended to be nervous and accepted his proposal with some conditions. It was to be as the Asura guru had instructed. They would only mate in the dark. Every day, she would take different female forms— human, animal, etc. He needed to take corresponding male forms. In addition to children, she would use her skills to create a community of people through the magical power of multiplying. She wanted to live like an empress. He should be a dedicated father and teach all the ways and techniques he knew to their children while allowing her to be the mother and share her values without interference from him as a father.

At this point, she could have said anything, and he would have accepted it all. It did not seem like a big deal to him. He just needed her physically and emotionally. The rest, she could have it all. He had no strong views on worldly matters, as he had lived all his life in a monastery. So, he had no personal, worldly ambitions. He was more than happy for her to experience these trivial things in life, so he thought.

They had a private ceremony, which suited them both. Kasiban was happy with simple things, and Surasi wanted it to be a secret to avoid attracting attention from both Devas and evolved humans who might see through her facade and disrupt her plan. The first night came. She gave him full physical and mental pleasure. He thought it was heaven. She was the first woman he had intimately connected to, and everything felt magical to him.

LEARNED BUT WEAK, MATING WITH IGNORANT BUT STRONG-WILLED, GIVES BIRTH TO POWERFUL BUT FETTERED SOULS

Surasi gave birth to a powerful son that night, using her and Kasiban's power. Asuras and Devas do not follow the human physical time cycle, including that of pregnancy. The following night, she took the form of a wild lioness. As promised, he took the form of a male lion, and they mated all night. On the third night, she took the form of an elephant, and on the fourth, she took the form of a goat. This resulted in three sons and a daughter. The sons were named Sooran (also known as Soora Panman), Singan (or Singa Muhan), and Tharahan (or Tharaka Asuran). Their daughter was named Asamuki.

Every night thereafter, they took the forms of various animals and creatures. To multiply their creations, each night they mated, Surasi grew longer nails and scratched Kasiban. From every blood drop, many sons were born through Surasi's magical powers. Within a few days, there were thousands in number. Using her magic powers, Surasi made them invisible before dawn. After a few weeks, she had created enough to make a strong army. They were to raise themselves with some support from members of the Asura community in exile. Surasi wanted to focus on her first three sons and her daughter. This also prevented anyone else from becoming suspicious and letting the Devas know.

The four children developed unique traits. Tharahan was extremely loyal to his brothers and fixed in his ways, like the elephant. He was not much of an independent thinker and had blind devotion to both his brothers. He would execute their requests wholeheartedly as though they were commands. Once he set his mind to something, he was unstoppable, like a charging elephant.

Singan was an independent thinker. He would point out any flaws as he saw them. He was impatient and could get angry quickly. But he, too, was very dedicated to his brothers and the welfare of his family. When all things were discussed, he would obey his older brother, Sooran.

Sooran was the most dominant and was evolving as a charismatic leader. He, too, loved his family very much.

Asamuki was the family pet, being the only daughter and youngest amongst the four of them. She loved her brothers. But she had a mind of her own. She was very ambitious and had the full support of her brothers to make her wishes come true. The only person who challenged and argued with her was Singan. If what she wished was wrong, he would be quick to point it out. But she would plead with her oldest brother and somehow have her way in the end.

They also had some of their father's traits. They were extremely good at meditation and yoga. But their mother made sure that they primarily identified with her values and ambitions to dominate the world—to become powerful, rich, and famous. Inheriting from both parents gave them the potential to become powerful forces in the universe.

Kasiban was a very contented man. All he had to do was a few hours of teaching, follow his routines during the day, and have all the pleasures of the world with Surasi at night. But he started to spend more and more time with her, even if it was just being around her during the day. The children were learning all the advanced ways of mind control and seeking boons from their father. But they continued to learn their values and approach to life from their mother.

CROSSROADS: SELF-PRESERVATION (CLINGING TO THE KNOWN) OR SELF-ACTUALIZATION (EVOLUTION)

Time passed by, and the children became young adults. In those days, it was customary for young men to venture out and become independent and evolved. So, the three brothers approached their parents and sought their advice on what they should be doing in their next stage—in their journey to leave the monastery and build their own lives.

They first paid their respects to their father. With genuine interest, they sought his advice. Kasiban was pleased and wanted to give his children the best advice he could.

He advised them that there were three key pillars in life. The *Ultimate Self*, the evolving *individual Self*, and the *fetters* that prevent the individual Self from evolving to become the Ultimate Self. The whole objective of life is for the individual Self to evolve and unite with the Ultimate Self. For this, they would need to go beyond the three fetters that impeded the process of this union.

The Ultimate Self is Siva-Sakthi with essence; Sakthi is self-actualizing power. Siva is a composition of Verity and Love. For the individual Self to unite with Siva, one needs to pursue the path of truth and authentic living (Verity). This journey needs to be fueled by Love, i.e., with benevolent intent. Each being also has an intrinsic power to know, the power to love, and the power to evolve. This aspect of Siva-Sakthi forms the more fundamental and intrinsic drive. It is also the ultimate purpose of life, i.e., to become fully realized as Siva-Sakthi in our conscious life (day-to-day living). This is called self-actualization and leads to the highest and lasting bliss.

When an individual Self is in pursuit of Verity, fueled by Love, following an innate tendency to self-actualize, it receives Divine Grace in the form of revelation or intuition. The more you pursue the path of self-actualization, the more there is the revelation of your true nature and the more the experience of bliss in your life.

The root cause for people being held back by the three fetters is ignorance. Awareness is the antidote for ignorance.

Sooran asked his father, "Can you please explain what you mean by ignorance?"

His father gladly explained that ignorance is not knowing your true and Ultimate Self, Siva. Instead, you cling to what you experience, via body and mind, as who you are—the flawed notion of "I am this." But in reality, your life is an evolving process of self-discovery and evolution, i.e., a process of self-actualization. The truth is "I am that I am," an evolving awareness. It is a process and not a fixed notion in terms of the body, mind, and experiences.

Then, the second son, Singan, asked his father to explain what the three fetters were and how they impede the process of self-actualization. Pleased by the quality of the questions, their father enthusiastically explained.

The three key fetters are:

1. **Kanmam**: The false notion that actions and outcomes are independent and ultimate truths.
2. **Mayai:** The false notion that the world experienced by the body and mind is an independent and ultimate truth.
3. **Anavam**: The notion that "I" is a fixed thing (i.e., an atomization of "I," as in "I am this"), based on Kanmam and Mayai.

They impede the process of evolution when one clings to them as the ultimate and independent truth. They are relative truths based on who one is at a given stage. For one to evolve, one needs to let the notions of relative truths go as one uncovers the higher truth of who one is. Not twist the experience to fit into a fixed notion of relative truth. What is useful as a scaffolding for day-to-day living should not become a self-imposed prison, preventing further evolution.

Singan continued with this line of questioning. "I am not sure I understand. Should I assume that any actions or outcomes are equally good? The world I see is void. What then motivates my actions?"

Kasiban looked at his second son with pride.

"Your questions show how deeply you are reflecting on my advice. At this young age, your interest and grasp of these concepts are admirable."

He expanded on the topic and said that in life, there is relative truth and ultimate truth. Relative truth is relative to your sense of awareness and being. What you see as a human is not necessarily true for bees, bats, or birds. Firstly, it depends on your physical capability. Then, your emotional and intellectual capability and orientation. The body-mind experiences changes based on body-mind capability. But that is the experience. The awareness that arises from the experience depends on your priority state of being. Collectivity, these relative or worldly truths are relative to your state of evolution as a whole—body-mind-spirit. You do not need to deny them; you need to live by them. But knowing that they are relative truths, do not cling to them. As your awareness evolves, let go of your previous view of the dualities of deeds and outcomes and that of the world and the sense of "I am." Evolve with awareness. Identify with the evolving awareness as "I am that

I am," as awareness evolves with the revelation of the Ultimate Self. Without relative truth, one cannot discover the ultimate truth.

The ultimate truth is that you are an evolving awareness, a spirit. You evolve toward uniting Siva-Sakthi. Siva is truth and love. Sakthi is the tendency to actualize your Self toward your Ultimate Self. You are not the body, mind, or your experience. They are instruments and experiences made available to you in your evolution toward self-actualization.

The pursuit of the ultimate truth needs to be fueled by love. If you cling to relative truth, which is only true to you at that moment, based on who you are, you cannot evolve. You need to take a higher path. On the one hand, live day to day with your relative truth. With each experience, meditate, evolve, and progress toward your ultimate truth.

Sooran then asked, "What is the root cause for getting fettered, and what sustains it?" Sooran always wanted to get to the bottom of things and get on with it.

Kasiban was brimming with pride at the nature of the questions. He went on to explain, "The root of all of this is ignorance of who you are. What sustains this is lust and anger. Ignorance leads to distorted experience. We then feel lust and anger toward something. This pulls you deeper and deeper into the way of ignorance."

As he was teaching his children, Kasiban began to become aware of his flaws. But he brushed those thoughts aside so he could focus on helping his children. He thought it was too late for him and that it was too painful to deal with.

Sooran then asked how one goes beyond the fetters. His father explained that the way to overcome ignorance is to become more aware of your true nature and evolve toward it, which is a three-step process.

1. Self-Discovery (Velvi) is a process of encountering the ultimate and receiving its blessings. The ultimate is Siva-Sakthi. Their blessing is a form of revelation of their true nature.

2. Evolution (Thavam) is overcoming the fetters with increased awareness.

3. Contribute toward the evolution of others (Thanam); when you help others evolve, you also evolve in that process.

Singan then asked how one practices awakening (Velvi). Kasiban advised that people, over a long period, defined a series of mental and physical activities that simulate the process of awakening. By practicing these, one creates a spiritual seal or outlook that can be practiced in life. He then went on to define the procedure.

- Establish a pit. Put in pieces of wood and set them on fire to create a small flame inside the pit.

- Think of Siva in your mind, utter spiritual phrases, and dedicate things to the fire that will keep it blazing. These can be some worldly things such as grains and oily things like ghee.

- When Siva-Sakthi is pleased, they will appear before you.

- You ask them for their blessings and a boon and evolve with it.

But the real meaning behind these actions is a process of self-actualization. When you perform this ritual with true understanding and genuine participation, you create a spiritual seal in your being that you can take to every subsequent moment of life as follows:

- The fire pit is the circumstances you encounter.

- You perform your best with equanimity.

- What you offer into the metaphorical fire is the expressions (deeds, words, and thoughts), outcomes, and experiences (via body and mind) that result.

- Fire is meditative awareness. It consumes everything you give it, and it grows from that.

- Siva-Sakthi is your Ultimate Self (that you may not be fully consciously aware of). When you meditate, the blessing comes in the form of revelation of truth and intuition. This intuition is seeing the Siva-Sakthi in action, i.e., the dance of Siva-Sakthi.

- Accept that intuition as evolving awareness and use that as a base for the next encounter in life. This is how you progressively become a part of the Siva-Sakthi dance.

- You will increasingly experience bliss, which, in turn, motivates you to progress further in this journey.

When you keep repeating this after every encounter and experience of the body and mind, your spirit will progressively evolve toward the Ultimate Self. You are becoming one with Siva.

Both Sooran and Singan were listening to this intently. For Tharahan, this was all too much. He only cared about fulfilling whatever his older brother asked him to do.

Surasi was patiently listening to all of this. Then, she decided to intervene.

"You have provided great advice to our children. I am very thankful for your advice, especially on how to invite Siva and seek his blessings. That is the most valuable advice. But the goal you have given our children is more suitable for those in the monastery than young men in their prime. They need to experience the world, create wealth, and experience power. After all that, should they seek a spiritual life, they can decide this when they are old and have passed on their assets and power to their children. That is the way of the world. They should not start with a monastic life."

She went on to say, "When we married, you made me a commitment that you would let me live like an empress and have children. You have kept that promise. You also promised to let each of our children evolve based on their aspirations, which may not be those of those living in a monastery. You also agreed to let me give them values and goals that they can pursue. I humbly ask you to keep those commitments."

Kasiban was taken aback. But he agreed to his wife's request, asked her to advise their sons, and stepped back to be a passive witness.

Surasi was now ready to execute the next phase of her plan. She said, "Learning the ways of evolved souls and highly sophisticated techniques are important. So please make sure you understand all that from your father. But for young men, the purpose of these is to create wealth and power. You should not live like the deprived and poor, living in suffering. What is the point of having all the evolution as a spirit and living a worldly life of deprivation or poverty regarding the body and with no authority regarding the mind? With great discipline and highly effective methods, you should perform a great Velvi toward Siva. Be relentless in your pursuit. But when He appears before you, seek wealth and power to rule the universe. You do not need Siva to tell you what your aspirations are. That is wasting His time. Instead, ask Him what you need to fulfill your aspirations."

Surasi was now ready for the final assault.

"I want you to understand who you are. I am an Asura princess. My father was defeated by the Devas and sent into exile. You are my children. That makes each of you an Asura prince. The Devas are your enemies. Your father, through evolution, has gained so many powers. You, as our children, can become much superior to the Devas with the blessings of Siva. Then, defeat them and win back everything that has been lost and all the Devas had in the first place. Rule the universe as undisputed power. Be relentless in this path. This is your destiny. Step forward and claim it."

Brimming with energy, wanting to make something out of their lives, with young and immature minds, the three of them looked at their father for approval. For Kasiban, it felt like the whole Himalayan Mountain range just fell on him. Everything Surasi said was true about the agreement they had made before their marriage, but he did not realize the scale of her ambition. He believed it was to evolve into a small tribe, not take over the universe with worldly ambition. He blamed himself for not realizing this early on. But for her part, Surasi had given him everything he wished from her. He realized that it was too late to do anything. He just needed to accept what destiny held for all of them. Their children needed to find their way to the truth in their lives. So, he said nothing and let the sons decide.

Surasi was in no mood to leave it to chance. She said, "So, it is settled. Now I will advise you on a few other things. Go to a place called Venom Island and follow the instructions that I will now give you."

She instructed them on how to set up the fire pits for Velvi. She warned that the Devas would come to know this and try to disrupt them, so she taught them the magical powers to repel any assault from the Devas and create a protective dome around the areas. She also said she would help them with all the material to be offered into the fire pit.

"For extraordinary power of body and mind, you need to give an extraordinary body and mind offering. I will give you the bodies of humans and beasts. Give these innumerable bodies and seek the most powerful bodies for the three of you. Offer their blood as oil to set the fire of Velvi ablaze so that it reaches the heavens. As for your mind, use all the training you learned from your father. Offer that to Siva. In return, you seek even more powerful minds."

She reiterated that they should be relentless until Siva appears.

"There is nothing else to be gained in your lives."

She instructed the two younger brothers to stand by Sooran no matter what. They needed to make this happen at any cost. She also asked the three brothers to meet with the Asura guru, Sukran, to receive detailed instructions on what to seek from Siva and to obtain the blessings of their grandparents, Asurendran and Mangalakesi.

She then brought all the other children, who had been kept invisible for all these years. They were now young, strong men, thousands of them. She instructed them to obey the commands of the three brothers and protect them from any assault. They all agreed and were excited to join their three brothers.

The three brothers obtained their parents' permission to leave and started their adventure.

Surasi sent their only daughter, Asamuki, to stay in exile with her grandparents and their community.

She then sat beside her husband and said, "You are a wonderful husband. You gave me everything I wanted. We have raised great children. Our sons will become the rulers of the universe. I now have to go. I need to help our sons get their Velvi started. Then I need to stay with my parents, who are now old. I need to look after them. Also, as the heir to my father, I need to look after the Asura community in exile as their queen until our sons return and take over. That is the right thing for me to do. I need to say goodbye and let you return to your monastic life and pursue your destiny."

Kasiban was heartbroken, but there was very little he could do. He tried to plead and persuade Surasi to stay with him but to no avail. He bid her goodbye and returned to the monastery. There, he confessed all that had happened to his teacher. His teacher advised him to use this life experience to develop an assessment of the courage of conviction in what he knew to be true and further enrich his awareness and evolve. So, he returned to his monastic life.

Before he met Surasi, with all his knowledge, he lacked life experience. There was no courage of conviction but just a collection of knowledge. That made him vulnerable and weak, allowing Surasi to do all she wanted even though Kasiban was learned and had many powers. But with this experience, he gained much life experience and decided to pursue his destiny.

Surasi, on the other hand, was preparing a Velvi of her own to protect her sons while performing their Velvi and amassed material to use as offerings. She planned to meet up with her sons in Venom Island shortly after.

"Velvi:" Encountering the Ultimate and Receiving Worldly Blessings

Along with his two brothers and a massive army, Sooran marched toward the exiled Asura. The earth shook, and the heavens began to tremble. The Asura guru, Sukran, and his old grandparents, Asurendran and Mangalakesi, gave him a very warm welcome. Their sister, Asamuki, was also there.

Sukran did not want to waste any time. He spent a day with Sooran and his brothers, who taught them some advanced magical powers and gave additional instructions on constructing and protecting the Velvi pit. He also warned that the Devas would come to know about this very soon if they did not already. He advised them to anticipate an attack from the Devas to disrupt the Velvi. So, he asked them not to waste any more time as they needed to reach Venom Island.

With the blessings of their guru and grandparents and loving wishes from their sister, they started their journey toward Venom Island. Sooran instructed Singan to lead the march and Tharahan to protect the rear of the formation of their army. He was in the middle. They were surrounded by their army. Before Deva's spies could reach Devendran, Sooran reached Venom Island. He picked the site for the Velvi ground. As per Sooran's instructions, his brothers and the Asura army built a huge wall around the Velvi site using mountains picked from the surroundings with the magical powers inherited from their mother.

Sooran then used the magical powers he learned from their mother and the guru to invoke protective energy fields to protect the sites from all sides, including from above and below. He then instructed them to build the structure of the Velvi pit in three concentric circles, with 1008 small pits in the outer circle, 108 in the inner circle, and a massive Velvi pit at the center. Then, they established a tall diamond pole at the center of the innermost pit and waited for their mother to provide the Velvi materials to be used as offerings. Surasi arrived just in time. She made a massive mountain of dead bodies of humans, animals, and all kinds of creatures, all soaked in fresh blood. She was thoroughly impressed with the inspection of the Velvi site. Then, she gave her blessings and returned to the exiled Asura community. There, she would eagerly await the outcome of these history-altering efforts along with her parents, guru, and daughter, Asamuki.

Sooran then lit the 1008 pits with fire and made an initial round of offerings in the outer circle. He invoked the magical spells he learned from his mother and the Asura guru as an invitation to Siva. Once the ritual was underway, he asked his younger brother, Tharahan, to continue the Velvi in the outer circle with the support of part of the army. He then did the same regarding the middle circle with 108 pits. This was meant to be a warm welcome to Siva when he arrived. He asked Singan to continue from there. He then went to the massive pit at the center, invoked the most powerful magic, and offered the best of meat and blood. This was to offer a place for Siva to arise and prove the worthiness of the three brothers.

Every day, the process continued from sunrise to sunset. The Devas learned about this effort and attacked the Velvi site from all angles. But it was well fortified. Also, the king of Deva, Devendran, was quite complacent by then. He thought these boys, driven by youthful excitement, were trying the impossible. He believed they might get some gold and beautiful women, which would hardly create a threat worthy of his attention.

Days went by, months passed, and the years progressed, but Siva did not appear. Tharahan and Singan were relentless and displayed full faith and love for the older brother, Sooran. They did not waver.

However, Sooran was becoming anxious. He did not want to walk away empty-handed. He felt the weight of all the expectations of his mother, grandparents, and the Asura guru. Above all, he did not want to disappoint his brothers and sister. He then thought about how the highest blessings needed the highest form of body and mind to be offered. Even if they were countless, the bodies of ordinary humans and beasts alone were meager offerings to Siva. Maybe that was why Siva had not appeared before Sooran. He then flew to the top of the diamond pole, cut his limbs one by one, and offered them to the central fire. His flesh and fresh blood fueled the fire. It grew into the dazzling glow of a blazing inferno. As he was born with the magical powers of Surasi, they grew back after he cut them off. But he was relentless. Another year went by with no sign of Siva.

One day dawned with an ominous feeling. Birds refused to leave their nests, animals stayed with their young and did not go to hunt, the Earth was shaking out of fear, and the air was still. Everything in nature subconsciously knew this day was very different, and something historic was about to happen. The two brothers were as dedicated as before. But they, too, felt that something was about to happen. However, they stayed the course, faithful to their older brother's instructions.

Sooran decided that it was the day. It was a "now or never" moment. He started flying higher and higher with increasing speed, calling out Siva's name. When he touched the heavens, he darted down at an even greater speed. He continued to call Siva's name all the way. Then he offered his body by letting the diamond pole pierce through it. His body reached the bottom of the central pit. The Velvi fire was set ablaze and became a humongous flame reaching from Earth to Heaven. It was as if the whole flame was chanting Siva's name.

Everything froze. The world froze with all its elements and creatures. Heaven froze, with the Devas in a state of shock. After a few moments, the Devas began to celebrate as they came out of their daze. Devendran felt justified for not taking the boys too seriously. He went back to merry-making. The earthly beings gave sighs of relief and returned to their normal routines. Everyone returned to their routines except the two brothers, the Asura army, and the exiled Asura community, including Surasi, Asamuki, Sukran, and Sooran's grandparents.

Singan saw this from the closest proximity and burst into tears. Many waves of sad thoughts and emotions ran through him.

"Is this the end, our brother? You were the greatest thing in our lives. You were very important to me. More than our parents and relatives. Even more important than God Himself. What do we do now? I cannot conceive of a life without you. Even if Siva appeared and gave all the boons, what is life without you at the helm of things? For me, life has no meaning without you. So, I will join you in death."

Singan started to fly past the 108 pits like a whirlwind. He was getting ready to run through the pit with his diamond-like body and offer his life in the final circle. There was no need to guess what Thraraka would do. He started doing the same across the 1008 pits in the outer circle. It was like a massive storm of two concentric circles, with the fire blazing in the central giant pit where Sooran's body was burning.

Heaven and Earth froze again, hoping this was the grand finale.

Siva and Sakthi patiently watched this from their abode. They looked at each other momentarily, then became one and appeared at the Velvi site disguised as an old man. Siva shouted, "STOP this nonsense."

Singan and Tharaka sensed a strange feeling running through their bodies and minds. They stopped everything and went toward the old man. The old man asked what they were doing, and they said they were scaring all the creatures in the neighborhood. They recounted the whole story and said they had no life without Sooran. Without Sooran, it was best to offer their lives to Siva and end theirs, too, as their brother did.

Siva then appeared in his form and said he was pleased with the Velvi of all three brothers. He revived Sooran, and the three brothers were restored to their normal, healthy bodies and paid their respects to Siva.

Siva spoke.

"I am touched by your earnest approach and dedication. Ask for what you need. I shall bless you with boons based on what you deserve."

The three brothers were ecstatic. Singan and Tharahan looked at Sooran and asked him to respond.

Sooran then spoke.

"Siva, the ultimate! Today, we feel deeply thankful and relieved. I ask of you four boons."

He then asked for the four boons the Asura guru and Sukran had advised him to seek.

1. "We want to win back the kingdom and that of Deva and rule the whole universe as a single empire.
2. I need a vehicle that can travel at the speed of thought from any point to any point in my empire.
3. I should not be defeated by any force.
4. We want to be eternal."

Siva smiled and agreed to give boons close to what was sought. But that which is born cannot be eternal. It will die one day. Impressed by their offerings, Siva offered the following four boons:

1. "You will rule all 1008 planets in this universe, across Heaven and Earth, for 108 yugas, each lasting many years.
2. I will grant you a vehicle called Indira Jalam. It can travel at the speed of your thought.
3. You will not be defeated by any force except my essence. I will give you all the weapons to meet these needs.
4. You will live very long lives. But my essence will end this if you go against my ways of truth and love.

These are very powerful boons. Use them wisely and for the welfare of the universe."

After giving these extraordinary boons, Siva disappeared and returned to His abode.

ASCENT TO THE PEAK IN ASURA WAYS

Sooran and his brothers hugged each other and celebrated this enormous event. They sang and danced along with the whole army. Everything else in Heaven and Earth felt like the world had ended. All the earthly beings lay in their homes as if they were in a state of coma. The Devas watched this with heavy hearts. The Deva king, Devendran, was in a state of shock.

Sooran was in no mood to drown in indulgence, as much was to be achieved. He ordered his brothers and their army to march toward the exiled Asura community, but news traveled faster. Their mother, grandparents, guru, sister, and the Asura community eagerly awaited their three heroes.

When the brothers reached the Asura community, their mother embraced them. With tears in her eyes, Surasi said, "Sons, you have fulfilled the purpose of my birth and started the journey for which you were born. I am very proud of you. But do not become complacent. Boons are potential at your disposal. They need to be actualized. Rest for a week and celebrate this monumental achievement with us, then go on to fulfill your destiny."

After their celebration and well-deserved rest, Sooran set out to actualize the Glorious Vision given to him by his mother and guru. With a strong army and divine boons, he set out to capture the city of Kuberan, the Deva of Wealth. They ransacked the city and took all its wealth but left Kuberan to rule his place as a colony. They did the same to all the Devas one by one. The final assault was on the King of Deva, Devendran. They attacked his city, Amaravathi. The Devas were helpless against Sooran and his army. Devendran, his wife Indrani, son Jayanthan, and guru Viyazhan, with a small community of Devas, went into exile. Sooran's army ransacked Devendran's city and took all its wealth. The fortunes had completely reversed. The Asuras became the rulers of the universe, and most of the Devas lived in colonies under Asura rule, while some were in exile with King Devendran.

Sooran called for a Deva builder and commissioned him to build cities for him and his brothers that would be worthy of their achievements and superior to what the Devas had. The builder established the most divine city for Sooran in the middle of a vast sea. His palace was built with gold overlay and glittered from dawn to dusk. It had a soft glow in the night with moonlight and light from lamps. It was named Veera Mahendram. "Veera" means brave, while "Maha" stands for grand, and "Indram" has two meanings: eminence or soul. It symbolized the grand and brave soul of the Asrura clan—Sooran.

The builder then established a city for Singan called "Asuram." The word "Asu" means protection. The word "Asuram" is also the first letter in Tamil. Singan's city was positioned as the ultimate defense of Sooran.

Finally, the builder established a city for the youngest brother, Tharahan. Tharahan, his forces, and his city were to be the first line of defense. As any enemy needed to overcome him before even reaching Singan, let alone Sooran, this needed to be fortified as instructed by Tharahan. He and his sister shared many traits with their mother and very few with their father. Tharahan was most meticulous when it came to the use of illusory power.

Let us look back in history for a moment and then come back to how his city was built.

Once there was an Asuran called Kravunja. He had many magical powers and had a strange hobby. He enjoyed misdirecting and confusing all passersby who went through his city. They were lured into a sophisticated, illusory maze, and almost all got lost. Most died out of thirst and starvation, unable to escape the illusory maze. What he enjoyed most was how people gave up.

At first, they became frustrated. Then, they became physically and emotionally tired. Their frustration escalated before their spirits gave up, followed by their minds. Finally, their bodies relinquished the fight to live. They died mental deaths before their physical deaths.

Once, a powerful saint crossed this path, and Kravunja played the same trick. The saint was very evolved and powerful, with many boons from Siva. He realized what was happening, so he cursed Kravunja to become a mountain range. This way, passersby could seek his structure and go around it. But Kravunja retained his magical power inside the tunnels and pathways within the mountain range.

The builder was instructed to build a city along the Kravunja mountain range. The city was called "Mayapuri," which means city of illusion. The three cities were built as concentric circles. In the outer city was Thrahan's Mayapuri and the Kravunja mountain range, while in the middle circle was Singan's city, Asuram. Singan had a very potent army, and he was very formidable, brave, and wise. The innermost city was Sooran's Veera Mahendram. It was built to make Devendran's capital, Amaravathy, look like a humble abode.

Sukran and Surasi's vision was finally actualized. The Asura community was elevated to power and wealth as never before. Devas were subservient or in exile. Life never stood still. It creates, evolves, and then dissolves various aspects. The Asuras had reached the peak of their evolution on the path they took.

After many years, they became complacent, and their founding principles of justice and ethics began to disappear completely.

Asamuki initially indulged in pleasing her brothers by selecting beautiful Deva ladies for their pleasure, but her interest was less about her brothers' pleasures and more about destroying any sense of pride amongst the Devas. When she learned about the defeat of the Asura clan under her grandfather, she vowed to humiliate the Devas once her brothers became the rulers of the universe. So, she set out to accomplish her mission on the side while the brothers ruled the universe.

The brothers married Deva ladies and had children. Sooran married the builder's daughter, Padhuma Komalai, and had a very powerful son called Banugopan. It is said that, even as an infant, he challenged the Sun god ("Banu" means sun, while "Gopan" means the one who got angry). Singan married the daughter of the Deva of Death called Vibuthai. Tharahan married Savuri, the daughter of the Deva of Disorder. These were strategic alliances. The builder's architecture was of utmost importance for the strategic defense of the empire. The alliance with the Gods of Death and Disorder gave the Asuras very strong alliances through marriage. Furthermore, marrying into a Deva family gave the Asuras an edge over Devendran as they could get insider information if a confrontation ever arose. But that felt like an impossibility in the current context, with the Asuras as the masters of the universe and Devendran hiding in exile. It felt like the Asuras were there to rule for eternity.

BEGINNING OF THE END OF ASURA WAYS

Life always has a cycle of creation, evolution, and dissolution of anything manifest, however great or small.

Individuals have two core features. The first is that they take the characteristics of what they identify with. The second is that they tend to augment and preserve their identity. So, the choice of what people identify with is the most important. Hence, "Who am I?" is the most fundamental question.

Asamuki felt unsatisfied with her contribution. The three brothers conquered the universe. What could she do to complete their victory? She decided to go after the Deva queen, Indrani. She thought the victory over Deva would only be complete if Indrani served as an object of pleasure for Sooran. That would not only make her brother feel happy but also deliver the final blow to Deva's pride for generations to come. But finding Indrani in exile was no small task. Asura spies could not succeed in this mission. But Askamuki, being the daughter of Surasi and taught in magical powers by Sukran, was not an ordinary person either. She eventually found where Indrani was hiding. But when she tried to arrest Indrani, Indrani's bodyguard, after repeated warnings, severed Asamuki's hand when she tried to grab Indrani by force.

While an expert in magical powers, Asamuki possessed no divine boons like her brothers. She should have been no match for the Deva guards. But she was no less in mental strength. She knew what should be done to completely subjugate the Devas.

Asamuki barged into Sooran's court. Sooran was engaged in his routine of gathering with his brothers, ministers, and young sons of the three brothers. Seeing Asamuki in tears with her severed hand, Sooran's eyes turned red and looked like a fire about to engulf the universe. Asamuki recounted what happened but emphasized that it was all an attempt to please her brother and ensure the Devas would never rise again. Instead, what she received was a severed hand and a crushed heart. Every council member drew their sword and awaited Sooran's order to imprison all the Devas in exile. There was one exception. Singan was always an independent thinker and preferred to do what was right.

Seeing Singan's sword still sheathed, Sooran asked for an explanation. Singan spoke.

"Brother and my king, we have received great powers from Siva. We have also been great at using them in the way that appeared right to us. But what our sister tried to do is not right. Trying to capture the Deva queen and make her an object of pleasure is wrong. It does not add to our glory. When they were in this position, the Devas did not do that to our grandmother or mother. They let them live in exile. For us to do that is unethical and unnecessary. Our sister was punished for a wrong deed. If we misuse our powers in the wrong path, we will set events in motion that may not be best for us in the end."

Asamuki and Singan debated on this. Sooran, seeing his only sister in tears and that she intended to please him, then spoke.

"My dear brother, even if our sister was wrong, the Devas should have complained to me. A warrior severing an Asura lady's hand cannot go unpunished. Asamuki is not any Asura lady. She is our sister. If an ordinary warrior dares to sever the Asura king's sister's hand, this is not an isolated event. This is a declaration of war, suggesting there is still strong resistance from Deva. Anyone who ignores a spark of flame in his house is ignoring the possibility of having his house burnt to the ground. This is more than a spark of resistance. I agree with you that we should leave Indrani alone. But I order that all of you imprison all the males in the Deva community in exile and severely punish them daily until their spirit is destroyed."

The king had spoken. Singan had to let events run their course. Sooran sent his oldest son, Banugopan, and a powerful army to imprison the Devas. Many Devas who were in exile, along with Devendran's son and heir, Jayanthan, were captured and sent to the harshest Asura prison in Mayapuri, Tharahan's city. They were physically and mentally tortured daily. But Devendran, Indrani, and a few Devas managed to escape. They had sought Siva's protection. Banugopan informed Sooran about the events. Sooran was very pleased with his son's success. He realized that anyone under Siva's protection could not be touched. But he was pleased that Jayathan was captured and that Devendran and Indrani would eventually need to surrender to see their son. At that point, Sooran was happy to close the matter.

Devendran and Indrani started their own Velvi. They prayed to Siva, who appeared before them. He reassured them that he would create a son from his essence and send him to release the Devas and end this matter. But things could only happen at the right time. Devendran and Indrani needed to be patient until then. In the meantime, Devendran and Indrani would be under Siva's protection, so Sooran would not capture them. They humbly accepted Siva's blessings and felt a great relief.

SILENT COMMUNICATION TO THE FOUR SAINTS

Upon returning to his abode, Siva found Four Saints requesting his blessings for their evolution. They were the most evolved and deserving of saints. They wanted to know the ways of actualization. There were four paths:

1. **The Way of Service (Cariyai)** — to use every engagement in the world as a service to Siva and evolve along this path. This is a process of spiritualizing the first fetter (Kanam), i.e., clinging to dualities of deeds and outcomes as ultimate and independent truth.

2. **The Way of Worship (Kiriyai)** — psychological evolution through worship of Siva and the use of that in engagement with the world as an act of worship. This is spiritualizing the second fetter (Mayai), i.e., clinging to the body-mind experience of the world as the ultimate and independent truth.

3. **The Way of Witnessing (Yoham)** — becoming a meditator. In this path, you evolve from being a witness to viewing what is experienced by the body-mind as an expression of Siva. The whole phenomenon of the universe as a whole

(external and mental) becomes like a Dance of Siva (and Sakthi). This brings the realization that the "I" is not a fixed ("I am This") but an evolving process of awareness ("I am That I am"). This state is a transition phase called "I am a Witness," where there are no fixed qualities of mind-body experience. However, you are still on the journey to unite with the Ultimate through the process of evolution.

4. **The Way of Unity** – this one is not about deeds, thoughts, or observations but about living as one with Siva (the Ultimate Self) in every worldly engagement. This is a wholesome living of life as a process of self-actualization, i.e., the notion of "I" as a process of evolving awareness toward union with the Ultimate—Siva-Sakthi. That is, "I" as a relative reality in the process of self-becoming, not independent of the Ultimate Self (Siva-Sakthi).

The first three could be explained and guided with principles, procedures, and guidelines. However, the last path is different and needs to be "seen" with inner eyes. The aspirant needs to be awoken to this path and instilled with sufficient faith. Hence, Siva transmitted this spiritual outlook via silent communication to the four great saints.

This lasted days. The Devas were getting impatient. They approached the God of Love and pleaded with him to get Siva's attention. With much reluctance but feeling sorry for the Devas, he relented. He took his arrow of love and directed it at Siva. When Siva opened his eyes, disturbed from his meditation, with one look, the God of Love burnt to ashes. His wife then pleaded with Siva and explained he was only trying to help the Devas. Siva then revived him. The Devas narrated the whole story and pleaded with Siva to end the Asura rule and restore the Devas to their previous glory. Siva agreed to help them.

Note: This form of Siva is called Thatchina Murthy. It is a symbolic story. In essence, silent communication refers to meditative awareness or intuition about who we are and what our response should be in a given situation. Until there is clarity and conviction in our mind, we should not act from memory or habit, especially in critical moments. Decisive clarity and conviction come as a flash of intuition. Hence, it is silent communication. We will discuss more of this in Chapter 2. It is enough to note that this is a key concept in the process of self-actualization.

BEGINNING OF DIVINE RESPONSE

Siva, from his eye of awareness (the third eye on his forehead, which is normally turned to look inward), created six sparks. They represented his essence, landed on a spiritual pond called Saravana Pond, and became six divine babies. Sakthi then embraced them to form one body with six faces and twelve hands.

Each of the faces represented a core aspect of Siva. The first two represented Siva as pure essence. The other four represented Siva as a process of actualization as follows: The first two represented Verity and Love, i.e., embracing truth and benevolence. The third represented the tendency for self-discovery. The fourth and fifth represented the tendency for self-evolution, the fourth represented the tendency to embrace evolution, and the fifth represented the removal of impediments or fetters to evolution. The sixth face represented a contribution to others for the Self's evolution. Collectively, they represented six facets.

He was named Muruhan. Siva looked at the Devas and said, "Muruhan is formed from Siva's essence. When the time is ready, he will defeat Sooran and restore balance."

The Devas were relieved and returned to their hiding place.

Six celestial stars were assigned to look after Muruhan. Time passed by, and Muruhan evolved into an adult. The time was right.

Siva summoned Muruhan and set out the plan to release the Devas and do what was needed to fulfill his mission.

Sakthi then materialized a weapon using her powers. It was a divine spear named Sakthi Vel, or Vel for short. It had the three powers of Sakthi unified as a weapon—the power to be aware, the power to love, and the power to evolve and execute. The power to be aware showed the truth, the power to love fueled the journey of actualization, and the power to evolve was to actualize the truth shown by the power to be aware.

With Muruhan as the essence of Siva and Vel as the weaponized form of Sakthi's powers, together, they were Siva-Sakthi in union for this mission.

Siva and Sakthi then created an army of soldiers to support Muruhan in his mission. The chief amongst them was called Veeravahu.

WAR: BATTLE BETWEEN THE WAY OF ASURAS AND DIVINE RESPONSE

As a first step, Muruhan, Veeravahu, and their army reached the Kravunja mountain range and Mayapuri of Tharahan. They sent a representative to advise Tharahan in negotiating the release of the Devas or getting ready for war.

The representative advised Tharahan that Muruhan was the son of Siva, formed from his essence. He carried Sakthi's weapon. It would be best for the Asuras to release the imprisoned Devas and preserve what they had gained. Tharahan found this extremely amusing. He thought it was a childish effort from an immature boy. By then, the Asuras had become the undisputed masters of the universe. Tharahan had completely forgotten the conditions and restrictions Siva outlined while giving them the boons. So, he declined and accepted the challenge. He did not think it was worth consulting his brothers. It seemed such a trivial matter that could be crushed in minutes.

The war began. It was intense and lasted for days. Tharahan soon realized this was no childish and immature adventure; it could be the beginning of the end of Asura's glory. But he was not done yet. Muruhan sent Veeravahu to capture Tharahan, who hid in the network of tunnels in the illusory Kravunja mountain. He created a maze of illusion and trapped Veeravahu and his men. They were confused and frustrated and eventually fainted.

Muruhan heard this. He realized that it was time to put an end to things. He directed his mother's gift, Vel, to kill Tharahan and destroy the Kravunja mountain. Vel did so. Before his death, Tharahan called one of his sons, Asurendran (who took the same name as his great-grandfather) and asked him to warn Sooran. His advice on his deathbed was not to take Muruhan lightly: "Release the Devas and save the Asura empire. Muruhan is the essence of Siva. Do not ignore his ability. He is very capable of destroying the Asura empire."

It was not worth the risk. It was better to release the imprisoned Devas and save the empire. Finally, he asked his son to accept his apologies that he could not dedicate a victory nor warn him earlier. But it was not too late to learn from Tharahan's death and save the Asura empire.

In the meantime, Muruhan and his army marched through Mayapuri and established a camp next to Singan's city, Asuram. He sent his representative to Sooran with the same message.

Asurendran, Tharahan's son, also reached Sooran's palace and informed him of all the events and Tharahan's advice. Everyone mourned Tharahan's death. But the threat to the Asura empire was at their doorstep in the form of Muruhan. Sooran called for a war council. Sooran's son, Banugopan, and his cousins laughed at the notion of surrender. They asked Sooran to give them the order to destroy this threat. While the death of their uncle was unfortunate, perhaps he was taken by surprise and did not have the support of the full Asura strength.

Singan called for reflection. He alerted Sooran to the context of Siva's boons. First, Siva had 108 yugas (each yuga consisted of many years) to rule over the universe, and that time was approaching its end. Second, Siva's boon was that they would not be defeated by any other force than Siva's own. Muruhan seemed to be born out of Siva's essence. More importantly, one should not dismiss Tharahan's death so lightly. It needed to be taken as the greatest evidence of the significance of the threat to their collective future. He then advised his brother to send his spies to learn more about Muruhan and his army.

Sooran agreed to take the advice of Singan as the first step and sent everyone back to their posts. He then asked Singan to return to Asuram, his city, and prepare for any eventualities. He then instructed Banugopan, Sooran's son, to mobilize an army under his command.

The spies confirmed the truth about the birth of Muruhan as Siva's essence, who carried a divine weapon gifted by Sakthi, and all the other events that Asurendran (Tharahan's son) recounted.

Sooran called upon Banugopan and asked him to attack Muruhan and his army. Banugopan was only too happy to oblige. He directed his army to strike Muruhan's camp. The war was intense and long. After a few days, Banugopan returned to Sooran and said, "Oh, my king and father, Muruhan is not a child with a youthful and immature mission! He is capable of destroying everything we have. I now see the wisdom of my uncle and your brother on his deathbed. I have faced it in the war over the last few days. Let us end this and save the empire."

Sooran smiled and said, "Son, you probably got frightened after a few days of intense battle. You are the victor over the Devas. We are all behind you when needed. We have boons from Siva. It is not Siva who is here, just his young son. If you are afraid, there is no shame. I will go to war myself. I will not only defeat and forgive him but send him back to his father alive as a token of appreciation for the boons he has given us."

Banugopan looked at his father in disbelief. He then agreed to go back to war. But, first, he made an earnest request. If he, too, died in the battle, at least his father should take this threat seriously and release the Devas. Sooran embraced his son and asked Banugopan to leave the final decision to him and focus on winning the next day's battle.

The battle continued with great intensity. Muruhan ordered Veeravahu to end the battle by killing Banugopan. Veeravahu executed the command. Soaked in blood, powerless against Veeravahu's attack, Banugopan died. But he sent a messenger to his father and king to remind Sooran of Banugopan's last words.

Sooran was heartbroken and deeply angry. He called upon Singan. Singan heard the whole story.

He reiterated his position, saying, "The deaths of Tharahan and Banugopan should have opened our eyes to what we are facing. Let us end hostilities now and save the empire."

Sooran was in no mood for a lecture.

He said, "To give up now means that the mighty Asura empire, with all its power and boons, is surrendering to a child of Siva and releasing the Devas who severed the hand of the king's sister. That is not needed or acceptable. Win the war and end this threat."

Singan, too, realized that no advice would change his brother's mind. He echoed Banugopan.

"Brother, I will go to the battlefield myself. I will not return to you unless I defeat Muruhan or am killed by him. But should I die, will that be the end? I love and revere you. What we have achieved has never before been done. Releasing the Devas is just a small price to pay; do not lose it all. You should live long and pass on our achievements to the next generation."

Sooran hugged his brother and said, "Singa, who can defeat you? I hear what you say, but that is most likely not needed. I will see you when you return victorious."

Singan knew that nothing was going to stop the inevitable end. He just needed to find peace in being there for his brother.

Singan fought furiously. His intensity was many orders of magnitude superior to that of Tharahan or Banugopan. He was like a lion among wild dogs. He destroyed many of Muruhan's army. He then had an intense battle with Veeravahu. Singan was way too powerful for all of them, and Veeravahu fainted and fell to the ground.

Muruhan knew that he was the only one who could stop Singan. So, he battled him, but every time his head or limb was cut, it regenerated immediately. No other weapon could even create a dent in Singan's forceful attack. Determined to put an end to it, Muruhan directed the Vel toward Singan, piercing through his chest. As Singan looked up to the sky, he said his final prayers for his brother's welfare and accepted his end.

The news reached Sooran. His wife pleaded with him to end the war. She said, "Now you need to think as a king. We have already lost our son. You have lost both your brave and mighty brothers. Muruhan cannot be wished away. He will see it through to its end as the essence of Siva with a weapon of Sakthi. But you can save the empire for your subjects. Releasing a few Devas from prison to save the empire is wise. It is never too late to make a wise decision."

Sooran looked at his wife momentarily and said, "Perhaps I should have done that and saved Banugopan, Singamuhan, and countless Asura soldiers. But we are Asuras. We live and die in certain ways. If our ways lead us to death, we should bravely accept it. After losing my son and my brothers, I will not just save myself. After ruling 1008 planes for 108 yugas, what kind of message would that send to our future generations if we surrendered to a child of Siva? I will have to go to the battlefield myself and then decide."

In the meantime, Muruhan revived Veeravahu, who had fainted in the battle against Singan. Then, along with their army, they marched through Singan's city, Asuram, and camped outside Sooran's city of Veera Mahendram.

The battle began the next day. There was a mountain of dead bodies everywhere, and blood flowed like a massive and forceful river. Sooran was at the peak of his power, and no one else could keep up with him. All the Devas who were released from the prisons in Tharahan's city (Mayapuri) and Singan's city (Asuram) joined the war and eagerly watched this final battle. Devendran came out of hiding and witnessed it with a hopeful heart.

After many days of intense battle, Sooran lost all of his weapons. There was nothing more to be done. He realized that he would not be able to defeat Muruhan. There was nothing more to be gained on the battlefield as his army was almost destroyed. All the boons Siva gave were powerless when directed against Muruhan, who was Siva's essence. For the first time, Sooran realized that this war was unwinnable. But he was not in a mindset to surrender and accept defeat.

Instead, his instinct was to use his mother's gift as a last resort. Sooran used the magic spell his mother taught him and disappeared from the battlefield. He took the shape of a mango tree in a forest beside the battlefield. He was not running away but needed time to think. He did not know what else to do and realized his powers were useless in this battle. So, he paused everything, took the form of a tree, and reflected upon Siva.

Transformation: Evolving toward the Ultimate, from the Ashes of the Fettered Self

Muruhan appeared before the mango tree and directed his Vel toward it. The Vel split the tree asunder into two pieces. Muruhan then showed mercy and grace. Through his transformative power, one part of the tree became a rooster, and the other became a peacock.

He instructed the rooster to become his flag, reflecting engagement with Murugan, as well as to become aware of one's true nature and evolve, then spread the good word for the benefit of others. This is one way of self-actualization—the spiritualization of emotions and thoughts through worship of the Ultimate Self. This is one way to progress along self-actualization toward the ultimate: via inner purification. That is, spiritualizing emotional needs and thoughts.

The peacock became Muruhan's vehicle. That is another manner of self-actualization—the spiritualization of deeds and outcomes. That is, worldly engagement is seen in a wider context as a service toward the Ultimate Self.

Muruhan then reinstated the Devas to their former glory. The wave of **V**erity and **E**volution fueled by **L**ove (VEL) spread across the universe.

Note that the title of this book is OM VEL Way. **VEL** is used as an acronym for Verity, Evolution, and Love, i.e., **E**volution of **V**erity (authentic living) fueled by **L**ove. We will discuss "OM" and "Way" in later sections.

(2) KEY TAKEAWAYS AND VISUALIZATION

HIGHLIGHTS

Self-actualization is a process of evolving toward the Self that we truly are, intrinsically and ultimately. This is this book's central subject, and we will progressively look at the details of various aspects of this process throughout this book.

In this chapter, let us look at some of the key characters and what they represent and try to illustrate the key aspects of the story through representations that we can intuitively grasp and recall—invokable representation (Visualisation, Matra).

The characters and the key aspects they represent:

- Siva-Sakthi represents a synthesis of two key aspects of the Ultimate Self: Siva as the ultimate essence and Sakthi as an actualization tendency. Sakthi enables the actualization of Siva in each being. When psychologically free to do so, every being evolves toward its ultimate nature.

    ◦ Siva represents Verity (Truth) and Love.

    ◦ Sakthi Represents the three powers—the power to be aware, the power to love, and the power to evolve. Together, they represent the self-actualization tendency.

- Siva-Sakthi are inseparable and form the most intrinsic and ultimate nature of living beings.

- Sooran and his brothers represent the three fetters that impede our evolution along with self-actualization.

  - Singan represents the Kanmam fetter: the falsehood that actions and outcomes are independent and ultimate truths.

  - Tharahan represents the Mayai fetter: the false notion that the world experienced by the body and mind is an independent and ultimate truth.

  - Sooran represents the Anavam fetter: the notion that "I" is a fixed thing, as based on Kanmam and Mayai.

- Surasi represents ignorance forged with lust and anger. This is the root cause of being a fettered Self.

- Kasiban represents the vulnerability of the Self. Without the courage of conviction, academic learning cannot withstand the ways of ignorance.

- Devas and Asuras represent the two approaches to life.

  - The Way of Asuras is that of self-preservation—to cling to a fixed notion and augment it. To be close to the new experience that carries with it an opportunity to be aware and evolve. But when we hold onto a fixed notion of Self, "I am This," we are not open to experience. Instead, we see what we want to see, distorting everything around us to preserve our definition of Self and augment it.

- The Way of Devas is that of self-actualization. To be open to new experiences and the opportunity for self-discovery that it carries with it. To be open to the experience, live fully in each moment, discover a higher truth, evolve beyond the experience, and engage the next moment as a more evolved being.

- Murugan represents the response of our Ultimate Self, a force of nature that we encounter when we stubbornly cling to and augment the Way of Asuras. Murugan, as the essence of Siva, carrying the weapon gifted by Sakthi (the Divine spear called VEL), represents the ultimate nature that we can progressively embrace in each moment so that we progress toward Siva-Sakthi eternally and ultimately. Vel represents the three powers of Sakthi.

- Murugan, with Vel killing the two brothers (Singan and Tharahan), represents the dispelling or weakening of the two fetters they represent.

- Without the two brothers, Sooran becomes weak and reaches a frozen state, unable to act or think (represented by Sooran taking the shape of a tree).

- Muruhan transforming Sooran into a peacock and rooster symbolizes the beginning of the journey toward self-actualization. They represent two of the initial ways of self-actualization.

  - The peacock represents the Way of Service.

  - The rooster represents the Way of Worship.

Let's look at some of these in more detail along with invokable representations—visualization and mantra.

INVOKABLE REPRESENTATION

As discussed in the Introduction, one must communicate an idea or concept in speeches or proposals to understand it. This way, the details can be discussed and understood. Once we reasonably understand these details, we need to practice them. If we don't, they remain gathered knowledge rather than living awareness. Prose is not that useful at the moment of truth or application. You cannot invoke the knowledge of ten thousand words at the moment of application in the here and now; it needs an invokable form. In various fields of study, across time and geography, people have devised various representations for practice. Some of the most common are as follows:

The idea of these representations is to invoke a state of awareness or being, here and now, of practice and truth. When the practice is repeated regularly, the underlying truth becomes part of one's being (i.e., second nature or a "spiritual seal"). Thus, when encountering a real situation, it becomes reflexive to process and respond to it with a certain state of being.

In this chapter, we will use some of these techniques to obtain an intuitive view of the key concepts described in the Epic and expand on the concepts themselves.

Visualizations

- Siva as the King of Dance performing the Dance of Bliss.
- Siva as Thatchina Murthy in Silent Communication with Four Saints.
- Muruhan, with Vel and Sooran, transformed into the forms of a peacock and rooster.

Mantra:

- The five letters Si-Va-Ya-Na-Ma (panchatcharam) are the five elements of self-actualization. Their sequence represents the dynamic interplay of self-actualization.

It is important first to understand the underlying concepts, then use the invokable devices above for practice and application. Otherwise, they become dry rituals or dogmatic notions. In this book, I am not using them in a religious context but instead for spiritual practice as invokable representations.

THE DANCE OF BLISS: THE ULTIMATE, INTRINSIC, AND ETERNAL NATURE OF THE SELF

The Dance of Bliss is an interplay of five elements.

Self-actualization is represented as Siva's Dance of Bliss. Siva's dancing form, devised during the Chola Empire, is one of his most recognizable forms. It is called "Anantha Kooththu" (also known as "Ananda Nanadam" and "Ananda Thanadavam"), meaning "the dance of bliss." It symbolizes more than a hundred aspects of life. However, for our purposes, we only need to discuss five.

These five aspects are also used in mantra form as five letters: Si-Va-Ya-Na-Ma (Panchatcharam). Their sequence represents four paths to self-actualization.

My focus here is not so much on religious practice but on a spiritual understanding that can be practiced by anyone of any or no faith, similar to using symbols in chemistry, where water is represented by H_2O. Here, however, the practice is not about chemistry or inanimate matters but instead about the lives of human beings. There are even higher aspects of subjective experience related to the individual and their spiritual evolution; it's not an objective science. In other words, we need to see what is useful and pick the methods that help. There is no standard cookie-cutter approach that works for everyone in the field of spiritual evolution.

Let's look at the concepts in mantra form and visual form. The purpose, again, is to get an intuitive sense of the concepts and an understanding of the details presented in prose form throughout this book.

The Mantra **Si-Va-Ya-Na-Ma** represents five aspects of life and their interplay as a universal rhythm of life.

- **Si** – Eminence (Sirappu): Siva is the **Ultimate Essence** of living beings. This is represented by the right side of the dancer. For the onlooker, it will be on the Self-side.

  - **Ultimate Self:** The Self that one truly is and forms the foundation and goal of self-actualization.

- **Va** – Grace (Vanappu): Sakthi is the **self-actualizing Tendency** (transformative power) of living beings. This is represented by the left side of the dancer. For the onlooker, it will be on the right side.

  - **Revealing Grace** – the flow of intuition that reveals the higher truth of our ultimate nature. This is often a progressive revelation of who we are and the truth about our lives as we become receptive (meditative receptivity).

- **Ya** – Evolving Self (Yappu): The flames across the arch represent an **Evolving Awareness** that witnesses both the dance of the universe (worldly experience via body and mind) and the King of Dance (spiritual experiences) within its awareness center (the lotus platform).

- ○ **Self as a Process Evolving Awareness:** A sense of Self that evolves with each experience toward its ultimate nature ("I am That I am").

- **Na – Worldly Experience** (Nadappu) (via body and mind): This is represented by the arch.

  - ○ **Concealing Grace –** the flow of ignorance forced into craving and resentment. This, in the short term, may be useful as a protective shield when we confront an overwhelming occasion. It triggers a way of self-preservation. But in the long run, what may appear as a scaffolding may itself become a prison and impede further evolution.

- **Ma – Fettered Self** (Maraippu): This refers to when the individual Self (Ya) clings to the worldly experience (Na) as the identity of "I," i.e., the body-mind experience is misidentified with the experience (who is a spirit/awareness) as "I am this." This is represented by the hideous demon at the feet of the dancer.

  - ○ **Fettered Self:** When the Self clings to a fixed notion as "I am This," based on the three fetters, the Self increasingly experiences suffering.

Image03: Dance of Bliss by the King of Dance

Image04: Five Aspects of the Dance Si-Va-Ya-Na-Ma

Now, let's look at each aspect in more detail.

The Ultimate Self: Both Intrinsic and Transcendental (Si-Va)

Together, Si-Va represents the Divine Dancer, or King of dance, dancing the Dance of Bliss, which sets a universal rhythm of bliss in motion. It fills the universe with the intrinsic essence but transcends universal experience. In Tamil, God is called "Kadavul," where "Kada" means transcend, and "ul" means intrinsic. Siva-Sakthi is the essence of all living beings and transcends worldly experience.

Image05: 5 Divinity that is intrinsic and permeates everything

Image06: 5 Divinity that transcends everything

"Si," representing Siva, is the potential essence of each being. Siva translates to "auspicious" or "sacred" and represents "Verity" (or the authentic) and "Love." To pursue the path of truth fueled by love is to progress toward Siva.

The ultimate truth is beyond the three fetters:

1. **Kanmam**: The false notion that actions and outcomes are independent and ultimate truths.

2. **Mayai:** The false notion that the world experienced by the body and mind is an independent and ultimate truth.

3. **Anavam:** The notion that "I" is a fixed thing (i.e., an atomization of "I," as in "I am this"), as based on Kanmam and Mayai.

We'll take a closer look at the fetters later in this chapter. Here, the key point is to see "I" as a process (not a product) of evolving awareness, in which the aim is the progressive discovery of the truth about the Ultimate Self (Siva) and our evolution toward it and that this path should be pursued with love. Together, this is referred to as a union with Siva, or self-actualization.

"Va" represents Sakthi. Sakthi is the actualizing tendency that helps individuals realize their ultimate essence in their daily lives (conscious living). Sakthi means power. There are three types of power: (1) the power to be aware, (2) the power to love, and (3) the power to evolve/execute.

If Siva is the potential essence, Sakthi is the dynamic essence. Siva and Sakthi are inseparable. Together, they form the most intrinsic and ultimate essence of every being. This is what is represented by the two letters "Si" and "Va."

When free, every being tends to evolve toward its Ultimate Self. This conclusion has been reached by various leading personalities in different fields of study, including cellular biology, neurology, philosophy, psychology, and spirituality. We will look at these studies in detail in subsequent chapters.

The Individual Self as Evolving Awareness (Ya)

The Self is not body or mind. These are instruments that are available for the Self to experience the world. The Self is the spirit or awareness—that which is aware of the experience and uses the instruments (body and mind). However, the Self is neither the experience nor the instrument itself—in other words, the experiencer should not cling to the experience or the instrument and think, "I am This." Rather, the Self is that which is aware of experience and evolves with it, by reflecting on the experience. In Hinduism, this notion of "I" as an evolving awareness is represented by the word "OM." We will discuss this in further detail in Chapter 6.

Self is represented as evolving awareness by a flame around the arch. The lotus platform at the base represents the awareness center. "I" as a process of evolving awareness is a witness to life as a whole (including body-mind experience) played out within our awareness center. We cannot experience anything outside our awareness (which may be conscious or subconscious). The dance of Siva-Sakthi represents being a witness to our awareness.

Image07: The Individual Self as Awareness

The Fettered Self: Clining to the Worldly Experience

The three brothers each represent a fetter:

- Singan represents the first fetter, Kanmam—to cling to the false notion that dualities of actions and outcomes are the independent and ultimate reality. That is to cling to the deeds and outcomes as who we are (a rigid form of "I am This").

- Tharahan represents the second fetter, Mayai—to cling to the notion that the world as we perceive it through mind and body is an independent and ultimate reality. That is to cling to the outlook and notion of the world as a way of describing who we are (another rigid form of "I am This").

- Sooran represents the third fetter, Anavam—to cling to the false notion that the Self is a fixed profiled and defined in terms of what we experience through body and mind (what we have, who we relate to, and/or what we are recognized as by the world around us). This is the final and dominant form of "I am This", that finitizes/atomizes the sense of Self (which is otherwise boundless) i.e. the three brothers represent the band of three fetters.

Surasi represents ignorance forged in craving and resentment. Her advice led her children down a path that eventually ended in destruction. Wanting to win back the lost kingdom is understandable; however, to be a great leader of the kingdom requires awareness of higher principles for the evolution of both individuals and the kingdom as a whole.

Kasiban's life indicates that learning alone does not automatically lead to evolution; it is only a means of gathering knowledge. What is needed is life experience and the true awareness that arises from it. This will lead to the courage of conviction. By simply gathering knowledge alone, one cannot withstand the onslaught of lust and anger that arise from ignorance; instead, one will succumb to it.

When the Self, due to ignorance of its ultimate nature, clings to the body-mind or its experiences as "the Self," it becomes a fettered Self. This leads to suffering, as worldly experience is ephemeral. If one is defined as a fixed notion ("I am this") in terms of the body-mind or its experiences, one cannot escape life's ups and downs, leading to a life of pleasure and pain. The overall trajectory is toward suffering due to the transitory nature of the world.

Image08: Individual Self as the Fettered Self, clinging to the Wordly Experience

Two Ways – Every Moment Is a Crossroads

Every moment of life is a crossroads. Do we be open and engaged at the moment and evolve with it? Or do we preserve the notion of "I" of the past and cling to this (i.e., closed to the new experience the arising moment brings with it. There is a decision to be made (consciously or subconsciously) about how to respond to the needs of the moment. Any given point passes by, but a series of such moments makes our life what it is. How we evolve from each moment makes us who we are along the way.

1. **Self-evolution** ("I" as a process of evolving awareness, i.e., "I am that I am"): Here, one starts with a view of the Self as a process of evolving awareness, not as a fixed profile of the body and mind or the experiences had through them. One is open to experiences and lives existentially (fully at the moment, "here and now"). One discovers the higher truth about one's nature by being aware of the experience, evolving from that moment, and facing the next as a more evolved Self. Here, "I" is an evolving process of awareness. Each experience is fully utilized as a steppingstone to go beyond it. This leads to a life of bliss, going beyond the pleasure and pain of the body-mind experience as an evolving awareness.

This path is called the Way of Devas in the story, or the path of enlightenment. Key aspects of this process include:

   a. Being open to experience.
   b. Existential living means living totally in the moment and progressively becoming aware of one's ultimate nature.
   c. Evolving toward one's ultimate nature as an evolving awareness so that the next moment is encountered with a more evolved awareness.

OR

2. **Self-preservation** (clinging to the fettered notion of "I am This"): In this approach, one engages in each moment with a predetermined view of "I" as in "I am this"—a fixed profile of the body and mind and/or its experiences. In this case, one is not open to the experiences and new revelations

SWIM (self-actualization)

Image10: Ultimate Essence

+

=

Image11: Self-Actualisation

i.e. I am one with Siva-Sakthi. The world has become a relative reality (based on who I am)

On each occasion, the Self is at a crossroads

Image09: The Individual Self as Awareness

SINK (Self – Preservation, i.e., clinging)

+

Image12: Worldy Experience

=

Image13: The Fettered Self

i.e. I am defined in worldly terms. I have lost the sense of Individual Self and Ultimate Self

the arising moment may provide. Rather, in this approach, one twists their experience to fit and further augment their predetermined view. New insights threatening this fixed notion of the Self are ignored or suppressed. There are no opportunities for transformation in this approach, only the preservation and augmentation of the fixed notion of "I am this." Here, one goes up and down with the pain and pleasures of the body and mind and its experiences.

This path is called the Way of Asura in the story, or the path of bondage. It not only torments the Self in suffering but also others under the Self's influence and control. This process can be visualized as follows:

SIVA AS THATCHINA MURTHY: SILENT COMMUNICATION WITH THE FOUR SAINTS

When the Asuras were tyrannizing the universe and the Devas were awaiting Siva's response, he took his time before meeting with Devas. He was silently imparting wisdom to the four evolved saints. This form of Siva is called Thatchina Murthy.

This silent communication is a symbolic representation of intuition or the grace of revelation. These four evolved beings represent the (1) emotional faculty, (2) intellectual faculty, (3) awareness center, and (4) sense of "I." These are collectively called inner instruments in Hinduism (Andha Karanam).

So, what is intuition? It is (1) the truth about our true nature ("who am I?") and (2) the organism's response to the arising situation ("what should my response be?").

The word "Thatcchinam" in Tamil has many meanings. Three of them include wisdom, right hand, and south. In this context, wisdom is the intuitive awareness (of who we are). The right hand refers to the action (what should my response be). South is symbolic of the manifest world. In Hinduism, it is also the direction of the God of Death (transient manifest). Wisdom here is the intuitive wisdom (silent communication or meditative revelation) that informs what actions are to be taken in each moment in a wider context of who one is (ultimate self). Each action should take us closer to self-actualization while also being an appropriate response to the worldly need 'here and now'. It should be a response of the whole being ("Organismic Response). The worldly context is represented by the "south-facing" postures.

Saint Manikka Vasahar beautifully described this concept. He illustrated it in his work (Thiru Chazhal) through a dialogue between two village girls, who discuss truth through a series of questions and answers.

> **The highly evolved, under the aura of the "sacred YES,"**
>
> **were blessed with the revelation of the four truths, starting with "Essence,"**
>
> **when they were poised. Can you reveal that to me?**
>
> **The highly evolved were blessed with the revelation of the four truths, starting with "Essence." Upon awakening to the true nature of the world, let us sing and celebrate.** [Thiru Chazhal #274]

The four truths are that of the Four Stages of Spiritual Evolution in Hinduism: (1) Essence (aka Aram or Dharma); (2) Application (aka Porul or Artha); (3) Experience (aka Inbam or Kama); (4) Transcending the (body-mind) Experience or Liberation (aka Veedu or Moksha).

The idea is that genuine or organismic response (of the whole being) needs to await the clarity of "who I am" and "What is my response" regarding the arising moment. Silent communication is the intuition that comes with the revelation of truth as a first step in mindful living. Before this clarity, if we act, we act from memory and habit—a machine-like "auto-pilot" response. The choice before us is to be a "living" being or life as a pre-conditioned object in motion.

We do this in our daily lives. Often, we say, "Let me sleep on it," or in a commercial context, we call it a "cooling period." In Chapter 4, we will look at the view of Carl Jung, a leading psychologist. His view is that the unconscious mind makes major decisions in our lives and that the conscious mind often succumbs to the unconscious mind when the stakes are high. The unconscious mind is far superior to the conscious mind in dealing with complex situations when the stakes are high. The unconscious mind communicates to the conscious mind via "intuition. The conscious mind needs to be receptive to the revelation of the flash of intuition coming from the unconscious mind. The conscious mind has four key faculties (- emotions, thoughts, etc. represented by the Four Saints. If the faculties are busy and engaged with the world, they will not be receptive to the unconscious mind. The faculties need to be still and receptive.

Carl Jung, an eminent psychologist, says that what he calls an unconscious mind is psychologically identical to what Hinduism and Buddhism call the universal mind. The techniques of Buddhism and Hinduism (meditation) expand the realm of the conscious mind to be more receptive to the unconscious mind. We discuss this in Chapter 4

The idea here is that what we do subconsciously can be done consciously as a way of Mindful Living. We will cover this in Chapter 5. The role of meditative awareness (or intuition) is crucial.

The Way of Devas is to wait until we get clarity of who we are and our response concerning the arising moment. The Way of Asuras is to act out of the memory of habit. It is a choice between way of self-evolution or self-preservation (clinging to the known).

Image14: Thatchina Murthy and the Silent Communication to the Four

The human figure under Siva's feet is a symbolic representation of the fettered self. It rushes to act based on a fixed notion of "I am This" guided by memory and habit. It is a knee jerk reaction to the rising moment. We will compare the two ways, Mindful Living and Mechanical Living in Chapter 5. The idea of Thatchina Murthy is to lead a Mindful Life – guided by intuitive/meditative awareness informing our other mental faculties.

HERE AND NOW:
THE FOUR-FOLD PATH

The life of the body-mind is transient. As Buddha pointed out, life is suffering due to the inevitable nature of sickness, aging, and death. Adding to this suffering is the transient nature of wealth, relationships, and fame. If one clings to these, one experiences pleasure and pain caused by the ephemeral nature of the body-mind and its experiences. Happiness in each stage is, at best, pain relief or temporary pleasure.

Through the ages, people have pursued the path of bliss, the idea that one can be happy, regardless of body-mind well-being or the dual experiences accompanying it.

A common phrase aptly describes life: "The way out is through." Any form of denial or escapism regarding where one is will not help; it will only further delay evolution. The only way out is to use every experience to evolve one's awareness of one's true nature and the nature of life. When one evolves from each experience, one goes beyond that experience. This process of evolving toward one's ultimate nature is self-actualization. The resulting experience is bliss. It depends not on what happens to us but on how we evolve from it. We will look at these concepts in further detail in later chapters.

As mentioned above, the three fetters are represented by the three brothers, and their root cause is ignorance forged in lust and anger, as represented by their mother, Surasi. Vel, the divine spear, represents the three powers of Sakthi: the power to be aware, the power to love, and the power to execute/evolve. Together, these are known as the tendency for self-actualization.

When the Vel was directed toward Tharahan and Singan, it killed them. One must go beyond the first two fetters: the false notion that dualities related to deeds and outcomes are independent and ultimate realities and the false view that the body-mind worldly experience is an independent and ultimate truth. Individuals need to see that their truth is relative to who they are at a given point in time. When one evolves, one must go beyond body-mind experience and recognize they are relative truths.

When the brothers were killed, Sooran became a tree. In other words, when the first two fetters are overcome, the Self is ripe for transformation, even if it holds the third fetter. It can no longer function in its previously fettered ways. Thus, when the Vel was directed toward Sooran, he was not killed when he became a tree (a frozen state, unable to act). Instead, he was transformed into a peacock and a rooster. The peacock represents the body, and the rooster the mind. From being fettered as an astonished Self, the Self is transformed. Muruhan, as the essence of Siva, represents ultimate potential.

The peacock, rooster, Vel, and Muruhan all represent the Four-Fold Path toward self-actualization:

1. **The Way of Service**, in which we spiritualize our physical and physiological engagement with the world within the wider context of self-actualization. This is the way of the peacock—to be the vehicle of action. This path is called "Cariyai" or Service.

2. **The Way of Worship**, wherein we spiritualize our emotional and intellectual activity within the wider context of self-actualization. This is the way of the rooster—to praise the lord as a way of self-purification and to spread the glories of this path. This is called "Kiriyai" or Worship.

3. **The Way of Witnessing**, wherein we witness life as the unfolding of the Self and evolve from the intuitive revelation of the truth. This is when one has evolved after following the way of the rooster and is looking beyond the emotional and intellectual realm toward the meditative or intuitive revelation of the truth. This path is called "Yoham" or Toward Unity.

4. **The Way of Unity**, in which our Self, Ultimate Self, and life are united in every moment—the here and now, and throughout our lives—eternally and ultimately. At this stage, the peacock, rooster, Vel, and Muruhan become a unified

process in the here and now, eternally and ultimately—in other words, they represent life as an evolving process. This path is called "Njanam," or Wholesome Awareness (Living in Union).

Siva-Sakthi's Dance of Bliss represents the eternal and ultimate process. Muruhan's war with the Asuras and the transformation of Sooran is an opportunity to be in the "here and now." Muruhan, as that which arose from Siva's essence and carries Sakthi's power in the form of the Vel, represents the potential of self-actualization in the moment of engagement. Serving Muruhan in every moment, here and now, is the same as serving Siva-Sakthi eternally and ultimately. This is similar to the biblical notion that the path to Our Father in Heaven is walked by serving Jesus, the Son of God.

We serve the Ultimate and Eternal through every arising moment, "here and now." The heart of self-actualization is comprised of existential and authentic living in every moment, and progressive enlightenment through meditating on this experience, and it allows the Self to evolve as awareness.

Thus, the essence of the story is that the Self is the process of self-becoming, here and now, eternally and ultimately. We will look at this in more detail in subsequent chapters.

Image15: Muruhan with Vel, Peacock, Rooster, and OM in the background

(3) SINK OR SWIM ACROSS THE VAST SEA OF LIFE

"Those who unite with the ultimate swim across
the vast sea of life; others sink." [TK10]

OVERVIEW

Life is like a vast sea with numerous waves of various goals, needs, and experiences. They arise as needs, we respond as expressions (thoughts, words, and deeds), and they culminate as experiences, only to rise again as new needs. This process is also called the birth cycle of the spirit. Each arising is a mini spiritual birth and goes through a full cycle. With their permutations and combinations, these arisings are numerous, like the waves of the sea.

Collectively, the path we take, by design or driven by circumstance, is the flow of our lives. Our awareness of this experience determines the content of our lives and how we evolve. Awareness includes that of the past, present, or future—our recollections of the past, awareness of the experiences of the present, and or anticipation of the future. The more we are aware of it, that is, the more we act mindfully, the richer and more wholesome our lives can be.

We cannot control what happens to us; it is not the primary factor determining our lives. The things that happen to us create occasions, but how we perceive, respond, experience, and subsequently evolve makes us who we are and makes our life what it is.

This Chapter deals with the following topics:

- **The Hierarchy of Needs:** Outlined by an eminent psychologist, Abraham Maslow, provides an overview of five categories of needs. They are organized in terms of a hierarchy, whereas lower needs are met, we become aware and pursue higher needs.

- **Sheaths of Experience (Kosha):** Outlined in an ancient Hindu Text (Taittiriya Upanishad). These are categories of experience a spirit goes through (Gross to Subtle) along its path to Bliss.

- **Happiness** – revisited in the context of the above two items.

- **Sink** – the process that leads to suffering.

- **Swim** – the process that leads to happiness.

THE HIERARCHY OF NEEDS

Goals and needs are innumerable. Their combination with environmental events and the resulting experiences can create infinite combinations. But for them to be useful, we need to be able to categorize them based on some core principles and understand their interplay.

Fortunately, a leading psychologist, Abraham Maslow, did just that. He used key goals as core principles and outlined a set of categories of needs. He then organized these categories as a hierarchy based on what he called pre-potency, gratification, and the evolution of needs.

- **The integrated wholeness of the organism** is one of the foundations of motivation theory. Classifications of motivations are based on goals rather than on instigating/ triggering events or motivated responses/behaviors.

- **Category:** Maslow categorized human needs into five categories: (1) physiological, (2) safety, (3) love and belonging, (4) esteem/legacy, and (5) self-actualization.

- **Pre-potency:** In Maslow's view, human needs can be arranged as a hierarchy of pre-potency; in other words, the arising of one need usually rests on the prior satisfaction of another, more pre-potent need. Lower needs are felt as urgent, finite, and necessary, while higher needs are more long-term needs—they are eternal, not-defined (infinite), and a possibility.

- **Gratification:** No need or drive can be treated as isolated or discrete. Every drive is related to the state of satisfaction or dissatisfaction with other drives. Maslow describes humans as perpetually wanting animals. As such, there is a natural flow of evolution through the hierarchy of needs.

- **Deficiency and Growth needs:**

  - Four lower needs are also called deficiency needs. These needs are deficiencies concerning the world or someone outside of the Self. As an individual satisfies them, the urge to satisfy more reduces.

  - The last need, the need for self-actualization, is called the "growth need." Here, the more the needs are met, the higher the motivation to pursue even more.

- **Quality and Scale:**

  - Higher needs provide deeper satisfaction (quality). They also last longer (scale – in terms of time) and impact more people (scale – in terms of scope).

○ Progress in self-actualization provides higher quality and longevity.

○ Self-actualization, the highest need, leads to the highest quality and longevity of happiness.

	Hierarchy of Needs (Abraham Maslow)	Expressions (Thoughts, Words, and Deeds)
Deficiency Needs	**Physiological:** These needs are biological requirements for human survival, for example, air, food, water, shelter, clothing, warmth, sex, and sleep.	• Physical and physiological expressions • An overlay of emotional and intellectual expressions
	Safety: People want to experience order, predictability, and control in their lives.	
	Belongingness and love: Belongingness refers to the human emotional need for interpersonal relationships, affiliation, connectedness, and being part of a group.	• Emotional expressions • An overlay of intellectual expressions
	Esteem: This need includes self-worth, accomplishment, and respect. Maslow classified esteem needs into two categories: (i) esteem for oneself (dignity, achievement, mastery, independence), and (ii) the desire for reputation or respect from others (e.g., status, prestige).	• Intellectual expressions • Physical, physiological, and emotional expressions are subservient
Growth Need	**Self-actualization:** This need refers to the realization of a person's potential, self-fulfilment, seeking personal growth, and peak experiences.	• Meditation - witnessing all other arising, evolving, and dissolving needs and expressions. • Physical, physiological, emotional, and intellectual expressions are in a still state
		• Organismic response, i.e., the expression of the Ultimate Self • All other expressions as subservient to this

In a hierarchy of needs, self-actualization is an ultimate and intrinsic need. Eminent neurologist and psychologist Kurt Goldstein first coined the term "self-actualization." He claimed that while there are many needs, as the most intrinsic and ultimate need, self-actualization is the only drive behind all the others. We will look at different views of self-actualization in Chapter 4.

SHEATHS OF EXPERIENCE

Long before Maslow outlined his theory of the hierarchy of needs, the *Taittiriya Upanishad* laid out a set of concentric sheaths of experience (Kosha). These sheaths of experience correspond to the hierarchy of needs; combined, they paint a more holistic picture of needs and experience. Maslow organized his hierarchy of needs based on goals; the *Taittiriya Upanishad* articulates the realm of experience as sheaths in pursuing the corresponding needs.

	Hierarchy of Needs (Abraham Maslow)	Expressions (Thoughts, Words, and Deeds)		Experience (Taittiriya Upanishad)
Deficiency Needs	**Physiological:** These needs are biological requirements for human survival, for example, air, food, water, shelter, clothing, warmth, sex, and sleep.	• Physical and physiological expressions • An overlay of emotional and intellectual expressions	**Fettered Life (Suffering)**	• Physical/ physiological sheath (Annamaya Kosha) • Experiences of the senses and body and its well-being
	Safety: People want to experience order, predictability, and control in their lives.			• Vital sheath (Pranamaya Kosha) • Experience in physical and physiological health and well-being
	Belongingness and love: Belongingness refers to a human emotional need for interpersonal relationships, affiliation, connectedness, and being part of a group.	• Emotional expressions • An overlay of intellectual expressions		• Emotional sheath (Manomaya Kosha) • Emotional well-being (or lack of it)
	Esteem: This need includes self-worth, accomplishment, and respect. Maslow classified esteem needs into two categories: (i) esteem for oneself (dignity, achievement, mastery, independence) and (ii) the desire for reputation or respect from others (e.g., status, prestige).	• Intellectual expressions • Physical, physiological, and emotional expressions are subservient		• Intellectual sheath (Vinjanamaya Kosha) • Intellectual well-being

Growth Need	Self-actualization: This need refers to the realization of a person's potential, self-fulfilment, seeking personal growth, and peak experiences.	• Meditation - witnessing all other arising, evolving, and dissolving needs and expressions. • Physical, physiological, emotional, and intellectual expressions are in a still state	Liberated/Transcendental Life	• Bliss sheath (Ananda Maya Kosha) as a liberated feeling (transcending the constraints of the world) • A natural state of happiness – uncausedhappiness
		• Organismic response, i.e., the expression of the Ultimate Self • All other expressions as subservient to this		• Experience of the Self in union with the Ultimate Self • Harmony or tranquillity (Santham) • Sacredness or sense of auspiciousness (Sivam) • Oneness (Advaitam) with the ultimate • (source: Mandukya Upanishad)

In its concluding remarks, the *Taittiriya Upanishad* states that fear drives our lives to the extent that we see ourselves as separate from that of the Ultimate. However, as we unite with the Ultimate Self (i.e., self-actualization), fear becomes less and less potent. Experiencing bliss helps us overcome fear by developing faith and courage of conviction.

- Self steps into each sheath of experience and, ultimately, into the sheath of bliss.

- If one finds a home (a resting place) in that Self (atman), which is invisible, indescribable, self-supported, and fearless, he attains fearlessness. But if one ever feels even the slightest apartness from it (the Self or atman), then fear arises in him.

- **He who is aware of the bliss of the ultimate does not fear other things.**

In a natural flow of evolution, human beings evolve from a lower form of experience to a higher form, initially driven by fear; over time, with the experience of bliss, they overcome fears and become self-driven. These are not all-or-nothing stages or rigid sequences. Anyone could experience a moment of bliss, even if much of their time is spent in the physical/physiological experience. But what makes life is what sheath of experience one is mostly in, and awareness of that experience can evolve an individual as a conscious Self.

HAPPINESS

Happiness can be categorized as **Ease, Peace, and Bliss**. The measure of happiness is in terms of quality and scale.

- Quality refers to the richness/intensity of the experience. As we evolve through the hierarchy of needs, the quality of happiness increases.
- Scale refers to longevity and scope. As we evolve through the hierarchy of needs, the scale of happiness increases.

Ease

Ease is an experience based on the correlation between our needs related to the external world and our ability to meet those needs. If most of the world's needs can be met by what we have or can obtain, then our daily life is hassle-free and goes smoothly from when we wake up to when we go to bed. This experience can range from reducing struggle in the world (pain relief) to happiness in the world (pleasure).

In terms of Maslow's hierarchy, this can range across the first four types of needs, from Physiological to Esteem. But the **emphasis is on effectiveness when we meet the world's demands**. The ability to have ease in our lives is called **competence**. It is the extent of our ability to meet worldly demands more effectively. The measure is mostly about the scale (longevity and scope).

Ease is a deficient experience in that the more we have, the less drive we have to keep having more. It is a relief from pain or transient pleasure. The quality of experience is lower compared to other categories of happiness. While ease seems like a well-defined and urgent need, it lasts the least amount of time. It is the most transient experience in terms of longevity. Once one is satisfied with the basic threshold, there are diminishing returns of happiness, making it a deficiency need. One may become habitually addicted or cling to ease. However, that would be to stay in the same state and not be motivated or driven to evolve. It is abnormal and pathological rather than natural and healthy. The more ease one has, the less one needs to consider meeting one's physiological or safety needs. We will discuss this more later.

These experiences are like journeys in shallow waters. They do not address deeper needs.

Peace

Peace, or internal joy, reflects the correlation between our expressions (words, thoughts, and deeds) and what we think of as internal measures (ethics, morals, our definition of success, etc.); for example, "I am a good parent, child, sibling, friend, etc.," or "I am a famous scientist." This has more to do with whether our expressions (deeds, words, thoughts) align with our inner standards. The experience ranges from momentary peace to sustained peace for a longer period.

In terms of Maslow's hierarchy, this can range across the first four types of needs, from Physiological to Esteem. But the **emphasis is on how we meet the world's demands compared to what we think is right.** The ability to have peace in our lives is called **character. The higher the character, the more we can be at peace.** The strength of our character is our emotional and intellectual well-being. By peace, I mean the experience that ranges from a reduction in guilt and disappointment to emotional and intellectual joy; in other words, this experience ranges from pain relief through reduced guilt to the experience of inner joy, both emotionally and intellectually.

With peace, the quality of experience is higher than in the first category—ease. It also lasts longer. But this, too, is a deficient need. Once one is satisfied with the basic threshold, there is a diminishing return on happiness. The more one has, the less one is driven to meet the belonging, love, and esteem needs.

These experiences are like undercurrents. They are deeper than source level or shallow waters but do not address the deepest needs such as, "Who am I?" and "What is the purpose of my life?"

Bliss

Bliss is a type of happiness based on how we evolve compared to our Ultimate Self. It is about progress in our ultimate nature. This refers to the questions of who we are and whether we are leading meaningful lives in the context of who we are. It is about discovering who we are and leading a meaningful life in that context.

In terms of Maslow's hierarchy, this form of happiness primarily deals with the highest need—self-actualization.

But the **emphasis is on who we are and how meaningful our lives are in that context.** The ability to have peace in our lives is called **clarity of awareness**. The higher the awareness and the evolution aligned to it, the more we can experience bliss. This is related to our spiritual well-being.

This form of happiness is the highest in terms of quality and scale. As Upanishads states, "He who is aware of the bliss of the ultimate does not fear other things", enabling the Self to progress along the path of self-actualization.

Increasing Quality and Scale of Happiness

Everything we do is to increase the quality and scale of happiness. Increasing quality means progressively experiencing richer and more intense happiness. Increasing scale means progressively experiencing happiness that lasts longer and/or across more situations, people, those we care for, etc.

In the ultimate analysis, the most intrinsic and ultimate form of happiness results as we progress along the journey of self-actualization—to progressively be the Self we truly are. Therefore, the highest gift we can give another is to contribute toward their self-actualization process.

In short, ultimately, we increase the quality and scale of Bliss by progressing along self-actualization. A sense of Ease and Peace clears the path as we progress to experience Bliss in our lives. Bliss is also underlying happiness that we become more and more conscious of. As such, it is both the most intrinsic and ultimate form of happiness. Each of us needs to arrive at our truth through the experiences of our lives and evolving awareness.

SINK

This is the Way of Asuras, as described in the Epic (Chapter 1). By exclusively focusing on lower forms of happiness (and needs), we progressively lose our ability and opportunity to meet higher needs and experience higher forms of happiness. Let us look at this in more detail.

We will sink if our lives are about meeting the expectations of others or some moral standard but lose our chance to become aware of who we truly are and lead a meaningful life based on that – if we exclusively focus on the body-mind well-being and ignore our well-being as a spirit.

So, how do we do this? The root cause is ignorance forged by lust and anger, making us cling to the body-mind experience.

In Buddhism, the "two-truth doctrine" is a crucial aspect of spiritual practice. Nagarjuna, considered to be the second coming of

Buddha, outlines it as follows:

- The Buddha's teaching of the Dharma is based on two truths: a truth of worldly convention (relative truth regarding our day-to-day living, based on our state of being at that moment and context of our environment) and ultimate truth (truth that is eternal and universal).
- Those who do not understand the distinction between these two truths do not understand the Buddha's profound truth (i.e., Buddha's teaching).
- Without a foundation in conventional truth, the significance of the ultimate cannot be taught. Without understanding the significance of the ultimate, liberation is not achieved.

The idea of evolution is not to deny the needs and experiences of the body-mind; that is just being disingenuous and living in deprivation rather than in an evolving state. You would simply be putting on the appearance of an evolved state. On the other hand, clinging to the body-mind experience leads to a fettered Self and impedes evolution. The middle path (or, as I prefer to call it, the "higher path") is a synthesis. Relative truths are needed for us to deal with day-to-day life. This is based on our state of being and the needs of the occasion/environment. The issue is when we exclusively focus on that and ignore the need to discover who we are and evolve toward our ultimate and intrinsic nature progressively. One does not cling to this truth while living day-to-day truth to meet worldly routines. As one evolves with awareness of the ultimate truth, one progressively elevates "relative truth," leading to a progressive transformation of day-to-day living. In a spiritual sense, ignorance is to cling to relative truth as the ultimate truth. In so doing, the Self becomes fettered (based on the three fetters described above).

How does this process work? In Buddhism, it is called the series of stages of dependent arising, that is, how ignorance leads to a life of suffering. This concept of dependent arising (Pratītyasamutpāda) is one of the cardinal concepts in Buddhism. It has been comprehensively described across twelve links or binds (nidanas). Let's look at a few of them:

- Ignorance (#1), through various links, results in distorting the experience of the world via the body-mind (#7).
- This, in turn, leads to clinging (#9), which then distorts the process of becoming (#10) and leads to a fettered being (#11).
- That, in turn, leads to suffering (#12).

Now, let's discuss this in plain English and common experience. To the extent that we are ignorant of our true nature, we develop a fixed notion of who we are: "I am this." This subsequently distorts the body-mind experience of the world; in other words, we distort what we experience to fit our definition of who we are. When we come across an experience that challenges our current notion of who we are, we suppress it or use a psychological defensive mechanism (denial, etc.). Instead, we use every experience to strengthen and augment a predetermined view of the Self by distorting how we see, process, and respond. The sense of craving and resentment toward body-mind experience further sustains and augments this process. This is called self-preservation mode, where the focus is to preserve a fixed notion of "I" ("I am This") rather than evolve with experience (as "I am That I am").

However, the body, mind, and experiences we encounter are transient. Holding onto something transient as a part of "who we are" leads to suffering. As Buddha pointed out, at the physical and physiological level, the body will go through sickness, old age, and death. Wealth is also transient. Clinging to these events and states by thinking, "I am this," will lead to inevitable suffering. The mind, as well as its experience, evolves. To hold onto relationships and legacy by believing "I am this" will also lead to suffering. The idea is not to run away, deny, or lead a life of deprivation. Instead, it is to experience things fully and evolve with experiential awareness to go beyond the body-mind experience at a given point in time.

1 Ignorance (Avidya)

Ignorance of nature of (true) Self, world, and life

2 (Faulty) Cognitive Constructs (Samskara)

Ignorance leads to faulty thought constructions about reality

3 (Faulty) Understanding (Vijnana)

Faulting cognitive constructs lead to faulty understanding

4 (Distorted and Rigig Notions of) Name and Form (Nama-Rupa)

Distorted understanding leads to distorted mental associations (names) and physical associations (forms) with the world

5 (Faulty Conditioning of) The Six Instruments (Ayatana)

This, in turn, leads to the incorrect conditioning of the five senses and mind, i.e., what to expect in the next encounter

6 (Wrongly Conditioned) Contact with the world (Sparsha)

This, in turn, leads to conditioned contact with the world

7 (Distorted) Experience arising from Contact (Vedana)

Leads to conditioned experience

8 Thirst (Tanha) for more

Gives rise to thirsting for what has been pleasant (which is already distorted)

9 Clinging (Upadana)

Clinging to what is experienced as a sense of "I"

10 (Distorted) The Process of Becoming (Bhava)

Distorts the process of Self-becoming, i.e., distorts Self discovery and self-actualization

11 (Fettered) Arising (Jati)

Distort every new arising of Self with subsequent experience

12 Suffering (Jaramaranam)

This will keep us trapped in suffering in the transient nature of the world (death, sickness, old age, etc.)

SWIM

This is the Way of Devas referred to in the Epic (Chapter 1). Swimming is about primarily focusing on self-actualization and experiencing increased quality and scale of happiness (Bliss).

What, then, is it to swim? The root cause for the path of "sinking" is ignorance. The antidote for this is awareness: to identify with

"I" as a process of evolving awareness ("I am that I am") and to progress along self-actualization (i.e., progressing toward the Ultimate Self). But this awareness is not about book-knowledge; it is gained through meditating on our experience.

So, how do we go about this? The twelve Sutras of Sinvajnana Potham eloquently outlines it. Below is my interpretation of the *Sivajnana Podham*, a core work with 12 steps. It describes self-actualization as follows:

An Intuitive Hypothesis - Overview

Twelve Sutras collectively outline the process of self-actualization. They are categorized into four parts, each with three Sutras as follows:

1. **Truth:** Three cardinal truths about the Self and their interplay
2. **Nature of the Self:** Nature of the Evolving Self
3. **Process of Evolution:** The Process of evolution (self-actualization)
4. **Outcomes:** Verity, Evolution, and Love (VEL)

(I) **Three cardinal truths about the Self and their interplay** • Fettered Self • Evolving Self • Ultimate Self	1	• **He, she, and it** (the Self as an evolving synthesis of the Divine, His Grace, and individuality) • (The Self) **becomes fettered in the three-pronged flow of actions - arising, evolving, and dissolving** • **The destination and source** (of the evolving Self) **are the same, say the wise**
	2	• **They** (he, she, it) **together are the** (evolving) **Self** • **Performing dual deeds that come and go** (as arising, evolving, dissolving) **according to the inseparable dictate** (of self-actualization as the most intrinsic drive)
	3	• **In saying it is and it is not, in saying this is my body** (it is my body, but not I am not my body) • **In being aware of stilling the five senses in** (deep) **sleep** (i.e., meditation), **where there is neither experience nor action** (only awareness of both as a witness) • **In being aware when awoken** (spiritual awakening) **in the illusory machine-like body, there is Self** (as underlying and evolving awareness across all the above)
(II) **Nature of the Evolving Self** as evolving states of awareness (OM) • Essence of Self (Sat, Chit)	4	• **(The) Self is not its inner instrument, which takes part along the way** (through mental experience) • **The fettered Self does not realize** (this distinction between the instrument and its user) • (The Self) **like the king, along with his ministry, evolves through the five states of awareness** (OM)
	5	• **In the same way that it is the mind that reveals the experience of the senses, which the senses themselves don't interpret or are not aware of** (they are just instruments), • **Self is enlightened by His revealing grace, which attracts the Self like a magnet** (toward the Ultimate Self)
	6	• **What can be experienced is manifest, and what is not experienced is unmanifest** • **Separate from these two is Siva Essence** (the Ultimate Self), **with its two attributes** (Sat and Cit) • **Unifies the world** (that we experience - the manifest and the unmanifest)

(III) **Process of** **evolution** **(The Way)** • They way – represented by the five letters ("Si," "Va," "Ya," "Na," and "Ma" (Panchatcharam)	7	• **Everything is empty before Sat** (the manifest has no independent truth outside the ultimate truth) • **Manifest (Asat) cannot know by itself** (is not capable of awareness) • **The** (evolving) **Self, which is neither, can become aware of both**
	8	• **When the senses are in a tranquil state** • **When one's ultimate (Self) becomes one's guru and awakens** (the Self) **in the process of evolution** (as a revealing Grace of Intuition) • **As the separation disappears, they unite**
	9	• **One cannot be aware of the Ultimate Self through the senses of the manifest** (the body and mind) • **Instead** (the evolving) **Self seeks** (the Ultimate Self) **via the eye of awareness** (meditative intuition) • **As the Self becomes aware of the ghostlike nature** (illusory) **of fetters, it transcends them** • **Embraces the way of five letters** (Si-Va-Na-Ma) **toward the cool shade of the Ultimate**
(IV) **Outcomes (VEL)** • Verity (V) • Evolution (E) • Love (L) Leading to an increase in happiness	10	• **In the path of "I am becoming Him," becoming a unity and acting in His Service without delusion, atomization of Self, and dualities of deeds** (i.e., the three fetters)
	11	• **In the same way, the mind interprets what the eyes perceive** • **It is the awareness that understands what the mind perceives** (the Self) **with relentless love evolves toward His feet** (self-actualization)
	12	• **Removing those fetters, that which impedes the evolution toward His lotus feet** • **Becoming one of the Beloved, with His Compassion and Grace** (of revelation) • **As darkness gets dispelled** (the Self, propelled) **with love, one becomes wholesome, worshipping the** (union of) **the temple** (circumstances), **the Self** (evolving awareness) **as one with the divine** (i.e., embracing life as a process of self-actualization)

Let us look at each section in more detail across the four parts.

(I) Three Cardinal Truths [#1 to #3]

- Fettered Self
- Evolving Self
- Ultimate Self

The first three Sutras outline the cardinal truth about oneself and life and their interplay.

1	• **He, she, and it** (the Self as an evolving synthesis of the Divine, His Grace, and individuality) • (The Self) **becomes fettered in the three-pronged flow of actions - arising, evolving, and dissolving** • **The destination and source (**of the evolving Self) **are the same, say the wise**
2	• **They** (he, she, it) **together are the** (evolving) **Self** • **Performing dual deeds that come and go** (as arising, evolving, dissolving) **according to the inseparable dictate** (of self-actualization as the most intrinsic drive)
3	• **In saying it is and it is not, in saying this is my body** (it is my body, but not I am not my body) • **In being aware of stilling the five senses in** (deep) **sleep** (i.e., meditation), **where there is neither experience nor action** (only awareness of both as a witness) • **In being aware when awoken** (spiritual awakening) **in the illusory machine-like body, there is Self** (as underlying and evolving awareness across all the above)

Highlights

- The Self is a process of evolving awareness toward the Ultimate Self ("He" or "Siva," the ultimate essence), with an inherent actualization drive ("She" or "Sakthi," the power of actualization). With the sense of "I am," the Self takes the nature of whatever it identifies with. (#1)

- As the Self participates in the universal process of creation, evolution, and dissolution, it clings to worldly experience.

This identification leads to an outlook of "I am this," a fixed product defined in worldly terms. In preserving and augmenting this notion, the Self is fettered to experience. As it is not its true or ultimate nature, this outlook impedes the evolution of the Self. (#1)

- Nevertheless, self-actualization is an intrinsic and inseparable drive that progressively steers the Self toward its true and ultimate nature. When the Self becomes aware of its true nature, after the painful experience of living, it lets go of the notion of "I am this." (#1)

- The true nature of the Self is its original nature in the first place; that is, the *destination* and *source* of the Self are the same. What came along in the journey was the experience of the physical and mental worlds with body and mind as instruments. (#1)

- The self-responds to worldly and psychological needs based on its nature and environment but the deeds and outcomes come and go. What is inseparable is the underlying need for self-actualization (#2).

- In this process, the Self begins to realize that it is not the body or the experience of this body. As it meditates on its experience by stilling the senses, the Self can stand apart from actions and their resulting experiences as a witness. It realizes that physical and physiological experiences are not an independent and ultimate reality. It is relative to who we are at a given point in time. (#3)

- Meditation prepares the Self to be more receptive to revealing intuitions as part of self-discovery. The Self realizes that it is a process of awareness that underlies all its actions and experiences and that the body and mind are only instruments. (#3)

- The Self recognizes that it is a process of evolving awareness. It is not a fixed product in terms of its physical, physiological, and psychological experiences (i.e., it does not have a fixed profile). It evolves from the notion of "I am this" through its initial clinging to its experiences, then learns to let go and evolves through the process of self-actualization with a new identification: "I am that I am." In other words, "I" is an evolving awareness (spirit) that underlies all physical, physiological, emotional, and intellectual experiences. (#3)

(II) Nature of Self [#4 to #6]

- Self as evolving states awareness (OM)
- Essence of Self (Sat, Chit)

Sutras #4 to #6 outline nature and describe the Self as states of awareness (aka OM). Self is something beyond body-mind and experience. Instead, it is that which is aware of the body-mind experience. The sutras refer to the two attributes that define the Ultimate Self (Sat - essence, which is a synthesis of Verity and Love, and Cit – actualizing tendency, i.e., Evolution).

4	• **(The) Self is not its inner instrument, which takes part along the way** (through mental experience) • **The fettered Self does not realize** (this distinction between the instrument and its user) • (The Self) **like the king, along with his ministry, evolves through the five states of awareness** (OM)
5	• **In the same way that it is the mind that reveals the experience of the senses, which the senses themselves don't interpret or are not aware of** (they are just instruments), • **Self is enlightened by His revealing grace, which attracts the Self like a magnet** (toward the Ultimate Self)
6	• **What can be experienced is manifest, and what is not experienced is unmanifest** • **Separate from these two is Siva Essence** (the Ultimate Self), **with its two attributes** (Sat and Cit) • **Unifies the world** (that we experience - the manifest and the unmanifest)

Highlights

Self as a state of awareness (OM)

- The Self is not the mind, either. The mind is also an instrument we use for the mental experience of emotion, intellect, and memory. (#4)

- As is the case with the body, the Self clings to the experiences of the mind by thinking, "I am this." However, by the same process of self-discovery via meditation, it realizes that the mind is an instrument at its disposal; it finds that "I am not my mind" but an underlying process of evolving awareness, like a king who becomes aware through the counsel of his ministers.

- "I am" is an evolving process of awareness that goes through five states that are collectively called "OM" (or "AUM"). We will discuss more of this in Chapter 6. (#4)

- There is a hierarchy of capabilities. The body can sense physical changes, but the mind (i.e., our emotions and intellect) interprets this sensation. But what interprets the experience of the mind? It comes in the form of revealing intuition as an "aha" moment. (#5)

- Through meditation, the Self becomes receptive to revelations about its true nature. The Self cannot make this intuition happen like other faculties; it can only be receptive to it. As such, meditation is a practice of stilling the physical senses, emotions, and thoughts of the body and mind and being receptive to the higher faculty of intuition. (#5)

- As it becomes increasingly aware of its true nature, the Self is more and more inspired to move through the process of self-actualization, like the iron before the magnet. (#5)

Self as Sat and Cit

- But what, then, is the Ultimate Self? In Hinduism, it is defined as Sat and Chit. Sat is the essence; it is Verity and Love. Chit is the actualization drive, a tendency to evolve toward Sat. (#6) Our most intrinsic and ultimate need is self-actualization. The ultimate experience we seek is bliss. The world we experience creates opportunities for self-actualization and, thus, the experience of bliss. (#6)

Siva, as the ultimate essence in union with Sakthi, is described in terms of two attributes: Sat and Cit. Sat is a synthesis of Truth and Love. Cit is the realization of it. We will look at this in detail in Chapter 5. (#6)

(III) Process of Evolution (Self-Actualization) [#7 to #9]

- They way - represented by the five letters "Si," "Va," "Ya," "Na," and "Ma" (Panchatcharam)

Sutra #7 to #9 outlines the process of evolution from going beyond the fetters and uniting with the Ultimate. It states that the process is described by the Mantra Sa-Va-Ya-Na-Ma.

7	• **Everything is empty before Sat** (the manifest has no independent truth outside the ultimate truth) • **Manifest** (Asat) **cannot know by itself** (is not capable of awareness) • **The** (evolving) **Self, which is neither, can become aware of both**
8	• **When the senses are in a tranquil state** • **When one's ultimate** (Self) **becomes one's guru and awakens** (the Self) **in the process of evolution** (as a revealing Grace of Intuition) • **As the separation disappears, they unite**

9	• **One cannot be aware of the Ultimate Self through the senses of the manifest** (the body and mind) • **Instead** (the evolving) **Self seeks** (the Ultimate Self) **via the eye of awareness** (meditative intuition) • **As the Self becomes aware of the ghostlike nature** (illusory) of **fetters, it transcends them** • **Embraces the way of five letters** (Si-Va-Na-Ma) **toward the cool shade of the Ultimate**

Highlights

- There are two notions of truth—the worldly or conventional truth and the ultimate truth. The Self is a process of synthesis through an evolving awareness. We will look at this in detail in Chapter 7. (#7)

- The stilling of the mind and body is the first step in meditation. Being receptive to revelation or revealing intuition is the real purpose. It is a process of self-discovery and evolution. (#8)

- This is a spiritual awareness that goes beyond bodily or mental experience. The role of the body and mind is to create an opportunity for meditation. (#9)

- The revelation of higher truth comes as a flash of intuition. Being in a meditative or receptive state to this revelation is stated as becoming aware through the "eye of awareness." (#9)

- This is a process of Si-Va-Ya-Na-Ma (Panchatcharam - the five-letter mantra). This was outlined in Chapter 2, but we will also look at this in more detail in Chapter 9. (#9)

(IV) Outcomes [#10 to #12]

- Verity (V) (#10)
- Evolution (E) (#12)
- Love (L) (#11)

Sutras describes the outcomes of pursuing this path of self-actualization.

10	• In the path of "I am becoming Him," becoming a unity and acting in His Service without delusion, atomization of Self, and dualities of deeds (i.e., the three fetters)
11	• In the same way, the mind interprets what the eyes perceive • It is the awareness that understands what the mind perceives (the Self) with relentless love evolves toward His feet (self-actualization)
12	• Removing those fetters, that which impedes the evolution toward His lotus feet • Becoming one of the Beloved, with His Compassion and Grace (of revelation) • As darkness gets dispelled (the Self, propelled) with love, one becomes wholesome, worshipping the (union of) the temple (circumstances), the Self (evolving awareness) as one with the divine (i.e., embracing life as a process of self-actualization)

Highlights

- As discussed earlier, Siva, in union with Sakthi, is called Sat-Cit. Sat is a synthesis of Verity and Love. Cit is the realization of it (Evolution).

  - **Verity:** The purpose of the pursuit of this path is to progressively live an authentic life without being shackled by the body-mind experience, i.e., Verity is to go beyond the three fetters as explained in earlier chapters (Chapters 1 and 2) – delusion (the false notion of body-mind experience – Mayai), atomization of Self (Anavam), and dualities of deeds (Kanmam). (#10)

  - **Love:** Such a life needs to be fueled by a progressive feeling of love toward this path, that is, toward the well-being of oneself and others. (#11) (#12)

- ○ **Evolution:** The emphasis is on the journey, not the destination, and on the Self as a progressive evolution of awareness and not a fixed state. As the Self evolves, there is increasing harmony between the evolving Self, the Ultimate Self, and life as a whole (with a series of occasions).

- Meditation awareness is the lever of evolution toward the Ultimate Self. The antidote to ignorance (of our ultimate nature) is the root cause of all three fetters. (#12)

- As fetters are dispelled when the conscious Self, the circumstances it is in (life occasions), and the Ultimate Self become a unity in harmony, we get closer to our ultimate nature. Progressively, the evolving Self is aligned with the Ultimate Self in responding to arising circumstances. (#12)

Conclusion

In short, to swim is to progress along the path of self-actualization and progress along the four aspects as follows:

1. **Progress in our Awareness of Cardinal Truth:** Three cardinal truths about the Self and their interplay (Fettered Self, Ultimate Self, and Evolving Self).

2. **Progress in our Awareness of the Nature of the Evolving Self:** Nature of the evolving Self and its progress toward the ultimate selves.

3. **Progress in executing Process or Evolution:** The Process of Evolution (self-actualization).

4. **Progress in experiencing the Outcomes:** Progressive bliss as a result of an increase of Verity, Evolution, and Love (VEL).

(4) MULTIPLE PERSPECTIVES ON SELF-ACTUALIZATION

OVERVIEW

This section presents multiple perspectives on self-actualization from various fields of study, including biology, neurology, psychology, philosophy, religion, and spirituality. They all have different emphases and ways of describing the concept, but collectively, they provide a richer and more holistic view of self-actualization.

I have provided an extract from source books (within the grey boxes) in each section. They are mostly direct quotes. But in some cases, I had to amend the sentences so that they collectively flow better rather than a set of disjointed statements. It primarily ensures that it captures the essence of the concepts outlined by each author.

For this book, I intend to outline my takeaway from the works of experts in different fields. Statements are selected from different chapters of their books. This is not meant to be an academic summary of their work, but rather my takeaway from them.

THE BIOLOGICAL VIEW: SELF-ACTUALIZATION AT A CELLULAR LEVEL

Hans Driesch (1867–1941) was a German biologist and philosopher. He is known for his early experimental work in embryology and his neo-vitalist philosophy of entelechy.

Driesch believed that the findings from his experiments challenged the contemporary mechanistic theories about the process through which individual organisms develop. He proposed that the autonomy of life deduced from this persistence of embryological development followed a directional and actualizing tendency in all organic growth.

Driesch learned how to tease apart the two cells formed after the first division of a fertilized sea urchin egg. If they were left to develop naturally, each of these two cells would have grown into a portion of a sea urchin larva as a part of a whole creature. Thus, the logical conclusion would be that when the two cells are skillfully separated, each will develop into part of a sea urchin. However, the cell developed into a whole sea urchin larva, a bit smaller than usual but normal and complete. This is an illustration of the drive to become a "whole" at a cellular level despite interference with the natural process.

THE NEUROLOGICAL/ PSYCHOLOGICAL VIEW: THE SELF AS AN INTEGRATED ORGANISM

Kurt Goldstein (1878–1965) was a German neurologist and psychiatrist who created a holistic theory of the organism. This theory focused on patients with psychological disorders, particularly cases of schizophrenia and war trauma, and their bodies' ability to readjust to substantial losses in central control. Goldstein's holistic approach to the human organism produced the principle of self-actualization, defined as the driving force that maximizes and determines an individual's path. Later, his principle influenced Abraham Maslow's hierarchy of needs.

In Goldstein's view, individuals, the environment, and their needs are all interconnected and cannot be viewed in isolation. According to Goldstein, the organism as a whole participates in every response in a natural state. While there may seem to be multiple needs, the underlying need and ultimate drive is self-actualization.

The list of statements in the grey boxes is paraphrased from the book *The Organism* by Kurt Goldstein. I am presenting this as my takeaway from the book rather than trying to summarize the whole book like an academic paper.

The Integrated Nature of Organisms with the Underlying Drive of Self-Actualization

- Reactions to stimulus do not happen in an isolated way. Changes in one area are followed by changes in other areas. Above all, the whole organism takes part in the response. Even in the simple response of the eye concerning light, in the act of seeing, a variety of phenomena happen throughout the body.

- In response to different environmental conditions, different responses come to the foreground. While they seem isolated and independent responses of different capabilities, they occur based on the nature of the underlying organism, per a process called self-actualization of the organism.

- Each organism is driven by a tendency to actualize its capability and its true nature in the environment. It is the most basic drive and, ultimately, the only drive by which the life of the organism is governed.

Goldstein goes further to say that self-actualization does not occur in a vacuum: As an organism becomes aware of higher challenges from the environment (either external or internal), it responds, consciously or unconsciously, within a holistic context. In this process, the organism becomes increasingly aware of its intrinsic and ultimate nature as a process of self-evolution. The higher the challenge, the more holistic the evolution.

Self-Actualization as a Natural and "Organismic" Response to Changes in the Environment

- In any given situation, what we call tendencies are a combination of the nature of the organization and the environment in which it is living.

- Each organism has a primal drive to actualize its nature. This need for such fulfillment is called the self-actualization of the organism.

- However, self-actualization does not happen in the seclusion of the environment. The shocks and demands of the environment create the trigger and opportunity for self-actualization. Hence, shocks and anxiety play a key role in drawing out the process of actualization of the intrinsic nature of the organism.

- In a healthy organism, self-actualization is a natural process of responding to various "disturbances" in the environment that trigger a response from the organism. What is inherent and intrinsic comes into the foreground as a result of a stimulus from the environment?

In contrast, Goldstein says, clinging to the known or preserving the existing state (i.e., self-preservation) is a response of a sick or weak organism. When the threat regarding the environment is overwhelming, and the organism feels largely inadequate to deal with it, its response is to go into self-preservation.

Self-preservation (Clinging), as opposed to Evolution, Is the Response of an Unhealthy Organism

- When the organism is sick or pathological, its response to the environment is to preserve its current state. When it finds that the demand of the environment is overwhelming and threatening its existence, the tendency to maintain (as opposed to evolve) takes over.

- This is a sign of sickness and decay of life. For the sick, self-preservation becomes a distorted form of self-actualization.

Goldstein also states that the level of an organism's evolution can be assessed by its courage to evolve in the face of adversity, in other words, how it rises to the challenge. It is venturing into the art of the possible as opposed to clinging to the current state as a measure of its level of evolution.

Courage of Conviction with a Healthy Attitude toward What Is "Possible"

- Courage is an organism's ability to deal with anxieties and shocks from the environment. True courage is a response of the organism amidst shock to its existence.

- To overcome this anxiety, an organism needs to look at every single experience in a larger context and take an "attitude toward possible," to have the "freedom of decisions" toward alternative responses.

- The way an individual cope with anxiety provides insight into the state of their nature. For a patient with brain injury, this is very low. For a healthy child, it is greater; for a creative person, it is the greatest. The creative person is more experienced with shocks and anxiety in the environment as he is not acting out of habit (self-preservation. But he/she can cope with it effectively and respond to environmental demands most genuinely.

THE PSYCHO-ANALYTIC VIEW: INDIVIDUATION – THE PROCESS OF BECOMING AN INTEGRATED BEING

Carl Jung (1875–1961) was a Swiss psychiatrist and psychoanalyst who was influential in the fields of psychology, philosophy, and religious study. Jung outlined a process similar to self-actualization he called "individuation," where the Self becomes an integrated unity. The Self has a conscious aspect to it. It also has a more powerful and capable unconscious (or yet-to-be-conscious) aspect to it. Jung observed that unconscious motives overrule that of the conscious in matters of vital importance.

> The list of statements in the grey boxes is relevant highlights from the books *The Archetypes and the Collective Unconscious* and *Psychology and Religion* by Carl Jung. I am presenting this as my takeaway from the books rather than trying to summarize the whole book like an academic paper.

> **The Unconscious Is a Significantly More Powerful Aspect of the Self**

> - Jung uses the term "Individuation" to denote a **psychological process where a person becomes "in-dividual," i.e., "indivisible unity or whole."**
> - There are conscious and unconscious aspects of the mind. Unconscious phenomenon is little understood, and most people deny its existence. But it manifests itself in individual behavior or response.

- But individuals as a whole include conscious aspects but unconscious. The unconscious is illimitable and far superior to the conscious mind.

- The conscious mind succumbs readily to unconscious influence, especially in matters of vital importance. The unconscious mind is often truer and wiser and overrules the conscious mind when stakes are high.

Jung defines the term "intuition" as a perception via the unconscious. He reiterates that the unconscious is more complete and superior in its insights than the conscious mind. Intuition does not come from the conscious mind, and they arise from the unconscious; however, the conscious mind can be receptive to it.

Intuition Is a Way of Perceiving via the Unconscious

- Jung defines "Intuition" as "**perception via the unconscious**."

- "My **psychological experience** has repeatedly shown that certain contents are from a psyche that is **more complete than consciousness**. They often contain a **superior analysis, insight, or knowledge that consciousness** has not been able to produce. We have a suitable word for such occurrences—**intuition**."

- "**You do not** make **an intuition. On the contrary, it always comes to you**; you have a hunch it has produced itself, and **you only catch it if you are clever or quick enough**."

In addition to being an eminent psychologist, Jung also had expertise in the study of religion and symbols. He concluded that through the systematic practice of yoga, one can make the conscious mind increasingly receptive to the unconscious. This, in effect, becomes a considerable experience of the conscious mind; it is the same notion of the self-actualizing individual self-evolving toward the Ultimate Self. As Jung admitted, what he called the "unconscious" is what Hinduism and Buddhism call universal consciousness (i.e., the Ultimate Self).

Training the Conscious Self to Be More Receptive

- "One hopes to control the unconscious, but the masters in the **art of self-control, the yogis, attain perfection in samādhi,** a state of ecstasy, which, as far as we know, is equivalent to a state of unconsciousness. It makes no difference whether they call our unconscious a 'universal consciousness.' The fact remains that, in their case, the **unconscious has swallowed up ego consciousness.**"

- **"Universal consciousness is logically identical to unconsciousness.** Nevertheless, a correct application of the methods described in the Pali Canon or the Yoga-sūtra induces a **remarkable extension of consciousness.**"

THE EXISTENTIAL PHILOSOPHY VIEW: A THREE-STAGED METAMORPHOSIS

Friedrich Nietzsche (1844 –1900) was a German philosopher whose work profoundly influenced contemporary philosophy. The following discussion is drawn from his great work, *Thus Spoke Zarathustra*.

Nietzsche outlines the process of self-actualization as a three-staged metamorphosis:

- **Stage 1:** For an individual in this stage, life is like a camel, the beast of burden. Worldly demands and expectations are the primary drivers for life. Fitting into the world is the primary goal, so the world's expectations and demands drive an individual's life.

- **Stage 2:** The suffocation of living as a beast of burden transforms the individual into a rebellious lion. This is the phase of the "Sacred No," in which the individual rebels against every worldly demand.

- **Stage 3:** In the rebellion of the "Sacred No," and in turning its back on the world, the spirit finds its sense of Self, not in terms of what the world wants but as an intrinsic sense of Self. Nietzsche calls this the "Sacred Yes" or the "child stage." This stage is a renewed innocence, a self-propelled wheel. "The **child is innocence** and forgetfulness, **a new beginning**, a sport, **a self-propelling wheel**, a first motion, a **'Sacred Yes'**...Yes, a Sacred Yes is needed, my brothers, for the sport of creation: the spirit now wills its own will, and the **spirit sundered from the world now wins its world."**

Interestingly, the word "OM" in Tamil also means "Yes," even in the most common usage of the word in day-to-day life. In a spiritual sense, it is a "Sacred Yes" to one's true nature. Embracing the way toward the ultimate nature of the Self, i.e., self-actualization.

THE HUMANISTIC PSYCHOLIGICAL VIEW: THE GOOD LIFE OF A FULLY FUNCTIONING PERSON

Carl Rogers (1902–1987) was an American psychologist and among the founders of the humanistic and client-centered approaches in psychology.

> This section is based on the book *On Becoming a Person*, which is a collection of essays by Carl Rogers. I am presenting this as my takeaway from the book rather than trying to summarize the whole book like an academic paper.

According to Rogers:

> "Good life is a process, not a state of being. It is a direction, not a destination. The direction that constitutes the good life

is selected by the total organism when there is psychological freedom to move in any direction.... [The] general qualities of this selected direction appear to have certain universalities."

- **Moving away** from being a facade and living a life based on thoughts and expectations. Rogers identified a few trends in how self-actualizing people move away from their world-bound ways as the primary form of living. This is similar to the stage of the "Sacred No" and the lion articulated by Nietzsche.

  ○ Moving away from facades: a tendency to move away from a Self that one is *not*, in other words, wanting not to be inauthentic.

  ○ Moving away from the "oughts:" moving away from the imposing image of what one "ought to be."

  ○ Moving away from pleasing others.

- **Moving toward** is a synthesis of three threads, (a), (b), and (c), as follows: This is similar to the stage of the "Sacred Yes" and the child articulated by Nietzsche.

  a. **Progressively becoming open to experiences:** Being open to the full richness of what life offers at each encounter, without distortion or suppression.

- A "fully functioning person" leading a "good life" can live free to live and experience one's feelings as they subjective exist in the Self, i.e., they don't shut down their feelings out of their awareness. This is the opposite of a psychological defensive mechanism.

- These individuals not only become more and more aware of their feelings and attitudes at a deeper level but also become aware of truths about reality outside. As they are open, they don't perceive reality in a preconceived and distorted way.

    a. **Progressively more existential living:** Engaging in each event totally as an organism in the "here and now." The person discovers more and more of their true nature in the awareness of the experience itself, rather than starting with a fixed position of the Self and fitting the experience within that definition.

- "Existential living means that the Self and personality emerge from experience rather than experience being translated or twisted to fit preconceived self-structure. It means that one becomes a participant in and an observer of the ongoing process of organismic experience rather than being in control of it...a discovery of structure in experience, a flowing changing organization of Self and personality."

Fully functioning people leading a good life:

- Have an inherent desire to be their true selves in each moment.
- To be open in each moment and discover in that present process the true nature of Self and what good life is. This is a progressive process of discovery of Self and truths about life and evolves along this journey. The "real Self" is discovered from each experience and not imposed upon it (distorting experience).

  - "Your job is just to discover it, and in the course of that, you will find yourself and your place. You must even let your own experience tell you it's meaning; the minute you tell it what it means, you are at war with yourself."

  - "He is more able to experience all his feelings and less afraid of any of his feelings; he is his own sifter of evidence and is more open to evidence from all sources;

he is completely engaged in the process of being and becoming himself; he lives more completely in the moment but learns that this is the soundest living for all time."

b. **Progressively trusting in the organism (i.e., the organismic response to a situation):** With wider awareness of the situation and the Self and total engagement, one is better positioned to make decisions as a holistic organism. The individual progressively finds that the integrated Self makes more trustworthy decisions than when relying on the ways of the world and trying to fit in and gain acceptance from others.

- "Individuals can trust their total organismic reaction to a new situation because they discover to an ever-increasing degree that if they are open to their experience, doing what 'feels right' proves to be a competent and trustworthy guide to truly satisfying behavior."
- A fully open person becomes aware of deeper and broader truths of life. As such, that person is also able to make decisions that are not only most genuine but also more effective in external situations.

- Fully functioning people can tap into more advanced intuitive capabilities in finding behavioral solutions to more complex and troubling situations as they are more open and fully present in each moment.

- With time, they progressively truth their deeper response than what is convenient or compliant to fit into the environment around them (ways of the world).

- "He can put more trust in his organism in this functioning, not because it is infallible but because he can be fully open to the consequences of each of his actions and correct them if they are less than satisfying."

In a "good life," a person views themselves as an evolving process, not a fixed product. They embrace self-discovery and evolution as a continuous and fluid process of life. The process of self-becoming is ongoing and is embraced, while the need to cling to the fixed notion of "I" is no longer there.

- "The individual seems more content to be a process rather than a product."

- "A person who is to live in this process is a participant in a fluid, ongoing process in which he is continually discovering new aspects of himself in the flow of his experience."

- "Each individual appears to be asking a double question: "Who am I?" and "How may I become myself?"

- "He is more able to experience all his feelings. Completely engaged in the process of being and becoming himself. He is becoming a more fully functioning organism, and because of the awareness of himself, which flows in and through his experience, he is becoming a more fully functioning person."

- "The individual moves toward being, knowingly and acceptingly, the process which he inwardly is."

- "He increasingly listens to the deepest recesses of his psychological and emotional being. To be what he truly is, this is the oath of life he appears to value most."

- "To be one's uniqueness as a human being is a positive, constructive, realistic, or trustworthy process."

- "It means taking continual steps toward being, in awareness and expression, that which is congruent with one's total organismic reaction 'to be that Self which one truly is.'"

- "Moving toward more openly being a process, fluidity, a changing...[He seems] more content to continue in this flowing current, beginning to appreciate himself as a fluid process."

- "The individual is constantly in the process of becoming and translates all his thinking in terms of process ... toward being a process of potentialities being born, rather than being or becoming some fixed goal."

This process requires faith and courage of conviction.

- "The person involved in the direction process...of the 'good life' is creative....He would not be a conformist...but live constructively in as much harmony...he would continue to move toward becoming himself and to have in such a way as to provide maximum satisfaction of his deepest needs."

THE PHILOSOPHICAL AND SPIRITUAL VIEW: MOTIVATION "TO BE THE SELF ONE TRULY IS"

Søren Kierkegaard (1813–1855) was a Danish theologian and is widely considered to be the first existentialist philosopher. In his great work, *Sickness unto Death*, he outlines the Self as a *spirit* becoming its Ultimate Self. He expresses the same sentiments as the *Sivajnana Podham* (outlined in Chapter 3), holding that the Self is a movement one makes exactly where one already is ("destination and source are the same").

The list of statements in the grey boxes is extracted from the book *Sickness unto Death* by Søren Kierkegaard. I am presenting this as my takeaway from the book rather than trying to summarize the whole book like an academic paper.

The Self as a Spirit in the Process of Self-Becoming

- A human being is a spirit or Self. It is a relationship of how it relates to itself. Self is a constant process of self-becoming. Becoming is a movement one makes where one is, i.e., it does not become something else.

- Every human, intrinsically, is driven to be the Self one truly is.

- "Despair" is an imbalance when:
  - One does not know who one is (Ignorance)
  - One does not want to be who one is (Distortion)
  - One is yet to be who one is (Drive)

Kierkegaard states that the Self is a synthesis between that which is worldly (the immediate, finite, and necessary) and that which is spiritual (the eternal, infinite, and possible). Genuine self-actualization is not escaping into a fantasy land by denying worldly realities; that would simply be putting up a reverential facade while feeling deprived inside. On the other hand, if all of one's life is about struggling to meet the needs of the body and mind—the deficiency needs or the first four needs of Maslow's hierarchy—one neglects or denies the Self's spiritual nature. Through Maslow's hierarchy of needs and the *Upanishads'* sheaths of experience, one becomes aware of the most intrinsic and ultimate need for self-actualization and its experience of bliss. This is a process of synthesis. As they say, the way out is through; in other words, self-actualization is a process of evolving awareness as one moves along the sheaths of experience of the *Upanishads* and evolves to meet the needs in Maslow's hierarchy.

Self Is a Synthesis of the Immediate, Finite, and Necessary and the Eternal, Infinite, and Possible. Despair Is an Imbalance. This Imbalance Triggers Evolution.

- Self is a synthesis of a notion of day-to-day Self and something more eternal/ultimate.
  - Finite and Infinite
  - Temporal and Eternal
  - Necessity and Possibility
- The environmental or worldly aspects give the Self a grounded perspective, and voids escape into fantasy.

- The Eternal and Ultimate nature drives the Self to evolve and not be held back to a rigid definition of the Self.

- "To despair is to lose the eternal...to lose the earthly is not in itself to despair."

- "Immediacy is like certain lower animals whose only weapon or defense is to lie quietly still and feign death...immediacy has no Self; it doesn't know itself. The immediate person helps himself in another way; he wishes he were someone else...."

  - "The Self becomes aware of itself as essentially different from the environment and the external world and their effect upon...The self that is won by infinite abstraction from all externalities...this naked Self and abstract, in contrast to the fully clothed Self of immediacy...the progressive impulse in the entire process through which Self infinitely takes possession of its actual Self along with difficulties and advantages Self infinitely takes."

  - "It is impossible to despair of the eternal without having a conception of oneself."

- "The possibility of this sickness is man's advantage over the beast, and it is an advantage that characterizes him otherwise than the upright posture, for it bespeaks the infinite erectness or loftiness of his being spirit. The possibility of this sickness is man's advantage over the beast; to be aware of this sickness is the Christian's advantage over a natural man; to be cured of this sickness is the Christian's blessedness."

Self's impediment and later evolution are due to despair. Initially, the Self clings to the experiences of the body and mind. It tries to fit into the ways of the world. This, Kierkegaard says, results from two types of despair: despair due to the ignorance of not knowing one's true nature and despair from denial, in other words, not wanting to be one's true nature and preferring to cling to a facade. However, there comes a time when the falsehood of these two types of despair and the suffering of clinging gives way to the true despair of wanting to be the Self that one truly is. Kierkegaard calls this possibility of despair man's advantage over the beast. Becoming aware of this despair is a Christian (or spiritual) person's advantage over others and represents progress toward self-actualization as Christian (or spiritual) blessedness.

Kierkegaard continues by saying that the initial tendency of most people is to cling to what is worldly—the finite, immediate, and necessary. The path to self-actualization is not for the faint-hearted. It requires courage of conviction. But the pain of clinging to our worldly ways and experience and denying one's spiritual and ultimate nature comes out either as a progressive suffocation reaching a threshold or as a life-changing event when these worldly ways are no longer able to meet the challenge that confronts us (i.e., an existential crisis).

The process of self-actualization requires the courage of conviction to stop clinging to worldly body-mind experience and evolve toward one's ultimate nature. Meanwhile, this courage of conviction evolves as one progresses toward self-actualization. Thus, it is a mutually reinforcing evolution.

Self-Actualization requires Courage and Faith

- "For if I have ventured wrongly, very well, life then helps me with its penalty. But if I haven't ventured, who will help me then? And when, into the bargain, by not venturing at all in the highest sense (and to venture in the highest sense is precisely to become aware of oneself), **I cravenly gain all earthly advantages – and lose myself!**"

- **"The biggest danger—that of losing oneself—can pass off in the world as** quietly as if it were nothing; every other loss, an arm, a leg, five dollars, a wife, etc., is bound to be noticed."

- "But with **petty bourgeois** vulgarity and triviality, which also essentially **lack possibility,** the case is somewhat different.

The petty bourgeois is spiritless, while the determinist and the fatalist are in a state of spiritual despair. But spirit lessness, too, is despair. The **petty bourgeois lacks any spiritual characteristic and is absorbed in the probable, where the possible finds its tiny place.**"

- "What we call worldliness simply consists of such people who...**pawn themselves to the world**.... They use their abilities, amass wealth, carry out worldly enterprises, make prudent calculations, etc., and perhaps are mentioned in history, but they are not themselves. In **a spiritual sense, they have no Self....**"

- "But to **arrive at the truth, one must pass through every negativity**; it is just as the old story says about breaking a certain magic spell: it won't be broken unless the piece is played backward."

- "The **despair, which is the corridor to faith,** is also due to the help of the eternal; through the eternal, the Self has the **courage to lose itself in order to win itself.**"

- **"The decisive moment only comes when a man is brought to the utmost extremity,** where there is no possibility in human terms. Then the question is whether he will believe that for God, everything is possible, that is, whether he will have faith. But this is simply the formula for losing one's mind; **to have faith is precisely to lose one's mind to win God.**"

- "In order to want in despair to be oneself, there must be consciousness of an infinite Self."

- **"Being a Self is the greatest, the infinite, concession that has been made to man, but also eternity's claim on him."**

- **"The only life wasted is the life of one who so lived it, deceived by life's pleasures or sorrows,** that he never became decisively, eternally, conscious of himself, as spirit, as Self."

Kierkegaard also proposes that self-actualization is an "infantilizing" process that aims toward the possibility of the Ultimate Self. It is also an ongoing process of evolution (the eternal). With its Ultimate Self, God, as its goal and measure, the world we experience through body or mind becomes an occasion for the evolution of the goal or standard.

Toward the Ultimate Self

- **"In relating itself to itself and wanting to be itself, the Self is grounded transparently in the power that established it**. Which formula, as has frequently been remarked, is the definition of faith."

- "The Self takes on a new quality and specification in being **the Self directly before God**. This Self is no longer the merely human Self but what, hoping not to be misinterpreted, I would call the theological Self, the Self directly before God. And what an infinite reality this Self acquires by being conscious of being before God, a human Self with God as its standard!"

- "Everything is qualitatively whatever it is measured by...and what is qualitatively its standard of measurement."

- **"The Self is intensified in proportion to the standard by which self-measured itself.... infinitely so when God is the standard."**

(5) MINDFUL VS. MECHANICAL LIVING

The Self that does not embrace the eight qualities
is like machines and planets. [TK-09]

MECHANICAL LIVING

Even inanimate objects, including planets, are in motion and have a lifecycle. They, too, undergo a process of creation, evolution, and termination. However, they are mechanical, and we do not call them living beings.

Mechanical living is leading a life based on a preconceived and fixed notion. At the heart of it is the ultimately fixed notion that "I am This." Defining a sense of "I" in terms of body-mind experience. It is described as "Sinking" in Chapter 3 or the Way of Asuras in Chapter 1.

Mindful living will draw us out of our comfort zone in our daily routines. It may not change what we do, but how we approach it. We cannot switch off our awareness and simply live from memory and habit. True living requires us to be mindful. It requires us to be aware and undertake self-discovery, meditation, and actualization. In other words, it requires us to live in a process of evolving awareness, not as a fixed profile responding to life in a predetermined way.

Mechanical motion may get us through the first two of Maslow's hierarchy of needs (physiological and safety needs). It may also start us with need three (love and belonging) and need four (esteem). Nevertheless, it cannot give a richer life when meeting needs three and four. It certainly falls short even of getting us started to meet the most intrinsic and ultimate need: self-actualization.

Self-actualization requires us to have a sense of courage and faith to become open to each experience and live existentially in each moment. We are required to discover the Self by meditating on the experience, to calibrate and evolve in the process of self-actualization, and to use every body-mind experience as a steppingstone toward self-actualization and not cling to them with the belief of "I am this."

Strangely, for children, it is easy and natural. It is very hard for adults because we have become fixed over time. The price we pay is leading a mechanical life. In the short term, the reward is pain relief by meeting our "deficiency needs" (as described in Chapter 3 – Maslow's hierarchy of needs).

To venture out internally and continuously discover our true nature is mentally threatening. It requires courage of conviction, but the reward is true and progressive bliss in meeting our "growth needs."

MINDFUL LIVING – SELF-ACTUALIZATION

Mindful living is living consciously along the path that is the most intrinsic and ultimate need of every being—self-actualization. This includes:

1. Self-discovery (Velvi in Tamil; Yagna in Sanskrit)

2. Self-evolution (Thavam in Tamil; Tapas in Sanskrit)

3. Contribution toward the evolution of others (Thanam in Tamil; Dhana in Sanskrit)

The Bhagavad Gita says that to do the above with faith is "Sat." Without faith, these are just empty rituals. One of the core mantras in Hinduism is Sat-Cit-Ananada, which translates to "essence-realization-bliss." Sat-Cit represents Siva-Sakthi in a union as the ultimate essence and actualization tendency of the Self.

Let's have a closer look at the Mantra "Sat-Cit-Anandam."

Sat-Cit-Anandam: Self-Realization is Bliss

Sat is the ultimate essence of the potential or subconscious Self. This essence is given many names with varying emphasis across different religions, spiritual practices, and philology. In Hinduism, Sat is defined as Verity and Love, represented by Siva. The Bhagavad Gita defines Sat as reality/truth (Sad Bhave) and good (Sadhu Bhave). Buddhism defines it as awareness (Pragyan) and compassion (Karuna). **Sat** is progressively evolving toward Verity (i.e., truth and authenticity), fueled by Love. Let's look at each phrase (Sat, Cit, Anandam) in more detail.

Sat (Essence) – Verity and Love

The Thirukural defines Verity and Love further. Verity is the state in which we are blemish-less in our awareness; in other words, we are progressively pure in our assessment. It is a more intrinsic assessment, not based on how others judge us or how we measure against established standards (e.g., those of psychology, religion, etc.). Kierkegaard calls it "transparently established before God." In this case, God is our Ultimate Self. Both the Bhagavad Gita and Kierkegaard describe "God" as a goal and measure in this process of evolving Verity. Hinduism, in general, and Siththantham, in particular, emphasize the intrinsic view of God as the Ultimate Self and its transcendental nature as the universal essence.

The Thirukural describes that truth washes off any blemishes inside in the same way that water washes off dirt outside. One of the measures of the evolution of the Self is based on how authentic one is (i.e., Verify).

Verity means being authentic, pure, and at one with truth. In this context, Verity is to go beyond the clutches of the three fetters as outlined in earlier chapters (Introduction).

Love: The Thirukural also describes love as something that fuels not only the path toward Verity (aram) but also the courage of conviction (maram) that supports this path. The second measure of evolution is love. In Buddhism and Hinduism, love is best defined via the four attributes of the Brahma Vihara:

- **Benevolence** (mettā or maitrī): A general sense of wishing well.

- **Sympathetic joy** (muditā): Being happy about others' happiness.

- **Compassion** (Karuna): Being empathic toward the sufferings of others.

- **Equanimity** (upuekkhā or upekṣā): Not being attached. Love is not clinging; love is freedom.

This love is not the same as falling in love with things, people, or ideas. It is an essence that one discovers and evolves, not an action or attraction directed toward something specific. However, if one must compare it to the common use of the word "love," this love is an attraction, in the broadest sense, to the Ultimate Self and its expressions in a holistic context. It is not something specific in isolation.

Cit (Realization): Actualization Tendencies (1) To be Aware (2) To Evolve, and (3) To Love

Cit is the intelligence or awareness principle. It is the transformative power to actualize the essence: It is the power to be aware, love, and evolve or execute. This is a three-step process performed with faith:

- Self-discovery (Velvi in Tamil; Yagna in Sanskrit)
- Self-Evolution (Thavam in Tamil; Tapas in Sanskrit)
- Dedication to the Evolution (Thanam in Tamil; Dana in Sanskrit)

Self-discovery is based on the tendency to be aware. Self-evolution is based on the tendency to evolve. Dedication to Evolution is based on the tendency to love.

Anandam: Bliss

Life is a process of evolving awareness with a progressively increasing quality and scale of happiness. As we saw in the discussion of Maslow's hierarchy of needs and the sheaths of experience of the Taittiriya Upanishad in Chapter 3, bliss is a form of happiness related to self-actualization.

Sat-Cit-Anandam is an invokable form of the whole notion of self-actualization. It helps us divert our awareness of life's most intrinsic and ultimate drive while interacting to meet our daily needs. In other words, it allows us to not lead a mechanical life but a mindful life, even when engaging in daily routines (i.e., meditative or mindful living).

MINDFUL LIVING – EMBRACING EIGHT QUALITIES

The Thirukural outlines eight qualities one should embrace to lead a mindful life and progress toward self-actualization. Here is the summary. We will look at each one in detail in subsequent chapters (specified within descriptions of each quality).

Q1: I am an Awareness [OM]

OM is the Ultimate Self. The world we experience arises from who we are. [TK-01]

The world we experience is dependent on who we are and what happens to us. The same events can be a threat or opportunity to evolve, depending on who we are. The world is experienced via the body and mind (physical, physiological, emotional, and intellectual). But we are, in essence, the experience (the spirit), not the experience itself or the instruments through which we experience it (i.e., the body and mind).

The spirit can be described in terms of states of awareness, which are represented by the phrase OM (a.k.a. AUM):

- A – Physical and physiological awareness: that which is aware of the external world.
- U – Psychological awareness. emotions, intellect: that which is aware of the mental/internal world.
- M – Meditative or intuitive awareness, i.e., revelations: that which is aware of one's nature and that of life as a whole.
- AUM – Wholesome or sacred awareness: This state is a synthesis of the above states applied to each moment, here and now, as a whole organism, not as an isolated capability, in other words, as a living awareness.

We will look at this in detail in Chapter 6.

Q2: "I am" an Evolving Process [VEL]

The purpose of all learning is to embrace the good path of the wholesome awareness. [TK-02]

While it is useful to understand the Self in terms of a state of awareness, the Self is more of an ongoing process of evolving awareness than a fixed state. Its evolution can be measured by the extent of its actualization toward its ultimate nature (i.e., wholesome awareness).

One of the key aspects of this process of evolution is self-discovery. The purpose of learning from every experience is to evolve toward the Ultimate Self. Life is a journey of evolving awareness and not a destination. The purpose of all the learning of life, via the body and mind, is to contribute toward evolving our awareness of the Self and who we truly are, in other words, self-discovery. It is a journey in which there is a progressive increase in authentic living (**V**erity), fueled by **L**ove as an ongoing **E**volution. I have used the Acronym VEL to represent this dynamic nature of the Self as an evolving process.

We will look at the detailed view of this quality in Chapter 7.

Q3: "I am" the Way

That which transcends the manifest and unites with the Ultimate leads a Heavenly Life on Earth [TK-03].

Clinging to the body-mind experience is about living a mechanical life with a fixed notion of the Self. It is clinging to what we experience as who we are and being ignorant about the distinction between what we experience and who we are. The most intrinsic and directive nature is evolving toward one's full potential. It is being as one truly, as we have seen across various fields of study.

The notion of life in Heaven on Earth means being able to live happily while engaging in grounded realities, in other words, full existential living. It is not about escaping into a fantasy land with a notion of heavenly life and living in denial and deprivation, representing the relative truth of the events we encounter. The Kingdom of Heaven, or the pure/sacred land, is one of the key ideas across Christianity, Buddhism, and Hinduism. In terms of humanistic psychology and existential philosophy, it is also the same as leading a life in the stage of the "Sacred Yes," as Nietzsche calls it: living a life of self-actualization, in Maslow's terms, or being a fully functioning person, as Rogers describes. We will look at this in detail later in this chapter.

Overview of the Remaining Five Qualities [(4) to (8)] and the Four-Fold Path to Self-Actualization

The above three qualities [(1) to (3)] define the overall nature of the Self. The next five [(4) to (8)] describe the dynamic attributes of a Self that evolve along the Four-Fold Path toward self-actualization. Qualities (4) and (5) represent the first path, while qualities (6), (7), and (8) represent the Self in evolution along the remaining three paths.

Each of the four paths can lead to self-actualization on its own. At any state of awareness, faith, and courage of conviction in the Ultimate Self, one can progress toward self-actualization. Thus, each path is considered a sacred path on its own; however, the degree of awareness and the size of the corresponding leap of faith that is needed varies across the four paths. The first path requires more of a leap of faith and less awareness, while the fourth requires more awareness and, as such, less of a leap of faith.

Each person takes a path as it suits their state of Self (i.e., their nature and stage in life) and evolves along a single path or across different paths as needed. The Judge of the choice of path is oneself. But, as the Self evolves, the choice also depends on the state evolution of the Self at any given stage.

Below presents a summary of qualities [(4) to (8)]. In the next chapter, we will look at them in more detail as part of the Four-Fold Path.

Q4: The Self transcends beyond the dualities of outcomes.

One goes beyond suffering by moving past the dualities of craving and resentment (outcomes). [TK-04]

Good and bad are relative truths based on who we are in each state of mind. As we evolve, our sense of good and bad also evolves. When we define ourselves in terms of good and bad experiences (via the body and mind) at a given point in time, it impedes our evolution through one of the fetters—Kanmam. This is not to say that we should have no view of good or bad outcomes; it is only to say that we should not cling to a given definition of good or bad outcomes. As we evolve, we should evolve our sense of "I" with the evolution of our awareness.

Q5: The Self transcends beyond the dualities of deeds.

Those who serve to glorify the Ultimate, unite with it and transcend the darkness-filled dualities of actions. [TK-05]

Qualities (4) and (5) represent the attribute of the Self that is the first path of self-actualization. This first path, Cariyai, meaning "service," is about disciplined engagement with the world, with "I" as a servant of the Ultimate Self. This path is about engaging with the world without clinging to the dualities of deeds and their outcomes. "I am" is not what I experience through the senses with the psychological overlay of emotions and thoughts. I am these experiences and evolve beyond each experience rather than clinging to or being imprisoned by them. In truth, the actions we choose depend on who we are and the state of the Self at that moment of truth. Outcomes, in turn, depend on our actions, not the other way around. In other words, experiences of actions or outcomes do not define us.

This path applies to most of us who cling to all three fetters: (1) the dualities of actions and outcomes, (2) an outlook of the world via the body-mind, and (3) the atomization of the Self as "I am this," in other words, based on the experience of (1) and (2). Here, an individual is operating at the level of physical and psychological awareness (i.e., the "A" in AUM).

The first path involves evolving, transcendental direction through dedicated actions and outcomes as an authentic and interim step toward self-actualization. It is sublimation and sensual engagement with the world with a psychological overlay, giving it a broader context of self-actualization. It is neither clinging to worldly engagement nor escaping from ground realities (i.e., dependent and relative truths). It is a synthesis found at a higher order of truth: It directly engages with each occasion and goes beyond them with a higher awareness acquired via the resulting experience.

This path is about providing a broader and deeper self-actualization context for fulfilling the first two of Maslow's hierarchy of physiological and safety needs. It is a way of transforming worldly engagement within a broader spiritual context.

Q6: The Self transcends beyond the outlook of the world.

To leave the sensual experiences with the senses and to lead a heavenly life by adhering to the discipline of truth. [TK-06]

The second path, Kiriyai, meaning "The Way of Worship," is about the inner psychological evolution (the emotions and intellect) of the Self, with "I" as a worshiper of the Ultimate Self (i.e., an heir to the Ultimate Self). This path is more about psychological evolution or inner purification. How we look at the world through our conscious or subconscious cognitive constructs at a given point in time is relative to and dependent on who we are (i.e., our state of being) at that moment of truth. It is not clinging to or escaping from that; instead, it reflects on the experience to form our outlook and continuously evolve it. This path is a synthesis found at a higher order of truth: It is being aware of our psychological profile and going beyond it with a higher awareness that is acquired via psychological experiences. An individual normally operates on this path with psychological awareness (i.e., the "U" in AUM).

This path applies to the method with two fetters. Individuals on this path have managed to loosen the first fetter because they don't cling to outcomes and actions. However, they still hold onto an outlook of the world based on body-mind experience and atomize the Self in the form of believing "I am this."

This is about providing a broader and deeper self-actualization context to the fulfillment of the 3rd and 4th of Maslow's hierarchy of needs, belonging/love, and esteem as a way of transforming psychological tendencies within a broader spiritual context, that is, an evolving state of awareness of the Ultimate Self.

Q7: The Self as the witness to the expressions of the Ultimate Self (the Divine Dance).

To transcend mental suffering is to identify with the essence of (the Ultimate), which is beyond description in terms of the body-mind experience. [TK-07]

The third path, Yoham, which is a path of meditation toward union, involves meditative reflection and receptivity to the intuitive revelation of the truth about the Ultimate Self and life. On this path, life is the lead "witness" of the Ultimate Self's expression of the demands of the moments of truth. Individuals on this path trust their organismic response (their response as a whole being) more than any individual capability of the body-mind; responding to life events has become a natural process. However, the individual's focus is being mindful of the process. In the same way, we don't do anything when seeing or hearing; responses simply happen when we are receptive. Similarly, responses to life events have become a response of the whole Self, but the individual just watches like a witness. In this meditative or mindful life, one evolves. This path is like the path of a friend or companion. On this path, an individual largely operates with meditative awareness (i.e., the M of "AUM").

Body and mind have become subservient to the meditative awareness of the spirit. As in the practice of meditation, sense, emotions, and thoughts become still, giving way to becoming receptive to intuitive revelations of truth.

Here, individuals are at the threshold of leading a life that consciously meets the highest of Maslow's hierarchy of needs: self-actualization. They directly engage in meeting their "being or growth" needs and have evolved beyond focusing exclusively on deficiency needs (the first four needs of Maslow's hierarchy). They experience true bliss in their lives as the innermost sheath of experience of the Kosha Upanishads.

In their daily lives, such individuals stand apart as witnesses. They do not identify with the world but are not yet in active union with the Ultimate Self. However, the Self begins to see the Ultimate Self as the primary reality and, hence, the experience of bliss. In the previous path, happiness starts as pain relief to be sublimated to bliss in the wider context of the

Ultimate Self. In this path, the individual has evolved beyond a life of pain relief, for they have gone beyond defining "I" by clinging to the two fetters of the body-mind experience and their outlook on the world. The atomization of the Self has become weak but still exists. They see themselves as witnesses. There is only progressive bliss: The more one is aware of the ways of the Ultimate Self, the more bliss one feels.

Q8: The Self as that which is in union with the Ultimate Self (Verity and Love).

Unless one is in union with that which is a synthesis of Verity and Love (Ultimate Self), one cannot swim across the worldly seas (body-mind). [TK-08]

The fourth path, njanam, which is the Way of Unity, means living with awareness, with the Ultimate Self at each turn of events. The sense of "I" can be compared to a spouse of the Ultimate Self: They are still separate but come together at each turn of events like a husband and wife making family decisions and taking joint action. The Self has no separate needs for engagement with the world; instead, it is in union with the Ultimate Self and has common goals toward each engagement. This path is one large, unified operation in the form of wholesome awareness (i.e., as AUM).

This path is being consciously in the state of Sat-Cit-Anandam (i.e., essence-actualization-bliss). If we view the previous third path as bliss at rest, standing apart as a witness, the fourth path is bliss in motion and rest—living awareness in union with the Ultimate Self through Verity and Love. In short, the mind and body have become completely subservient to the needs of the spirit. Bliss is not a separate experience but a natural experience in one state of being.

(6) Q1: "I AM" AN AWARENESS [OM]

OM is the Ultimate Self. The world we experience arises from who we are [TK-01]

STORY: IN SEARCH OF THE ULTIMATE

The story of two gods, Brahma and Vishnu, contending to determine who among them is superior and the ultimate form of divinity, holds significant importance in Hinduism.

Siva is considered the Ultimate God in Sivaism, a tradition within Hinduism. He orchestrates the entire universe, performing the five acts: creation, preservation, dissolution, concealment, and revelation. However, he also directly deals with the dissolution of the universe. Creation is delegated to a god named Brahma, while Preservation/Evolution is entrusted to Vishnu.

I am not presenting this as an academic and precise representation of the story or its traditional interpretation. I have used this as the foundational story, infused it with my perspective, and offered my interpretation at the end. The purpose of its inclusion here is to provide an intuitive and initial overview of what we will discuss in the remaining parts of the chapter. The intent is not solely academic knowledge transfer (i.e., sharing stories of Hinduism) but rather a way of looking at life.

Story

One day, Brahma began to wonder who among them was the greatest. He became convinced that creation is the most supreme divine act. So, he approached Vishnu and shared his views. Vishnu became drawn into the same line of thinking. His view was that while creation and dissolution are important activities, it is the preservation and evolution of the universe that are the most sacred acts. So, he concluded that he was superior among them. They both debated for a long time.

Siva was passing by; knowing the reason for their debate, he suggested a contest. He said he would take the form of a column of fire that spread across the universe as a universal flame. Whoever sees the top or bottom of the flame first is the Supreme God among the three. Brahma and Vishnu agreed to the contest.

Siva then took the form of a flame of blazing fire in the form of a column that cut across the universe. It was so bright and great that the whole universe was lit. Brahma was quick to react. He took the form of a celestial swan and ascended to see the top of the flame. Vishnu took the form of a Divine Warthog and started to "dig" through the universe to see the bottom of the flame.

During their first travel segment, they saw physical and physiological expressions of the universe. Bodies, alive and dead; beings in motion; assets, beings with plenty and others suffering deprivation; and beings that were beautiful and beings who were unattractive. Brahma was looking for Siva's head and Vishnu's feet. Brahma, as a celestial swan, could fly around. Vishnu, as a divine warthog, could dig through and was looking for Siva's feet. They could see Siva's presence everywhere but not his head or feet.

They then moved on to the second segment. They both hoped they would find Siva's head and feet there. They were exhausted, but neither wanted the other to win. They saw the emotions, thoughts, and memories of beings in that segment. They saw sensual experiences and all kinds of emotional experiences, including anger, lust, and love. In other areas, they saw basic and advanced thoughts. However, like before, they saw Siva's presence everywhere except his head or feet. Like before, Brahma ascended higher and higher, and Vishnu dug deeper and deeper. But neither with success. They kept going, but Brahma was losing his patience and thought he could use his creativity to win.

Then Brahma saw a flower descending from the skies. The flower belonged to the species called "Thazhampoo" in Tamil and "Fragrant Screw Pine" in English. Brahma intercepted the flower and inquired about its origin and the purpose of its journey. The flower said its purpose was to decorate Siva's head, but its time had come; hence, it had fallen off his head.

Brahma saw an opportunity. He proposed that the flower provide a false witness to Siva, confirming that Brahma saw Siva's head. In return, he would reward the flower once Brahma was accepted as the supreme. The flower was hesitant at first, but Brahma used his creativity to persuade the flower. Brahma then called upon Siva.

Vishnu's situation was different. Vishnu realized that Siva's feet could not be found by digging through the universe, realizing his limitation. However, Vishnu saw this, with humility, as an opportunity to evolve, and so he meditated on Siva and called upon him.

Siva appeared before Brahma, the flower, and Vishnu. Brahma executed his plan and told Siva that he had found Siva's head and that the flower was the witness. The flower went along as planned. Siva, being omniscient, saw through his lie and punished Brahma, stating that no one on earth would have a temple for him or offer worship again. He also punished the flower so it would never be used as an offering to Siva.

However, Vishnu accepted his limitations and apologized to Siva. Siva embraced him and appreciated his authenticity.

Image16: Brahma and Vishnu in search of Siva's Head and Feet

Key Takeaways

- Our Ultimate Essence (represented by Siva) cannot be found in physical, physiological, or psychological experiences (emotions, intellect, or memory).

- The body-mind experience is a steppingstone to realizing that ultimate essence.

  ◦ By realizing the limitations of the body-mind experience.

  ◦ By meditating (calming/stilling body-mind senses) so that one can be receptive to intuitions/revelations of truth regarding the nature of the Ultimate Self (Siva appeared before Vishnu when he realized the limitations of his experience and meditated on Siva).

- Vishnu, as a warthog digging through the universe, is a symbolic representation of beings engaging with the world through physical senses and deeds.

- Brahma ascending as a celestial swan is a symbolic representation of engaging with the world through our thoughts and emotions.

- Brahma asking the flower to provide false witness is a symbolic representation of when we cling to our body-mind experience as the independent and ultimate truth. Instead of relative truth based on who we are at a given point in time, when we cling to the notion of "I am this," we tend to twist and distort reality to fit within our line of thinking. This leads to inauthentic living.

- Brahma and the flower being punished is a symbolic representation of dismissing the habit of clinging to the body-mind experience as independent truth. Instead, use the body-mind experience as a steppingstone to understanding its limitations, meditating on what lies beyond the experience, becoming aware, and evolving.

- Conversely, Vishnu realized the limitations of his past views and body-mind experience. He was receptive to the revelation of higher truth (the appearance of Siva) and evolved with it. Hence, he was embraced by Siva (representing the Ultimate Self).

OM: STATES OF AWARENESS

We briefly discussed OM as states of awareness in the earlier sections. Now, let's delve into it in more detail.

In Hinduism and all major religions that originated in India, including Buddhism and Jainism, OM is a sacred and revered phrase. From my studies, I have found that it is comprehensively defined in the Thirumandhiram (a part of the Saiva Siththantham) and summarized in the Mandukya Upanishad. Let's explore the concept of OM based on the Thirumandhiram and a complementary view from the Upanishads.

Again, my objective is not to provide a translation of spiritual or religious works. Instead, I aim to use my understanding of them to offer my perspective on aspects of self-actualization that enable us to find happiness and bring happiness to others.

OM represents states of awareness. Awareness is the self: The Self is not the body, mind, or what we experience through them, but rather our awareness of all our experiences. There is nothing we can experience outside of our awareness. The past, present, and future are all within the realm of awareness: The past is a recollection, the present is what we experience "here and now," and the future is what we anticipate and experience. But it all exists within our awareness. Even our religious experience of God is within our awareness. If something lies beyond our awareness—whether conscious or unconscious, at some level within the body, mind, and spirit as part of our memory, current experience, or future anticipation—we cannot experience it.

Siththantham, a Hindu tradition, outlines five states of awareness (the Upanishads talk about four). The fifth state is where individuality is meant to be inexplicable. So, for this book, I primarily focus on the other four states and only mention the fifth state for the sake of completeness.

While we have explored these states previously, let's summarize them here as a refresher before we delve into further detail.

The three states of awareness are represented by the letters A, U, and M; the fourth state is the synthesis of the other three states to form AUM (or OM). The fifth state is not represented by letters but by their absence.

1. A – Physical and physiological awareness: That which is aware of the external world.

2. U – Psychological awareness: Emotions, intellect; that which is aware of the mental/internal world.

3. M – Meditative or intuitive awareness, i.e., revelations: That which is aware of one's own nature and that of life as a whole.

4. AUM – Wholesome or sacred awareness: This state is a synthesis of the above states applied to each moment, here and now, as a whole organism, not as an isolated capability; in other words, as living awareness.

Here are some extracts from the Mandukya Upanishad that add flavor and complement our understanding (Sloka #1 and #2):

- Everything is OM. That which has become, that which is in the process of becoming, and that which will come into being are all OM. Past, present, and future are all OM.

- The Self is Ultimate, and the Self has four states.

Thirumandhiram states that because all physical and psychological phenomena arise within ultimate awareness, it is as if the Ultimate

Self, which has neither shape nor form, has taken embodiment (name and form) everywhere.

> **From the body, mouth, eyes, nose, and ears** (instruments & experience) **is the physical arising.**
>
> **Overlaid with the inner instruments** (emotional and intellectual faculties, etc.) **is our universe.**
>
> **As the universe and every being in it dance as per the orchestration of God,**
>
> **It is as if, that which has neither form nor name took embodiment Everywhere.** [TM-2586]

Let's now look at each state in more detail.

"I" as Physical and Physiological Awareness (The "A'" of "Aum")

Let's start with a verse from the Thirumanthiram:

> **Perceived via five and engaged via five.**
>
> **Along with the inner four to experience**
>
> **As awareness of the manifest expanded across the universe**
>
> **Be there as Self.** [TM-2153]

The first state of awareness is also called the waking or worldly state (Nanavu in Tamil; Jagarita in Sanskrit). This state involves an awareness of physical and physiological experiences with an overlay of psychological awareness through emotions and intellect. It is experienced through 14 instruments, including:

- Five instruments of perception—eyes (seeing), ears (hearing), tongue (taste), nose (smell), and skin (touch)

- Five instruments of action or interaction with the world— hands (grasping), legs (walking), mouth (eating), genitals (procreation), anus (excretion)

- Four inner instruments—emotional center (feeling), intellectual center (rational thoughts), awareness center (being receptive to revelation or intuition), and a sense of "I"

For physical and physiological awareness, the experience occurs through the five instruments of perception and the five instruments of action. There is then a psychological overlay that completes the experience. This includes emotions and thoughts that overlay the physical and physiological experience, defining it as either good or bad. Here, the awareness center is, by default, the memory, which provides a sense of continuity. The sense of "I" is defined in terms of the physical and physiological experience, such as gender, height, strength, wealth, or speed.

This state of awareness deals with the first two of Maslow's hierarchy of needs: psychological and safety needs, along with the corresponding two physical and physiological sheaths of experience in the Upanishads.

"I," by default, is a fixed notion in physical and physiological terms (i.e., "I am the body and its experiences"). All experiences are distorted to fit this definition. The spiritual awareness of "I" is at the lowest level. "Who I am" is confused with "what I have" or "what I can physiologically do or experience." This state of awareness tends to be bound by all three fetters.

The spiritual experience in this state is called "darkness" (Irul in Tamil). If one lives only with this awareness, one can gain mastery over the external world but will surrender the Self to it by conforming to the world's expectations of what is considered good and great. There will be no sense of the true Self or one's ultimate and eternal needs beyond the "here and now."

Here are some extracts from Mandukya Upanishad that add flavor and complement our understanding (Sloka #3):

- in this state, our awareness is outward-directed (Bahis Prajna).
- What we experience are gross matters - that which is experienced by the body, i.e., physical and physiological (Sthula Bhuk).
- It is a state of the universe or a worldly state (Vaisvanarah).

The Evolving Self is not what is experienced through the body, but rather what is aware of the body's experiences within the larger context of the Ultimate Self.

"I" AS PSYCHOLOGICAL AWARENESS (THE "U" OF "AUM")

Letting go of the ten instruments and the sense of "I" that is identified with them and

(Living) **based on the remaining four** (inner instruments)

World blended with the mind (emotions, thoughts, etc.)

Experiences the Dreams in the mental realm (i.e., psychological living). [TM-2154]

The psychological experience primarily involves emotions and thoughts. The awareness center provides the continuity of psychological memory through emotions and thoughts. The sense of "I am" is defined in terms of a psychological profile or its application—for example, I am affectionate; I am a parent, child, sibling, spouse, and friend; or I am a great thinker, known for my achievements, including my positions and legacy as a whole.

In this state, psychological awareness still defines "I" as the "other." In psychological terms, as opposed to physical or physiological terms, "I" by default is a fixed notion (i.e., a psychological profile). The many psychological profiling methods used in the workplace, such as DISC, are a good example. As they appear in the Bhagavad Gita, the four castes of Hinduism are a psychological profile, which was later distorted to become a social or birth-based class structure.

This awareness is related to the third and fourth levels of Maslow's hierarchy of needs: belonging and esteem, along with the corresponding emotional and intellectual sheaths of experience in the Upanishads.

All experiences are twisted to fit this definition. The spiritual awareness of "I" stands apart from the physical experience (i.e., I am not the body or its experience); instead, it is identified with the psychological experience (i.e., I am the mind and its experiences).

The spiritual experience in this state of awareness is referred to as "murky" (Marul in Tamil). While it sees "I" beyond the body and its experience, it still views "I" in terms of the experience of the mind as a psychological profile. This state is called a dream (kanavu in Tamil; Swapna in Sanskrit). While the Self goes beyond the limits of the external world, it is limited by the mind via the emotional and intellectual constructs of memory, which provide a sense of continuity.

Here are some extracts from the Mandukya Upanishad that add flavor and complement our understanding (Sloka #4):

- In this state, our awareness is directed inwards (Antar prajnaḥ).

- What we experience are finer things in life, i.e., emotions and thoughts (pravivikta-bhuk).

- In this state, one experiences items that are brighter, i.e., intellect, etc. (Taijasah).

The Evolving Self is not what is experienced through the mind, but rather that which is aware of the experience of the mind within the larger context of the Ultimate Self.

"I" AS MEDITATIVE AWARENESS (THE "M" OF "AUM")

Letting go of possessions, finding solitude in the heart.

Letting go of the mind, transcending emotions and intellect.

In the vast space of being without a body (beyond the physical or mental body, i.e., as a spirit)

Is to exist in meditative awareness. [TM-2155]

In meditative awareness, one goes beyond clinging to the experiences of the body and mind. Most people would have some experience or knowledge of meditation, with so many meditation centers around. Even in basic meditation, we learn to quiet the senses, emotions, and thoughts and simply focus on our breath. This is just a preparatory discipline. As one advances, one uses that stillness of body and mind to become receptive to intuitive revelation; one carries that mental stillness into day-to-day life, into the here and now. This means bringing what is otherwise a background but a far superior process of intuition into the foreground.

In this state, one works with three instruments:

1. The awareness center
2. The sense of "I"
3. The view of the body-mind experience as an expression of the Ultimate Self

It is not my intention to give the impression that this is a purely Eastern or religious view. Here is an extract from eminent psychologist Carl Jung, who studied various religious practices and tried to give them a psychological perspective.

> "Consciousness succumbs all too easily to unconscious influences, and these are often truer and wiser than our conscious thinking. Also, it frequently happens that unconscious motives overrule our conscious decisions, especially in matters of vital importance. ...I have defined intuition as 'perception via the unconscious'.... One hopes to control the unconscious, but the past masters in the art of self-control, the yogis, attain perfection in samādhi, a state of ecstasy, which, as far as we know, is equivalent to a state of unconsciousness. It makes no difference whether they call our unconscious a 'universal consciousness'; the fact remains that in their case, the unconscious has swallowed up ego-consciousness."

In the state of meditative awareness, the third instrument, the awareness center, is much more than a simple memory dump: It becomes a center that is receptive to flashes of intuition or revelations and progressively becomes aware of the true nature of the self. "I" is no longer a fixed notion regarding physical, physiological, or psychological awareness. "I am" is a witness to physical and physiological experiences and evolves from there.

It is the commencement of life with "I" as a process of evolving awareness. In other words, "I am that I am." As such, it is the conscious beginning of life as a pursuit of the fifth of Maslow's hierarchy of needs, self-actualization, and the corresponding sheath of experience of the Upanishad, bliss. This state relates to growth needs (rather than deficiency needs) and experience.

This state is a meditative state where the senses and mind are still as if one is in deep sleep (aRivu in Tamil; Sushupti in Sanskrit). There is no direct construction of reality from the experience of the body or mind. It is holistic awareness, not formed by denying the body-mind experience but founded upon the higher truth of spiritual awareness that is experienced as intuition or meditative revelations, from them and beyond them as intuitive awareness. The spiritual experience is one of clarity (Thelivu in Tamil).

We do this all the time subconsciously. For instance, after an in-depth sensual, emotional, or intellectual interaction, we often say, "Let me sleep on this," or we need a "cool off" period. While the "cool-off period" includes a period of contingency for anything we have not become aware of as experience or awareness via the body and mind, it also means that when we no longer actively focus on something, our subconscious is actively working on it. This is especially relevant if it is a matter of significant importance, whether choosing a life partner, a place to live, a school for a child, or our career. Most decisions are not exclusively made based on sensual, emotional, or intellectual capabilities alone. After going through all these experiences, we eventually have an inner intuition, and we are psychologically free to make a decision. We call this a hunch, something that "feels right," or our "inner voice." Even when we are not psychologically free, and whether we are externally or internally compelled, we still know that we are going against something intrinsic. In some cases, we may be ignorant of what we need, but life quickly reveals it soon after. It is often us choosing to be compliant with or please others or what we are nurtured with.

As we have seen before (e.g., Goldstein, Rogers), being closed to experience and twisting the experience to fit a fixed notion is an unhealthy, unnatural response from a living being. The natural flow is to be open, discover, and evolve. However, as modern living becomes more layered and sophisticated, self-actualization requires us to be even more trained in techniques such as meditation. In less complex living forms, from single cells to animals, self-actualization is much more straightforward and more of a biological or simpler psychological evolution, for example, seen in more advanced mammals. Given the increasingly shrinking psychological distance between various parts of the world, cultures, and ideas, to stand apart as a witness requires people to have an even higher level of discipline. With the evolution of technology and the increasing power of artificial intelligence, people and organizations with power and resources can find sophisticated ways to dictate our needs and influence, orchestrate, and control individual behavior. To the extent we are less clear about who we are and what we need, the world around us is only pleased to dictate that to us, thus reducing us to a beast of burden or mere order taker. Our primary drives then get distorted in a crowd-pleasing pursuit, so that we can fit into the worldly order, where means are mistaken for the end (spiritual need of self-actualization).

On the other hand, it requires a sense of awareness and courage to step back and discover who we are and what we need. It does not require sophisticated technology or resources; rather, simple techniques that have been developed since ancient times are necessary. It requires an element of courage to go into Nietzsche's lion stage of the "Sacred No." When we do that, what was pushed into the background, or our subconscious activity, is progressively brought to the foreground as a way of living. This only happens when the senses, emotions, and rational thinking processes are at rest. By rest, I do not mean suppressed but calm and receptive; I mean that they have done their part and let a higher faculty take it from there. As Carl Jung and countless sages and saints have found, revelation or intuition is much superior to the common body-mind perceptions, especially in matters of very subtle and great importance. Self-actualization is the most foundational and ultimate need, as we have seen across many fields of study.

However, this process is not limited to Hindus or Buddhists. The below describes this process given by two great saints in Christianity.

St. Augustine (354–430 AD)

St. Augustine is regarded as one of the key personalities in Christianity. He extensively wrote across many fields of study: philosophy, psychology, theology, history, political theory, and other subjects. His *Confessions*, from which the following passage is taken, is widely recognized even today.

- "I entered into the innermost part of myself.... I entered and I saw with my soul's eye (such as it was) an unchangeable light shining above this eye of my soul and above my mind.... He who knows truth knows that light, and he who knows that light knows eternity. Love knows it. O eternal truth and true love and beloved eternity!"

- "And I often do this. I find delight in it, and whenever I can relax from my necessary duties, I have recourse to this pleasure. [I experience] a state of feeling which is quite unlike anything to which I am used—a kind of sweet delight which, if I could only remain permanently in that state, would be something not of this world, not of this life. But my sad weight makes me fall back again; I am swallowed up by normality."

St. Teresa of Avila (1515–1582 AD)

St. Teresa was one of the most prominent figures in Christianity. Her books are widely recognized. Here are some excerpts from her works.

- "My soul at once becomes recollected, and I enter the state of quiet or that of rapture so that I can use none of my faculties and senses…"

- "Everything is stilled, and the soul is left in a state of great quiet and deep satisfaction."

- "From this recollection, there sometimes springs an interior peace and quietude that is full of happiness, for the soul is in such a state that it thinks there is nothing that it lacks. Even speaking—by which I mean vocal prayer and meditation—wearies it: it would like to do nothing but love. This condition lasts for some time and may even last for long periods."

The state of awareness described in this section is known as "clarity" (Therul in Tamil). It represents the dawn of conscious and holistic spiritual awareness. In the previous categories, awareness results in engagement and experiences through the body and mind. In this state, one acts as a witness to the unfolding of life as a continuous process. It witnesses the experiences of the body and mind as aids, steppingstones, and subjects of meditation for intuitive awareness.

Here are some extracts from Mandukya Upanishad that add flavor and complement our understanding (Sloka #6):

- In this state, what we experience is bliss (Ānanda bhuk).

- This state of awareness is the Lord of all manifestations (Sarvesvara), one who governs from within (antaryami), aware of all (sarvajna), the womb of all, where all things arise and dissolve (yonih sarvasya prabhavā apyaya).

Self is not what happens in life but that which is aware of what happens in life within the larger context of the Ultimate Self.

"I" AS WHOLESOME, LIVING, OR SACRED AWARENESS ("AUM" AKA "OM" AS A SYNTHESIS)

In meditative awareness, witnessing through three aspects-

Awareness Center, Life (experience), **and Sense of "I,"**

Evolve (beyond this meditative state) **from within the inner lotus** (awareness center).

The sense of "I" embraces the "Ultimate" (Self). [TM-2156]

Here, one is letting go of the awareness center as a separate instrument. It is a continuous evolution of wholesome or living awareness, not living from memory. This does not mean that we live as if we have an empty brain, but rather that the Self does not allow memory to distort the experience of the arising moment. One is fully open to experience and lives existentially in each "here and now." This is ongoing proof, "eternally and ultimately;" it is a sense of "I am," not as a fixed notion but as a continuous evolution, not just as a witness but as a union of the Self and the Ultimate Self on each occasion. It is more of meditation in action than sitting down to witness. It is a process of self-discovery, evolution, and contributions in each occupation. This is a state of wholesomeness (seRivu in Tamil; Turiya in Sanskrit).

The instruments used in this state are:

1. The Ultimate Self
2. The evolving Self (as a sense of "I") in union with the Ultimate Self impinges on the center of awareness.

In this state, life is experienced as an interplay between "I" and the "ultimate" Self, coming together in unison, in every here and now, on all of life's occasions. It is a state in which the Ultimate Self is the primary reality, and the individual Self is an instrument that becomes the awareness center for divine expression. In this state of awareness, the primary trajectory of life has become an evolving process of self-actualization: The Self is evolving awareness toward the Ultimate Self, with increasing authentic living (Verity) fueled by an increasing sense of love.

We discuss the details of what this means in real life in Quality (8) as a part of Path 4. We have already seen a summary of all eight qualities in an earlier section.

The spiritual experience in this state is called "blessedness" (Arul in Tamil). It is bliss as an inherent state of who one is, not just as an experience.

In short, "I" is an evolving awareness. Progressing toward its ultimate state, using every experience as a steppingstone to engage, experience, reflect, discover, and evolve.

Here are some extracts from the Mandukya Upanishad that add flavor and complement our understanding (Sloka #7,#8, and #12):

- This is the essence of the Self (eka ātma pratyaya sāraṃ).
- It is tranquil (Śāntam), auspicious, and the ultimate essence (Śivam), a unity i.e., non-dual (advaitam).
- OM is the Self (aumkaara atmaiva).
- In this process, the evolving Self reaches the ultimate Self (samvlshaty atmana atmaanam).

Self is not the unfoldment of life itself, but an awareness that evolves through the unfolding of life and progresses toward its Ultimate Self.

MEDITATIVE AWARENESS AS THE STRATEGIC LEVER OF SELF-ACTUALIZATION

Archimedes (an ancient Greek mathematician and physicist) said "Give me a lever long enough ... and I shall move the world". In the self-actualization context, Meditative Awareness is that lever for self-discovery and self-evolution along the journey of self-actualization.

Let's take a closer look at this starting with a song from Thirumanthiram

There is a deep field and two barren fields.

Then, there is an intrinsic field that permeates all.

For those who cultivate the deep field,

(The permeated field) **flourishes like a fertile and irrigated field.** [TM-2871]

The first two fields, on their own, are spiritually barren by default. The physical/physiological and psychological fields are relative i.e. "I" with respect to other things or beings. They deal with the first four needs of Maslow's hierarchy (physiological, safety, belonging, and esteem needs) and the corresponding sheaths of experience (Kosha) in the Upanishads (physical, physiological, emotional, and intellectual). The third field (deep field), represents meditative awareness and has the potential to become directly and consciously aware of the true nature of the Self as a spirit. In this field, "I" is viewed in the context of the Ultimate Self (not in relation to the world i.e. not in terms of body-mind experience). It is a spiritual sense of Self. As we cultivate this awareness through meditation, the Living Awareness (OM or AUM) permeates all others and evolves as a synthesis of them. The Self becomes a wholesome or living awareness.

As we have seen, the root cause of suffering is ignorance. We can best cultivate our meditative awareness by transcending this state of clinging to body-mind experience (as "I am This") and leading a life of happiness by embracing the journey of self-actualization (with I as an evolving awareness i.e. "I am that I am"). This, as we have seen before, requires a sense of courage of conviction. As we have seen in Chapter 3, Taitarya Upanishads say that to the extent we have a sense of separation from the ultimate, to that extent we have fear. But as we progress along self-actualization and experience true bliss, the fear (of the other) begins to fade away. As we have found a new anchor, beyond the body-mind experience.

The pivot for transformation is meditative awareness that goes beyond the first two states of awareness and lays the foundation for wholesome awareness. It takes us beyond the deficiency needs (i.e. first four needs in the hierarchy of needs, as discussed in Chapter 3) and growth needs become the new predominant motivation.

This is why meditation was the most critical life skill in ancient India when India was the superpower economically and culturally (before 1 B.C. and even very much up to 1000 AD). Ideas and practices of meditation spread right up to East Asia including China to Japan. For instance, the word "Thyanam" in Tamil and "Dhyana" in Sanskrit means to meditate, which became "Chan" in Chinese and "Zen" in Japanese. It is said that the first Patriarch of Zen Buddhism, Bodhidharma, was a Tamil prince from Kanchipuram (present-day Tamil Nadu, India).

Being mindful in the "here and now," but within a wider context of the "eternally and ultimate", helps us use every occasion as a steppingstone to progress along self-actualization.

Let's look at a brief story expressed as a song from Thiru Kalitruppadiyar (part of Saiva Siththantham of Hinduism). There was a devotee called Senthanar. He was considered a low cast from a social perspective. As such he was not allowed to dedicate any food to God (Siva) in temples. The story goes that he packed some rice in a piece of cloth. Untied the cloth and placed it on the ground outside the temple. Siva came out and ate it with great joy. Senthanar experienced great bliss.

The grain of rice from the unfolded cloth

Untied by the detached mind of Senthanar.

Offered with genuine love.

It became a joyful feast for the king (Siva) whose hair was let loose [Thiru Kalitruppadiyar, #53]

Regardless of its historical aspects, it is highly symbolic from a spiritual perspective. The offered grain of rice is a body-mind experience (the happening in the external or internal world). Senthanar is the evolving awareness. His act of offering to God is the process of meditation, where the senses, emotions, and mind are made calm and receptive. Sethanar untying the cloth, humbly placing it on the ground, and waiting for Siva's response, is symbolic of meditative awareness, receptive to the revelation of the truth about the ultimate self ("Who am I?"). The act of Siva accepting the offering and bestowing blessings is the intuitive revelation of higher truth (of the true nature of Self and life as a whole). Senthanar then evolves from being a low cast (limiting to body-mind experience) to a seer of Siva (evolving awareness reaching toward the Ultimate Self). This is an eloquent way of saying how meditative awareness acts as a cardinal lever in the process of self-actualization.

In short, "Self will enjoy a blissful experience of being blessed whenever one can look as a detached and joyful witness at things and events happening to him with a mind free of defined preconceptions and in a state of surrender to His Grace ". On a personal note, the words in quotes were those of my fathers. This was one of the key topics via email exchanges I had with my father in May 2002, the year before he passed away. I am using this as an opportunity to take a moment to reflect and appreciate his role in my life.

The culminating experience in this process of self-actualization is beautifully outlined in another song from Thirumandhiram.

> **When the expressive letters (A, U) unite with the silent letter (M)**
>
> **Like the limbs are withdrawn** (as separate entities) **into the tortoise** (unity), **the five senses unite within** (the self)
>
> **OM has become all permeating; the inner light is received.**
>
> **I am unaware when and how the** (individual) **Self has ceased to exist** (as separate from the Ultimate Self) [TM21-58]

The union of the Individual Self with the Ultimate Self-i.e. self-actualization is a very subtle and iterative process. It is not a single event when I have become the Ultimate. It is a progressive self-discovery and self-evolution. While the trigger to switch to pursue self-actualization as a deliberate need, may occur from pivotal moments in life (existential crisis from a life-changing event), the process of self-actualization is progressive and subtle.

(7) Q2: "I AM" AN EVOLVING PROCESS [VEL]

The purpose of all learning is to embrace the good path of the wholesome awareness [TK-02]

STORY: BRINGING THE SKY-RIVER TO THE EARTH

The story of Bageerathan is also well-known in Hinduism.

Again, I am not presenting this as an academic and accurate representation of the story or its traditional interpretation. I have used it as the base story, added my flavor, and provided my interpretation at the end. The purpose here is to provide an intuitive and initial view of what we will be discussing in the remaining parts of the section.

Story

King Sagara wanted to perform a Velvi, a procedure of dedication to God, to receive great blessings regarding the increase in the prosperity and well-being of his kingdom. Part of the offering included the use of a royal horse. Deva King Devendran of heaven was jealous of King Sagara's progress in the Velvi. Devendran wished to disrupt the Velvi. With such malicious intent, Devendran hid the horse in the dark recess of the universe, where a powerful sage was meditating. Firstly, this made it difficult to find the horse, and even if someone found it, retrieving it without disturbing and thereby offending the sage would be impossible. If the sage were disturbed while in his meditation, the consequences would be devastating.

The king sent his able sons in search of the horse. They eventually found it, but in their attempt to retrieve it, they offended the sage. Disturbed from his meditation, the sage cursed the princes and reduced them to ashes. The redemption of the princes and the completion of the efforts started by King Sagara then passed on to the next generation. There were a few attempts, but all failed during the following generation. Then it was the turn of King Bageerathan, the great-grandson of the former King Sagara.

The redemption required the holy river Ganga to wash away the cursed princes' ashes so that they could gain liberation and ascend to heaven. Bageerathan prayed to Ganga in an intense meditative form. At that time, the Ganga was a holy river in the sky and did not flow down to earth. In response to Bageerathan's prayers, she appeared in celestial form and asked what blessings he wanted. Bageerathan humbly requested Ganga to flow down to earth and redeem his ancestors. Ganga was ready to bless him as he requested. However, there was a problem. If Ganga descended directly from the sky to the earth, the force of her flow would destroy the earth. So, she advised him to seek the help of Siva. Only with his help could Ganga flow gently to the earth.

Bageerathan thanked Ganga and began to meditate on Siva. After an intense meditation, Siva appeared before Bageerathan and agreed to help. Siva let the Ganga flow from his head, such that Siva's hair helped slow down the force of the flow of Ganga between the sky and the earth. Ganga then started flowing gently as it touched the earth. Bageerathan's ancestors were redeemed, and his kingdom was prosperous again under his rule.

Key Takeaways

- Ganga, the flow of the sky-river to the ground, represents the revelation of higher truth (the flow of intuition revealing the higher nature of the self) to the conscious Self (earth—as the manifest reality experienced by the body and mind).

- Intuitions are deep communications from our Ultimate Self (or what Carl Jung calls the unconscious), symbolized by Siva.

- The Ultimate Self is far more powerful than our conscious selves (beings on earth). If intuitions are revealed in all their force and glory, i.e., in their raw form, they will disorient our day-to-day living.

- Siva's blessing of letting Ganga flow from his head, from the sky to the earth, to slow down the flow of Ganga, is the mediation process of using the revealing intuitions in a usable way that benefits our day-to-day living.

- The ancestors' sins symbolize our past habits, outlook, or orientation to cling to the body-mind experience as the ultimate and independent truth.

- The powerful sage cursing the princes and reducing them to ashes is symbolic of the idea that before the reality of life, all false notions will be reduced to ashes. At some point, even in a remote corner of our lives, truth will come to the foreground, and then falsehood will fall apart. The idea of Velvi is symbolic of self-discovery, and the blessings one seeks are self-actualization. If we distort that for external prosperity as the end (not the means), life will show us the hollowness of that pursuit.

- Ganga flowing to earth and cleansing the ancestors' sins is the use of the revelation of truth (intuition) to evolve our current awareness toward the Ultimate Self in the process of self-actualization. Meditate, become aware, and evolve beyond experience so that we meet the next occasion as more evolved beings. To continue this process of Self as evolving awareness (not clinging to the body-mind experience) and to progress toward self-actualization is the Mindful Living we discussed in Chapter 5.

Image17: Bageerathan bringing the Sky River, Ganga, to the Earth

OVERVIEW

As we have seen in Chapter 4, Carl Rogers, an eminent psychologist, states that people who are progressing in self-actualization ("fully functioning person," "Good Life") view themselves as a process, not as a fixed product. In Hinduism, the Self is seen as an evolving process of awareness. Clinging to the body-mind experience leads to a fettered life (3 fetters). In this chapter, let's examine this process of evolving awareness in more detail. In the previous chapter, we discussed self-awareness that evolves through four states, with the highest being wholesome awareness. We also discussed that the strategic lever for self-actualization is meditative awareness. In this chapter, let's take a closer look at how meditative awareness helps the Self transcend the clutches of the manifest (clinging to the experience of the body and mind) and evolve toward the Ultimate Self, wholesome awareness. The summary of topics we will discuss is as follows:

- **SYNTHESIS:** Use of Relative Truth as a steppingstone toward Ultimate Truths
- **"VELVI":** Discovery of the Ultimate Truths about ourselves
- **ENLIGHTENMENT:** How awareness of the Ultimate Truth dispels Ignorance
- **EVOLUTION:** Toward Self-Actualization
- **"KAIVALYAM":** Culmination - Transcendental Aloneness (going beyond the body-mind experience as the primary reality) & Union with the Ultimate

Let's examine each one in this chapter in more detail. Starting with authentic/existential living, meditating on the resulting experiences, and then emerging as a more evolved Self from each experience is an ongoing process of self-awareness. This is self-actualization, with life as an ongoing homage to the Ultimate Self. If life is an evolving union of the Self at any given point in time, progressing toward the Ultimate Self, then it is a continuous process of evolution.

This outlook is further elaborated in the following song (from Thirumandhirtam):

> **Awareness and Divinity are not two** (separate) **things.**
>
> **Divinity is revealed in our awareness.**
>
> **As awareness becomes clearer and clearer,**
>
> **Divinity takes residence within our awareness.** [TM-2853]

Our Ultimate Self is divinity. Evolution is embracing this divinity in our life, i.e., becoming divine (consciously or unconsciously). That is the process of self-actualization—to become the Self that one truly is and evolve transparently/consciously before the notion of the Ultimate Self, with Divinity as the goal and standard. That is how Soren Kierkegaard describes self-becoming, as seen in Chapter 4.

SYNTHESIS: USE OF RELATIVE TRUTH AS A STEPPINGSTONE TOWARD THE ULTIMATE TRUTHS

In life, there are two truths. The first category is that we use in our day-to-day living, which is relative to who we are at that moment. These are called conventional truths or worldly truths that guide our day-to-day living. Then there is a second category of truth called ultimate truth. They do not change with time or geography; they are eternal and universal.

To lead an authentic life (Verity), one needs to recognize both truths and lead a life of synthesis, i.e., applying ultimate truth to the moment of need here and now, to the extent we can. Evolution progressively uses the demands of the here and now as an occasion to respond with ultimate and eternal truths. With each moment, one lives existentially (without distortion) and evolves from the experience to meet the next moment as a more evolved being. In this process, we evolve our notion of conventional truth (what we consider our day-to-day truths) with each occasion.

The Self is a process of evolving synthesis. It does not run away from relative truth, as it is the only truth it can live by at any moment. However, as it evolves and becomes more aware of the ultimate truth, it should not cling to past relative truths. One should let go of them and evolve one's life with evolving awareness.

The idea of evolution is not to deny the needs and experiences of the body-mind. That is just being disingenuous, and living in deprivation or denial is not the same as evolution. It is merely putting up an appearance of the evolved state. On the other hand, clinging to the body-mind experience leads to a fettered Self and impedes evolution. The middle path (or what I prefer to call the higher path) is to realize that:

> **"He" and "I" are two truths.**
>
> **Once seen that "He" and "I" are in one's awareness,**
>
> **Once one dedicates "I" as the flower at the feet of "He,"**
>
> **To say "He" and "I"** (as two separate things) **is not sensible.**
> [TM-1607]

Self is an evolving process of awareness and a progressive synthesis of the relative with the ultimate along the path of self-actualization. This means that one progressively brings the ultimate and eternal nature into day-to-day and conscious living, leading to increasingly authentic living. This process is fueled by love, serving as a worship of the Ultimate Self in an ongoing process of evolution.

The evolution leads toward progressive Verity in one's life, filled with love for this way of living (VEL). This does not involve dogmatic or fanatical living, but instead, it involves experiential and evolving awareness of truth. In short, it is about living an evolving authentic life, fueled by love, with an increasing quality and scale of happiness.

Various religions eloquently describe this idea as follows:

Two-Truth Doctrine of Buddhism

Buddhism provides another way to understand this idea, i.e., transcending the manifest and uniting with the ultimate.

The "two-truth doctrine" is a critical aspect of spiritual practice in Buddhism. Nagarjuna considered the second coming of Buddha, outlines it as follows:

- The Buddha's teaching of the Dharma is based on two truths: a truth of worldly convention and ultimate truth.

- Those who do not understand the distinction between these two truths do not grasp the profundity of the Buddha's teachings.

- Without a foundation in the conventional truth, the significance of the ultimate cannot be taught. Without understanding the significance of the ultimate, liberation is not attained.

The middle path, a core concept of Buddhism, is a synthesis. It involves living a mindful life in which one does not deny the place of relative truth in day-to-day existence. However, we should not cling to that relative truth as we evolve. Instead, as we progressively experience and understand more of the ultimate truth, we evolve with it.

Christian View – Soren Kierkegaard

As we have seen before, Soren Kierkegaard outlines the Self as a synthesis of immediate necessity and eternal possibility. He says that the drive (or despair) toward the ultimate is humanity's blessing over the beast. Progressing along this path is what he calls "Christian Blessedness."

Kierkegaard also shares this notion of synthesis. He states that immediate necessity gives us a sense of the grounding reality as a confining factor, preventing us from getting carried away with fantasies. However, if we limit ourselves to that, we lose a sense of Self and continue living our lives just to meet other people's expectations and fit in.

As we saw in Chapter 4, he outlines that the notion of ultimate possibility is the "infinitizing" factor. Self-becoming is an ongoing and evolving synthesis.

Two-Birds Notion of Upanishads (Hinduism)

A similar idea is outlined in the Muṇḍaka Upanishads. The two notions of truth are symbolized as two birds. One bird experiences the world and represents the fettered Self when it clings to the experiences through the body and mind. It remains ignorant of its ultimate nature and suffers from worldly ups and downs as a result. The other bird watches the former and represents the Ultimate Self. When the ignorant bird realizes that its true nature is that of the Ultimate Self, it no longer suffers from the body-mind experience. It evolves toward becoming one with the Ultimate Self and experiences progressive bliss.

> a. "Two birds, bound to each other in close friendship, perch on the self-same tree. One

eats the tree's fruits with relish, while the other just looks on without eating."

b. "Seated on the same tree, one of them—the ego—sunk in ignorance and delusion, grieves for his impotence. But when he sees the other—the Lord, the worshipful one with His Glory—he becomes free from dejection."

c. "When the seer realizes the self-effulgent supreme Being—ruler, maker, and source of the creator even—then that wise one, shaking off all deeds of merits and demerits, becomes stainless and attains the supreme state of equipoise."

Two Beings and their Synthesis of Bhagavad Gita (Hinduism)

a. There are two beings in the world—the Perishable (**kṣaraḥ**) and the Imperishable (**akṣaraḥ**). All manifestations (body-mind) are perishable, and the immutable (underlying awareness) is called the Imperishable. (15.16)

b. But distinct is the Supreme Self, called the Ultimate Self, the indestructible Lord, who pervades and sustains the three worlds. (15.17)

c. As I transcend the Perishable and am even above the Imperishable, therefore, I am known in the world and the Veda as 'Purushottama,' the Highest Self. (15.18)

d. d. He who, undeluded, knows Me as the Highest Self knows all, and worships Me with all his heart. (15.19)

The perishable Self is the notion of "I am this," defining "I" as a fixed profile in terms of the experience of the body-mind: physical, physiological, emotional, and intellectual experiences. The

Unmanifest is a potential and has no manifest qualities. The Self is an evolving awareness. It is not an unmanifest (or unconscious) foundation like underlying awareness. Nor does it cling to the manifest. It is an evolving awareness that uses the body-mind experience to evolve toward the Ultimate Self. It is a synthesis of the two notions of a living and evolving self.

"Velvi": Discovery of the Ultimate Truth

Let's now revisit the idea of "Velvi," which we discussed in Chapter 1 as part of the story. The process of evolution is symbolically represented in the ritual of Velvi (or Yagna in Sanskrit).

- The fettered Self is represented by the one performing the Velvi (i.e., dedicating worldly things to the fire).

- Evolving awareness is symbolized by the fire that grows from what is offered.

- The Ultimate Self is represented as the divinity toward which the Velvi is dedicated.

- The worldly things that are offered are the body-mind experience.

- Blessings are revelations of higher truth as intuitive wisdom (to the questions - Who am I? What is the purpose of my life?)

- Accepting the blessings allows the Self to evolve as an evolving awareness ("I am That I am") rather than clinging to the body-mind experiences of the past ("I am This").

Growing fire is considered the greatest wealth,

Becoming the guiding Guru,

Comes to me as awareness that governs the world (that I experience).

That which is harmful departs, as I become a witness. [TM-1041]

In most religions that originated in India (and across other religions as well), there is a high emphasis on using Tantras. Tantras are a set of physical/physiological and psychological (emotional, intellectual) procedures/outlooks, meant to be an aid used to create a given state of mind. As we have seen in the story in the first chapter, conducting Velvi is defined as a set of body-mind rituals simulating what needs to happen in life. Velvi is a process of training oneself to become a part of our being, a part of our muscle memory that we can take to day-to-day life as a way of self-discovery and evolution, using every experience as a steppingstone. The following extracts from the Bhagavad Gita describe the symbolic representation of Velvi as a self-actualization process.

Image18: Velvi

- "The oblation is the Ultimate (Brahma); the clarified butter is the Ultimate, offered by the Ultimate in the fire of the Ultimate. Unto Brahman, verily, goes the one who recognizes the Ultimate alone in his actions." (4.24)

- "As the blazing fire reduces fuel to ashes, so does the fire of awareness reduce all actions to ashes." (4.37)

- "Certainly, there is no purifier in this world like awareness. He who is himself perfected in yoga finds it in the Self in time." (4.38)

- "The yogi, abandoning attachment, performs work with the body, the mind, the intellect, and the senses only for self-purification." (5.11)

- "He whose happiness is within, whose delight is within, whose illumination is within only, that yogi becomes the Ultimate (Brahman) and gains the liberation of the Ultimate (Brahman)." (5.24)

- "Let a man raise himself by himself; let him not lower himself. For he is himself his friend, himself his foe." (6.5)

- "Of one unattached, liberated, with the mind absorbed in awareness, performing work for Yajna alone, his entire actions melt away." (4.23)

- "When the mind, disciplined by the practice of yoga, attains quietude, and when seeing the Self by the self, he is satisfied in the Self." (6.2)

- "Fix your mind on Me; be devoted to Me; sacrifice to Me; prostrate before Me; so shall you come to Me. This is My pledge to you, for you are dear to Me." (18.65)

ENLIGHTENMENT: HOW AWARENESS OF THE ULTIMATE TRUTH DISPELS IGNORANCE

We do not need to fight that which is false. The antidote for ignorance is to develop awareness. As we become aware of our true nature, ignorance about our true nature is dispelled. Truth prevails over falsehood in the same way that light dispels darkness.

The Mundaka Upanishad states (Book 3, Chapter 1, Sloka 6):

"Truth alone prevails, not untruth.

By Truth is laid out the path divinity,

along which the seers, free from desires,

reach the highest abode of Truth."

In Chapter 3, we explored a key Buddhist concept called dependent arising, which outlines the 12 links of dependent arising. The arising of ignorance leads to a life of suffering. This is referred to as "Anuloma" or going with the grain of dependent arising.

The reverse flow is called "Pratiloma," which is going against the grain or in reverse order to dependent arising. As awareness dispels ignorance, the reverse flow is initiated. When ignorance ceases, the remaining links also cease, leading to the cessation of suffering. Buddha states this as follows:

> **"When this exists, that comes to be; with the arising of this, that arises. When this does not exist, that does not come to be; with the cessation of this, that ceases."**
> (Samyutta Nikaya 12.61)

As awareness dispels our ignorance, the cessation of ignorance sets in motion a domino effect regarding the cessation of the other links, ultimately leading to the cessation of suffering.

1 CESSATION of Ignorance (Avidya)

Cessation of the ignorance of nature of the (true) self, the world, and life

2 CESSATION of (Faculty) Cognitive (Samskara)

Cessation of ignorance leads to the cessation of faculty thought constructions about reality

3 CESSATION of (Faculty) Understanding (Vijnana)

Cessation of faculty cognitive constructs leads to the cessation of faculty understanding

4 CESSATION of (Distorted and Rigid Notions of) Name and Form (Nama-Rupa)

Cessation of distorted understanding leads to the cessation of distorted mental (names) and physical associations (forms) with the world.

5 CESSATION of (Faulty Conditioning of) the Six Instruments (Ayatana)

This, in turn, leads to the cessation of the incorrect conditioning of the five senses and the mind, i.e., what ti expect in the next encounter.

6 CESSATION of (Wrongly Conditioned) Contact with the World (Sparsha)

This, in turn, leads to the cessation of conditioned contact with the world.

7 CESSATION of (Distorted) Experience Arising from Contact (Vedana)

This leads to the cessation of conditioned experiences.

8 CESSATION of Thirst (Tanha) for More

This leads to the cessation of thirst for what has been pleasant (which is already distorted)

9 CESSATION of Clinging (Upadana)

This leads to the cessation of clinging to what is experienced with a sense of "I"

10 CESSATION of the (Distorted) Process of Becoming (Bhava)

This leads to the cessation of a distortion of the process of becoming one's self, i.e., the process of Self discovery and self-actualization.

11 CESSATION of (Fettered) Arising (Jati)

This leads to the cessation of distorting every new arising of the Self with subsequent experiences.

12 CESSATION of Suffering (Jaramaranam)

This leads to cessation of suffering

EVOLUTION: TOWARD SELF-ACTUALIZATION

The purpose of evolving awareness is to live with true conviction throughout our life journey, not merely to exist in a mechanical life or meet the expectations of others. As we observed in Chapter 4, self-actualization, evident across various fields of study, is not for the faint-hearted. It requires courage and conviction. Leading a life of habit or compliance may be easier, yet it places us in a more vulnerable position to live mindfully and with conviction. The difference in outcomes is stark: one can live mechanically, thus experiencing a limited sense of life, or cultivate a progressively evolving sense of self. The former often results in a trajectory of suffering, whereas the latter may lead to progressive bliss. The intellectual or emotional analysis we do only prepares the ground for conviction but does not arrive at it.

This intellectual and emotional process helps to eliminate options. But the decisive moment of conviction only comes as a flash of intuition. When all other senses, emotions, and intellect are calm and receptive, a higher insight flashes as intuition. This is the primary training provided by meditation. To train our body and mind (senses, emotions, thoughts) to be calm and receptive to intuition.

Recollecting the silent communication between the "Thatchina Murthi" form of Siva and the four saints. Siva's communication represents the revelation of two truths: (1) the Truth of Self (Who am I?), and (2) the Truth of how to respond to each occasion (organismic response). These truths are communicated to the four inner faculties: (1) the emotional faculty (manam), (2) the intellectual faculty (buddhi), (3) the awareness center (Siththam), and (4) the sense of I (ahankaram). These faculties represent the spiritualization of inner capabilities, culminating in the courage of conviction. From this seat of courage of conviction, one can holistically engage the world—self, Ultimate Self, and life in harmony; head and heart aligned.

Kurt Goldstein observed that the whole organism participates in every response, consciously or unconsciously.

Carl Jung proposed that intuition is the communication of the unconscious. In his view, the unconscious is far superior to the conscious mind. Furthermore, he suggested that the conscious mind can be trained to be more receptive.

Training the Conscious Self to be more Receptive

- One hopes to control the unconscious, but the past masters in the **art of self-control, the yogis, attain perfection in**

samādhi, a state of ecstasy, which, as far as we know, is equivalent to a state of unconsciousness. It makes no difference whether they call our unconscious "universal consciousness"; the fact remains that, in their case, the **unconscious has swallowed up ego consciousness**.

• **"Universal consciousness" is logically identical to unconsciousness**. Nevertheless, correctly applying the methods described in the Pali Canon or the *Yoga-sūtra* induces a **remarkable expansion of consciousness**.

The Yoga Sutra outlines eight steps for mindful living. The last three (6 to 8) are collectively called **Samyama**. It is a process of self-discovery and self-evolution with each experience. Looking at the eight steps:

Preparation

1. Removal of blemishes (Yama)
2. Embracing "purity" (Niyama)

Engagement & Disengagement

3. Seat (of action) (Asana)
4. Total life engagement (pranayama)
5. Withdrawal from body-mind experience, i.e., not clinging (Pratyahara)

"Samyama" – toward actualization

6. *Hold (Dharana)* – *behold the body and mind experience as a subject of meditation.*
7. *Meditate (Dhyana)* – *meditate on the body-mind experience, leading to the revelation of truth to the point of conviction.*

8. **Actualization (Samathi)** – *transcend the experience as a more evolved being guided by the revelation of higher truth via meditation. Engage the next moment as a more evolved being, i.e., not cling to the body-mind experience and define Self as a fixed notion ("I am This") but keep evolving with each experience via meditation (i.e., as evolving awareness, "I am That I am").*

Steps (1) to (3) are preparatory steps for action. Step (4) involves total actions (existential living) in the here and now. Step (5) is a preparatory stage for meditation—stilling the senses, emotions, and thoughts by not clinging to the body-mind experience, i.e., withdrawing from the body-mind experience. Steps (6) to (8) are collectively called "Samyama" and include meditation (leading to the revelation of higher truth) and actualization, i.e., making this higher truth part of one's conscious being.

"Kaivalyam": Culmination – Transcendental Aloneness (Non-Clinging) and Union with the Ultimate

Kaivalyam is one of the cardinal and culminating concepts in the Yoga Sutra.

There are traditional definitions. As I have mentioned many times before in this book, my interest is not in knowledge transfer with academic compliance to traditional interpretation; it is more about what I have learned in my life and how I have interpreted it.

This topic is one of the focused subjects I discussed with my Guru and father 21 years ago (December 2002) when he was in his mid-sixties and I was in my early thirties. In this chapter, I want to quote my father. For the reader, I am not quoting this as a quote from a source of widely accepted authority. It is the world's misfortune that he never took to public life. But it is my fortune that there was an intense period of a few years where he and I were fully engaged in an intense spiritual exchange, with him being the Guru and I being the disciple.

I am reproducing these out of respect and love for him and the journey he started me on. I would like some of his words to be included in this book as my way of profusely thanking him and for the reader to understand this in his words.

The following are extracts from email exchanges in December 2002, one year before he passed away.

> The essential meaning of Kaivalyam is "de-linking" - de-linking means "non-dependence." So, it should be correct to say that one has attained Kaivalyam in relation to anything with which he has no dependent relationship—a relationship where one is not affected or disturbed by whatever the other does or whatever happens to the other. The Kaivalya Upanishad gave me this insight. It uses Kaivalyam to describe the state of "witness," which is not affected by what it witnesses. The ultimate state of Kaivalyam dealt with in the Upanishad is the state where one is not affected by anything manifest to his senses, mind, and intellect - at this stage, one is supposed to be at "oneness" with Brahman - it is at this stage one is supposed to be eligible to exclaim the two famous Vedic Mahavaakyas*: "Tat tvam asi" - you are that; and "aham bramasmi" - I am Brahman!
>
> The ultimate state of Kaivalyam described in Yoga Sutra - Vibhuti patha verse 55 is also the same. It says that one is deemed to have attained the ultimate Kaivalyam when he attains the same purity as the purushaa/Brahman - purity

meaning freedom from any dependency or affliction in relation to anything manifest to the senses/mind*/intellect - anything of the manifest world*.

The road to spiritual growth, therefore, lies in the progressive growth of non-dependence on the manifest world - on the progressive withering away of the significance of the manifest world in one's life - on the progressive growth of the significance of the unmanifest reality in one's life filling the void created by the withering away of the role of the manifest - on the progressive growth of the significance of "what is yet to be" as against "what had already been" - on the progressive growth in the capacity to "kick the manifest past" and to say "the race is not yet over" in relation to the "unmanifest" - on the progressive growth in one's capacity to "not to say die till one is manifestly dead!" - on the progressive growth of the reality of "He and I" partnership in our lives!

So, Kaivalyam is indeed the noblest of concepts taught by our scriptures for a life of faith and hope in relation to the future, unaffected by anything of the past. The God to be served - in fact, served by all living beings - is the "unmanifest" waiting to "manifest" – the tomorrow. The pooja to God, all of us are performing all the time, with or without our awareness, is our deeds in the present moment directed toward the creation of the tomorrow awaiting manifestation!

Note

- Please note that there are four great sayings in Hinduism called Mahavaakiyas.* Two of them are listed in the email above.

- In this book, the term "de-linking*" has the same meaning as "non-clinging."

- I am using the word "emotions" to refer to what he calls "mind."*

- The term "Manifest world"* is what I refer to as a "body-mind" experience.

I then asked my father and guru to interpret verse 34 from the last part of the Yoga Sutra by Patanjali. A traditional interpretation of the Sutra goes as follows:

"Thus, the supreme state of independence manifests while the guṇas reabsorb themselves into Prakṛti, having no more purpose to serve the Puruṣa. Or [to look from another angle], the power of pure consciousness settles in its own pure nature." (#4.34, The Yoga Sutras of Patanjali: Commentary on the Raja Yoga Sutras by Sri Swami Satchidananda)

The Sanskrit verse is as follows:

Puruṣārtha śūnyānām guṇānām pratiprasavaḥ kaivalyam svarūpa pratiṣṭhā vā citi śakter iti. (#4.34)

Here is an excerpt from his email with his interpretation:

The meaning I ascribe to this Sutra is as follows: "When the purposes of an embodied soul (purushartha) to be served by the Gunas (psychological qualities) come to an end (sunyaanaam), the Gunas return to their original state of equilibrium in the prakirthi (the embodiment ends) or get established (prathishta/ prathishtai in Tamil) (the embodiment continues) with the Gunas in their ultimate nature (svarupa) as pure awareness - cit Sakthi – jnana sakthi. This is Kaivalyam."

This essentially means that when a soul has reached its end in active engagement in worldly life (sansara) - where it no longer cares for anything in the world - it either ceases to be embodied - it attains nirvana, or it continues its existence as a "pure witness" - as an "ava thutha" who enjoys every dance of Mother Nature without the need to dance with his own! His continued existence is to "see" and to "sing" the glory of the

Divine dance through his purification via his power to be aware (Gnana Sakthi – all "doings/doers" have come to an end, and only "seeing/seer" is left as a continuing last thread until the total elimination of existence occurs at the ordained end of the embodiment. [To sing your glory is why you created me – a saint sings as a purpose of his life.]

Here again, the essence of Kaivalyam is total indifference/non-dependence in relation to the manifest world.

Now let us attempt to reconcile this essential meaning with the verbal meaning quoted by my son, perhaps from a Sanskrit dictionary. This reconciliation is a "must" because otherwise, any reader of any scripture will claim "unbounded license" to give any meaning as his "moods" may dictate from time to time. The meanings for Kaivalyam given by my son are as follows: Isolation, transcendental "aloneness," and absolute unity. How is "non-dependence" related to the above? All relationships between beings are based on "mutual expectations" - "mutual dependence." If there are neither expectations nor dependence, there is no relationship. Where there is no relationship, one is in a state of "isolation."

Anything not dependent on anything else is beyond the influence of that other thing - it cannot be affected by the other thing. Hence, if anything has attained total non-dependence on all else, it has achieved an "aloneness" beyond the reach of all else - "transcendental aloneness" (transcend = go beyond).

Anything seeks to connect with anything else only because its integrity/unity is incomplete without a link with the other – hence, its unity is dependent on the other – hence, it is not absolute. Its integrity/unity becomes absolute only when it is not dependent on anything else to complete itself. Hence, the "attainment of Kaivalyam" from all else and the attainment of "absolute unity" are, in fact, two sides of the same coin.

I hope we have satisfied the need for reconciliation of the "essence" and "form" of Kaivalyam!

SUMMARY

In short, "I," as a process of evolving awareness, discovers the truth to the point of conviction and engages in the present moment, "here and now."

This is a continuous process of evolution, repeated at every moment of engagement. To engage, experience, meditate, and evolve is a continuous journey toward self-actualization. Thus, transcending a particular body-mind experience can be seen as a mini "kaivalyam." The progressive evolution of life follows a trajectory that increasingly advances the state of "kaivalyam" toward self-actualization.

The emphasis is on acting with progressive clarity and conviction, as opposed to from memory or a pre-defined fixed notion of Self and response to the world.

Thirumandhiram describes this as follows:

> **To become the celebrated spirit** (the rest of the faculties) **and become a** (part of a) **band of spirit.**
>
> **Expressions bow down** (to the essence). **He has blessed it to be so.**
>
> **Here onwards, "I"** (Evolving Self) **will not bow down to the external gods; I have arrived at clarity in my awareness.**
>
> **"I am That"** (Ultimate Self), **to which "I"** (Evolving Self) **reaches and bow down.** [TM-2674]

This is also the stage of pursuing the final need in Maslow's hierarchy of needs. When all other needs are experienced, one begins to see their relative nature and that they are void without the context of the Ultimate Self. Then self-actualization needs to come to the foreground as the real/direct need, and all other needs become subservient to this ultimate need.

(8) Q3: "I AM" THE WAY

That which transcends the manifest and unites with the
Ultimate leads a Heavenly Life on Earth [TK-03]

OVERVIEW: TRANSCENDING THE MANIFEST AND UNITING WITH THE ULTIMATE

> **"I am the way** and the truth and the life. No one comes to
> the Father except through me." (John 14:6, Bible)"

In the previous two chapters (Chapters 7 and 8), we discussed two qualities of the Self as an evolving awareness (Chapter 7) and the Self as a process (Chapter 8). This chapter deals with the notion that the Self is in harmony with how life unfolds. The Self, as an unfolding along an evolutionary path, aims to be progressively authentic (Verity) with its pursuits fueled by love, i.e., Self as VEL WAY.

But what is the overall trajectory of VEL Way? It is to transcend the manifest and unite with the Ultimate. To go beyond the body-mind experience by becoming aware of higher truth (i.e., via meditated/intuitive awareness of who we are), as lessons learned from each experience and to evolve toward the ultimate.

In Chapter 6, we explored "I" as a state of awareness (OM). In Chapter 7, we examined "I" as a process of Evolution ("VEL"). In this chapter, we will explore "I" as a path, a trajectory for transcending the manifest (body-mind experience) and uniting with the Ultimate.

To use this evolved awareness to progress toward the ultimate, which is the way of self-actualization. In the chapter "Self-Actualization Epic," the author of the Hindu Epic (Kantha Puranam) states that the benefit of reading his work is targeted as follows:

> **To become heavenly beings on earth, to be blissful, and to pursue the good.**
>
> **Let that which arises in awareness find its fulfillment in the State of Siva** (Ultimate Self)

The overall dynamics of the way, as we have discussed, involve the interplay of five aspects, as previously mentioned. In Chapter 2: Ultimate Self (Si), Revealing Grace/Awareness (Va), Self as a process of evolving awareness (Ya), Concealing Grace/Ignorance (Na), and Fettered Self (Ma) (collectively represented as the five-letter Matra in Hinduism – Panchatcharam).

Let's unpack this and discuss the following aspects of this trajectory.

The rest of the chapter outlines the following sections:

    a. **SPIRITUAL SEAL/RESOLVE (CIN):** Visualization of this trajectory and an intuitive way to understand this path as a Mudra (hand gesture).

    b. **LIVING A HEAVENLY LIFE ON EARTH:** Look at how various religions (Christianity, Buddhism, and Hinduism describe this idea).

    c. **OM TAT SAT:** Inner dynamics of the path toward the Ultimate Self.

    d. **SATHYAM SIVAM SUNDHARAM:** Dynamics of the path in terms of the execution of each step.

Before we move on to the next chapter, it is useful to recap some of the key concepts discussed:

- **SELF-ACTUALIZATION** – Revisited to refresh our minds and also look at it in the context of the ideas discussed in this chapter.
- **PRACTICE** – via Existential Living, i.e., apply what we know here and now, living totally in the moment.
- **GUIDED BY MEDITATIVE AWARENESS** – INTUITION: To learn from our experience, evolve, and meet the next moment as a more evolved being.

(A) Spiritual Seal/Resolve (Cin Mudra)

Therefore, there are three categories of the self:

1. **Ultimate Self** – This is the true north star or represents the destination in the journey of self-actualization.
2. **Fettered Self** – This is where one is at any point in time and the extent to which it clings to the three fetters (during evolution). It is the Self that exists until that arising moment.
3. **Evolving Self** – This is the Self that is present in the arising moment. It is receptive, let's go of what it was before the moment (the fettered self), and aspires to evolve closer to the Ultimate Self.

Life is ultimately an eternal process of evolution across a continuum of moments, the "here and now," serving as steppingstones toward that which is "ultimate and eternal."

This process of letting go or transcending the notions of the fettered Self and aspiring to unite with the Ultimate Self is represented by a hand gesture called "Cin." It is one of the aids that help in the practice of meditation or meditative living. It serves to remind and invite the unconscious mind to participate in the self-actualization process. It is like a call to the whole being to align around a mental seal, to let go of the fetters, and to unite with the Ultimate Self.

Cin Mudra – a visual representation in the form of a hand gesture

- The three fingers (pinky/little, ring, and middle fingers) represent the fettered self, which is shackled by the three fetters.
- The pointing/index finger represents the evolving self.
- The thumb represents the Ultimate Self (or divinity).

Image19: Cin – The Spiritual Seal

Following are some extracts on the Cin Seal from Thirumandhiram:

Self-aware and united with Siva (Divine Self),

Letting go of the fetters progressively and going beyond the fetters,

Achieves liberation and acquires great (inner) **light** (of awareness),

Conferred by the Awareness Seal when embraced. [TM-2331]

Many concepts have been discussed in previous chapters. The purpose of this is to bring them together as they relate to this chapter in terms of "I am the way." The first song highlights that "I am" the way that leads to Self-Actualization. Being authentic "I" (Verity) is to evolve toward the Ultimate Self. Using intuitive/ meditative wisdom, one transcends the body-mind experience. That pattern is Cin Mudra or Awareness Seal. The second song outlines Siva-Sakthi (i.e., the ultimate essence with three powers – to be aware, love, and evolve) as the seed of our self. It takes part in worldly engagement with five activities - creation, preservation, dissolution, concealment, and liberation. The silent beings are stilled inner faculties (emotions, intellect, awareness Centre, the sense of "I") that received the revelation intuition (of the truth of Self and how to respond to the occasion). Then, the Self is ready to engage in the arising moment with the Cin Seal.

Let's further look at the overall structure as outlined in the Gita.

(B) LIVING A HEAVENLY LIFE ON EARTH

Living a life of a fettered Self leads to suffering. Living a life that progresses toward one's ultimate nature leads to a more blissful life. But, as we discussed before, it is not about escaping from worldly realities into a fantasy land. It is about living in this world but not being fettered by worldly experiences and using them as a steppingstone to evolve toward the ultimate.

This idea has been a common and important notion across various religions. In Christianity, it is called the Kingdom of Heaven on Earth. In Buddhism, it is called Sukhavati (the place of bliss). In Hinduism, it is called Sivapuram (the domain of Siva).

The idea here is to have a spiritualized view of worldly engagement. Yes, you engage with the world in a day-to-day manner. But the perspective with which you engage is different. It is viewed within a wider context of self-actualization. We will look at the four ways of doing this in the next chapter, but this chapter gives an overall flavor of this idea.

To transcend the manifest and unite with the ultimate in every engagement. Not to cling to the body-mind experience but to evolve from that toward the ultimate. In this perspective, what happens to you is not good or bad. What matters is how you respond to it.

We looked at multiple perspectives (Chapter 4) of evolution as a holistic and authentic response to the challenges and opportunities. Kurt Goldstein and Kierkegaard point out that the challenges trigger the evolution of the self. Rarely do people evolve toward the highest, except as a series of responses to major challenges in life. Carl Rogers states that we discover our true selves in the very experience. It is not based on what I wish or learned from books. He emphasizes the experiential notion of self-discovery.

Hinduism, Buddhism, in general, and Siththam, in particular, have also emphasized the experiential way to evolve. All the learning and deduction are preliminary steps. To experientially and intuitively see, let's look at each to get a richer view of this idea.

Kingdom of Heaven on Earth in Christianity

Following are some excerpts from the Bible:

- Jesus was once asked when the kingdom of God would come. The kingdom of God, Jesus replied, is not something people will be able to see and point to. Then came these striking words: "Neither shall they say, Lo here! or, lo there! for, behold, **the kingdom of God is within you**." (Luke 17:21)

- And he said: "Truly I tell you, **unless you change and become like little children, you will never enter the kingdom of heaven**." (Matthew 18:3)

- He told them another parable: "**The kingdom of heaven is like a mustard seed**, which a man took and planted in his field. Though it is the smallest of all seeds, when it grows, it is the largest of garden plants and becomes a tree so that the birds come and perch in its branches." (Matthew 13:31-32)

Jesus teaches that the kingdom of heaven is within each of us. It is not an escape from the "here and now," where we seek something outside of the life before us.

He then states that one must become like little children to enter the Kingdom of Heaven. This is similar to Nietzsche's view of the final stage of evolution, the "Child Stage" or the "Sacred Yes." To be open to experience and become a self-propelled wheel along the path of self-actualization. We should not view life as a burden, doing things to please others or conform to externally dictated norms. Instead, we should be open, discover our truth, and be willing to live by it.

This is also what Carl Rogers explains as a fully functioning person – being open to experience and fully living in each moment.

Pure Land/Land of Bliss (Sukhavati) of Buddhism

Buddhism describes the Pure Land (Sukhavati) as follows:

> "At that time, the Blessed One addressed the Venerable Śāriputra: 'To the west, Śāriputra, there is a Buddha-field, a world system named Sukhāvatī, which lies beyond countless hundreds of thousands of other Buddha-fields. At present, a Tathāgata, an Arhat, a perfectly awakened Buddha named Amitāyus dwells there, teaching the Dharma. Why do you think, Śāriputra, that world system is called 'Sukhāvatī,' the '**Realm of Happiness**'? In that world system, Śāriputra, in Sukhāvatī, living beings experience no physical or mental suffering, and there are endless causes of happiness. This is why that world system is called 'Sukhāvatī,' the 'Realm of Happiness.'"

A place beyond physical and mental suffering, a realm of happiness where awakened beings live and teach Dharma.

As we evolve in the process of self-actualization, we can move beyond the clutches of the body-mind experience. We learn to be happy regardless of what we experience through the body and mind. This is not an exotic or fantastic notion, nor is it an escape from reality. It is the ability to fully experience and use that experience to elevate our awareness and transcend the experience as evolving beings. Yes, the body and mind may still experience pain and pleasure, but that does not necessarily mean our life as a whole needs to be suffering with it. The spirit can transcend the body-mind experience and find bliss by redirecting its attention to the primary flow of life – self-actualization.

Many have transformed diversity into evolving opportunities. Most of us passively let time heal and learn. What is called for here is to actively pursue this path as a continuous and mindful way of living.

Sivapuram of Hinduism

Saint Thirumoolar described the nature of evolution in the following way:

> **No one can harm me.**
>
> **Once the wholesome Lord** (Ultimate Self) **entered my awareness** (i.e., wholesome awareness),
>
> **I celebrate and roam there** (heaven on earth).
>
> **I am awakened to the wisdom of not clinging to anything else.** [TM-2960]

Saint Manikka Vasahar described the more advanced stage of the evolution of the Self as follows:

> Eradicator of a suffering-laden life,
>
> Those who praise the inexpressible one.
>
> The song that is woven into the journey, the one who realizes its meaning,
>
> Will enter **Siva Puram**, to live the auspicious path,
>
> To humbly serve in the evolution of many.

(C) Om Tat Sat: Inner Dynamics of the Path toward the Ultimate Self

Let's examine the inner dynamics of the Self as an evolving trajectory through the Hindu Mantra OM Tat Sat. It is another invocable representation (mantra) and is hailed as the triple designation of the ultimate. It is a condensed form of a composite concept that can be invoked to create a state of mind.

- **OM** – We have covered this as evolving awareness across four states. The Evolving Self is OM.

- **Tat** is an outlook of directing the Self toward self-actualization (or liberation from the body-mind experience). That is, moving away from clinging to the experience and toward becoming the true self—toward the Ultimate Self, and not becoming a fettered Self and clinging to the body-mind experience of the world.

- **Sat** (the essence) has two definitions in the Bhagavad Gita:

  - We have looked at Sat as the ultimate essence (as Verity and Love).

  - The second definition is the essence in action, i.e., performing the following with conviction and performing this directed toward the ultimate (self-actualization):

    ◊ Self-Discovery (Yajna or Velvi): We have covered this in the previous chapter.

    ◊ Self-Evolution (Tapas or Thavam): This is about evolving oneself toward self-actualization (Being Happy).

◊ Dedication to the Evolution (Dana or Thanam): This is about evolving to help others with their self-actualization.

◦ When the above is not performed with faith, i.e., done as mechanical motion or compliance, that is not Sat. It is the opposite (Asat).

Another way of looking at the process is a three-step and progressive evolution — "discovery, evolving to be happy, and evolving to make others happy." These three steps are iterated to progress holistically along the path to self-actualization.

The following is extracted from the Bhagavad Gita.

- "Om Tat Sat" has been declared as the triple designation of Brahman. (17.23)
- Therefore, with the utterance of "Om," the acts of yajna, tapas, and dana, as enjoined in the scriptures, are performed. (17.24)
- Uttering "Tat" without aiming for the fruits, the acts of yajna, tapas, and the various acts of dana are performed by the seekers of Moksha. (17.25)
- The word "Sat" is used in the **sense of reality (i.e., Verity) and goodness (i.e., Love)**; similarly, the word "Sat" is used in the **sense of an auspicious act (i.e., Evolution toward self-actualization)**. (17.26)
- **Firmness in yajna, tapas, and dana is also called "Sat," and action for the sake of the Lord is also called "Sat."** (17.27)
- Whatever is sacrificed, given, or performed and whatever austerity is practiced **without faith** is **called Asat**. It is of no account here or hereafter. (17.28)

Another way to understand the quality of being the "way" is to consider the perspective from which we live our lives in this world. It is not about escaping reality into a fantasy land or being mere beasts of burden or machines. Instead, it is about living and evolving beings striving toward their ultimate selves and gaining awareness through life experiences.

This transcends the worldly experience and leads us toward union with the Ultimate, allowing us to live as heavenly beings on earth. Many religions describe this quality as living the life of a heavenly being on earth. Here are summaries of this view across Christianity, Buddhism, and Hinduism. The striking similarities in how various religions arrive at the same view are amazing. However, each religion also highlights certain nuances, which widen and enrich our perspective, giving us a more complete understanding of this idea.

(D) SATHYAM SIVAM SUNDHARAM: THE RESPONSE AND THE INTERPLAY OF THE STEPS

Let's now look at the dynamics of the execution of tasks in our path, i.e., how we respond to each arising moment (here and now). Kurt Goldstein describes the dynamics of a healthy organism in Chapter 4, where the whole organism participates on every occasion (the "Organismic Response"), not as an isolated response of the individual faculties.

In Hinduism, this is described with Siva as Thatchina Murthy, where Siva as the Ultimate Self enlightens the four saints through silent communication before responding to the world (creating Muruhan as a response to Sooran tyrannizing the world). The world (Devas and Humans) had to wait until this communication was complete. The four saints are the Emotional Faculty (manam), Intellectual Faculty (buddhi), Awareness Center (siththam), and the current sense of "I" (ahankaram). This was described in Chapter 2.

Now, let's delve into this in more detail, as described in another Hindu Mantra.

SATHYAM (Truth): Our response should always be rooted in truth, i.e., Verity. What does truth mean in terms of responding to a situation? One needs clarity on "who am I" concerning this situation? and "what is this situation in relation to me". How does this situation fit in within my life? As the underlying drive in my life is self-actualization, how does it all fit together? This is the holistic truth about oneself, the situation, our life within the context of self-actualization. It is about looking at each "here and now" directly on its own merits and also looking holistically within the context of the "eternal and ultimate" nature of self. This is the Thatchina Murthi's silent communication to the four saints i.e. meditative/intuitive revelation of truth to the four faculties of the mind (emotional, intellectual faculties, awareness center, and sense of "I"). Then one is ready for an "organismic response."

SIVAM (Auspicious): Truth can tell you what needs to be done. But to mobilize ourselves to action, we need clarity around the question "WHY?". This will help us find clarity on what are we willing to commit and concerning what, whether we have the courage of conviction? Only a sense of Love can answer that. May that be love towards our welfare, that of others (as an extension of who we are), or regarding an idea (such as nationhood, religion, culture, or belief system, which are even further extensions of who we are in our view). We need a sense of love to give the broader truth, that we have become aware of, a concrete view in the form of courage and commitment. Let us look at what others have said about this topic.

Thirukural states that "Not only does a virtuous life (Verity) lean on Love, but also that of Courage (of conviction)" [TK-76]. Love is the backbone for both.

In the Bhagavad Gita, Lord Krishna says that the ignorant (fettered self) acts due to their attachment (clinging to the three fetters). But those who are aware (enlightened) act out of love for the welfare of other beings (3.25). Krishna then goes on to say that there is nothing "from" the world that he requires for his personal needs (he has transcended the world). Yet he acts for the welfare of other beings, i.e., his state of self-actuation has entered the extended phase (of scale, i.e., scope and longevity) to help others in the process of their self-actualization. The welfare of other beings ("**loka saṁgraham**") has become part of Krishna's view of his self-actualization.

Thirumandhiram states:

Only the ignorant say that Love and Sivam are two separate things.

Few are aware that Love is Sivam.

Once one is aware that Love is Sivam,

One becomes a personification of Love and an actualization of Sivam. [TM-270]

In simple terms, we act because we care about the well-being of ourselves, someone else, or a way of life – i.e. the wellbeing of ourselves, the people around us, or an idea that represents the wellbeing of people beyond our time. Having clarity about what is relevant and where we have conviction, regarding the need of the moment helps us shape an optimal (useful and practical) response.

As we have seen before, Siva is a synthesis of Verity and Love.

"Sathyam" (Verity) gives clarity about the "WHAT." Sivam (Verity along with Love) gives clarity regarding the "WHY" of the situation.

SUNDHARAM: Sundharam translates to beauty or grace. This is the "HOW and WHEN" of our response.

Once we have clarity on the "WHAT" and "WHY" of our response, we still need to know the "HOW and WHEN." We are acting to address a need - may that be our own need (self-actualization) or an extension of that (scaling self-actualization) to address the need of someone else. So our response needs to be in harmony with our awareness of who we are and the needs of the situation. That is the essence of beauty or grace.

Having harmony between who we are, and our response is called Dignity (inner beauty or grace). The harmony between our response and the need for the situation is called Empathy (beauty or grace regarding the other). Having dignity and empathy in our response is the essence of beauty/grace i.e. Sundharam. This then guides the choices of "How" and "WHEN."

REVISITING SELF-ACTUALIZATION

In the previous chapters, we discussed self-actualization as the most intrinsic and ultimate need of living beings. Similar ideas can be found across various fields of study, including biology, neurology, psychology, physiology, religion, and spirituality.

Let's revisit some of these key ideas before delving into the details of the four-fold path toward self-actualization.

Self-Actualization and the Most Intrinsic and Ultimate Need

Self-actualization is the ultimate need in Maslow's hierarchy theory, which leads to true bliss, as discussed in the *Taittiriya*

Upanishad and covered in Chapter 3. We then examined multiple fields of study in Chapter 4.

- Hans Driesch's research suggests a cellular-level drive toward self-actualization in cellular biology, as demonstrated in his Sea Urchin experiments.

- Kurt Goldstein, a neurologist and psychologist, posits that self-actualization is the ultimate drive, with all other drives acting as precursors. He argues that the tendency to cling to or preserve oneself arises when an organism is threatened, which he calls a pathological tendency. However, he believes the natural course of life is for an organism to evolve toward its most intrinsic and ultimate nature.

- In psychology, we studied:

  ◦ Abraham Maslow's theory is that self-actualization is the ultimate need in the hierarchy of needs. According to him, as we meet a series of deficiency needs (physiological, safety, belonging, and esteem needs), we move closer to realizing our ultimate need: self-actualization. While the other needs are deficiency needs (their drives decrease as they are met), self-actualization is a growth need (the drive increases as we progress).

  ◦ Carl Jung's concept of individuation is where humans evolve toward becoming an integrated whole. He argues that the unconscious is more powerful than the conscious Self and that the conscious mind makes all major decisions, which ultimately succumbs to the unconscious. According to him, intuition serves as a communication channel with the conscious self. Techniques like meditation can train and extend the scope of the conscious mind, making it more receptive to the unconscious.

- ◦ Carl Rogers highlights the process of self-actualization (becoming a fully functioning person, leading a good life) as a series of three iterative/cyclical steps: (1) being open to experience, (2) living existentially (fully engaging at the moment), and evolving from that, and (3) trusting in the ways of the total organism (organismic response). He portrays the Self as an ongoing process of evolution, not as a fixed product.

- In philosophy, Friedrich Nietzsche outlines three stages of metamorphosis. In the first stage, the Self lives as a beast of burden (Camel), living solely to please the environment and fit into it. In the second stage, it defies worldly impositions and explores its own needs and nature (Lion Stage, the Sacred "NO" Stage). In the third stage, it becomes self-aware and engages the world with its own spiritual needs (Child, the Sacred "YES" Stage). It interacts with the world based on its inner values as a self-propelled wheel instead of being driven by external forces.

- In spirituality and religion, we discussed:

  - ◦ Soren Kierkegaard's description of the Self as the eternal process of becoming the true Self it aspires to be. With the Ultimate Self (God) as its goal and standard, it evolves consciously and transparently toward it. The Self is seen as a synthesis of immediate/immanent needs and the eternal/ultimate possibility.

  - ◦ The concept of life as a middle/higher path of synthesis between worldly truth and ultimate truth. This view neither denies worldly truth nor ignores ultimate truth. It advocates using worldly truth to experience, meditate on, and evolve toward the ultimate truth. The key concept of dependent arising is discussed, where awareness can lead to bliss and ignorance to suffering.

- ○ Several Hindu perspectives, which include:

    - ◊ Two notions of the Self (worldly and ultimate) with the evolving Self as their synthesis.

    - ◊ The outline of four states of awareness (Chapter 6).

    - ◊ The importance of meditative awareness in self-actualization and the concept of Velvi (self-discovery) (Chapter 7). Also discussed is the way to transcend each worldly (psychical, physiological, and psychological) experience and use it as a steppingstone toward self-actualization in an experiential/existential manner.

    - ◊ The concept of fetters and self-actualization as transcending the fetters and aligning with the Ultimate Self (Cin Spiritual Seal) in Chapter 8.

There are many more detailed nuances we discussed. The above summary serves to refresh our minds on key ideas before we delve into the four paths.

In this chapter, exploring these concepts through songs might be useful. While logical thoughts are helpful for in-depth examination, songs, visuals, and mantras can intuitively capture these concepts in more condensed forms.

Thirumandhiram outlines the life of self-actualization as follows:

Being self-aware, there is no suffering.

Without self-awareness, one suffers.

Once one is aware of the need.

To be aware of the (ultimate) self,

(Life becomes) **the worship of** (the ultimate) **Self by (the conscious) Self.** [TM-2355]

GUIDED BY MEDITATIVE AWARENESS – INTUITION

Recalling the concept of silent communication from Siva to the four saints in Chapter 1 and described in Chapter 2.

In Hinduism, Siva is symbolized as the essence (Ultimate Self), and Sakti represents the tendency to actualize the power of transformation: (1) to be aware, (2) to love, (3) to evolve/execute. Self-actualization is symbolized by the Self breaking free from the three fetters through the compassionate grace of Sakthi, allowing the Self to unite with the ultimate Self (Siva). The ignorant Self (unaware of its true nature) is likened to a blind, weak old man. Sakthi wishes to reveal the truth of the Ultimate Self, so the Self can progress toward self-actualization. But one can only gain awareness through personal experience (sufferings arising from clinging to the fetters).

The old lady was in the corner of a dark room,

Aiming to unite with the blind old man.

She cured his blindness, displaying various qualities (8 qualities),

She terrified him, and then they married. [TM-1514]

We discussed the three fetters and meditative awareness (revealing grace) through life experiences as a means to transcend the grip of these fetters. This process unfolds in three experiential stages:

1. Transcending the duality of actions and outcomes (going beyond the Karma fetter - clinging to the outcomes of actions) to achieve unity beyond the duality of deeds and outcomes ('iruvinai oppu').

2. Freeing oneself from the illusion of the world (both mental and physical) as the ultimate truth ('mayai') and weakening the hold of the first two fetters ("mala paripaham").

3. Channeling the Self toward the Ultimate Self through revealing grace (Sakthi nipatham) and transforming the final fetter - the atomization of the Self in terms of physical and psychological attributes (anavam).

4. Experiencing transcendence. This is a progressive process, where each experience in the present moment leads to eternal and ultimate transcendence.

Blessed Sakthi resides in the unity beyond the dualities of actions (and their consequences).

She manifests as the Guru and eliminates the qualities (that cause attachment to three fetters).

Through the awakening of revelation, one transcends (attachment to) **actions (and their outcomes).**

When the three fetters are dissolved, "I" becomes "Siva." [TM-1527]

Practice – Via Existential Living

Hinduism, in general, and the Siddhanta tradition (of Tamils), in particular, highly emphasize evolution through experience. Academic learning (knowledge) is considered only a preliminary step. One cannot self-actualize through academic learning alone.

Thirumanthiram describes this as follows: "It symbolizes the grace of revelation through living experience as Sakthi. It is she who can show the way to Siva (the Ultimate essence)."

Feet and head, these fools do not know.

Feet reveals Sakthi's grace (through experience).

Transcendental awareness is (represented by) **the head** (Siva).

When the feet (path) **take you to the transcendental awareness, then there is liberation** (Sakthi helps establish Siva in every being as a union of Siva-Sakthi-Self). [TM-2425]

Hinduism is a highly symbolic religion with advanced techniques for harnessing the power of the unconscious mind. Some misunderstand this as Hindus having thousands of gods and angels. The highest forms of Hinduism emphasize that God is one and that God is both within each individual and transcends all. It emphasizes many experiential ways of evolution, recognizing the limitations of a formed being in easily relating to the Ultimate Self, which has no name, shape, or form. As such, it encourages people to relate to God through a wide variety of forms and symbols, each representing an eternal principle or feature. The idea is not to be dogmatic about God having a specific shape, color, or name but to engage with the Ultimate Self through a symbolic representation that one finds easy to relate to.

The following song, Thirumanthiram, beautifully explains this:

> **From the body, mouth, eyes, nose, and ears arises the** (relative) **truth of the manifest.**
>
> **Then the inner instruments** (emotions, thoughts) **give a sense of reality to the universe.**
>
> **As every soul dances according to the orchestration of the Ultimate,**
>
> **It is as if the wholeness that has neither hands** (deeds) **nor mouth** (words/thoughts) **becomes embodied everywhere.** [TM-2586]

The idea here is that every encounter in life and the resulting experience presents an opportunity to discover a higher truth. While books, advice, and experiences through the body and mind are all useful as preparatory steps, each of us must be intuitively aware of who we are and the truths of life. This awareness cannot be handed over; it is a process of ongoing evolution of awareness with each experience. This is a pivotal state of the awareness of transformation. Here, the Self begins to see the experience of the body and mind as a secondary reality, as a subject of meditation, rather than as a primary reality to deal with. The Ultimate Self is the primary reality.

This is beautifully illustrated by the following song that everyone can relate to.

> **Only fools limit their sight to the eyes on their face.**
>
> **Bliss is when you can perceive with your inner eyes.**
>
> **Same as, a mother cannot truly make her daughter** (a virgin bride) **understand the conjugal bliss that she enjoyed with her husband.** [TM-2944]

The inner eye is a symbolic representation of intuition or meditative awareness. A mother cannot explain the experiential joy of conjugal bliss to her daughter, a virgin bride about to get married. The mother can explain the mechanics or what to expect, but the virgin bride needs to go through the conjugal experience herself before she can truly understand what it means.

Invokable Representation

To enhance our day-to-day practice, prose alone is not sufficient. It is challenging to recall detailed and highly nuanced ideas in prose. While prose may assist in academic learning, it is insufficient for practical application in daily life.

As we discussed earlier, various forms of invokable representation (such as mantras, visualizations, etc.) are crucial for progress along the path of self-actualization. We have covered many of these throughout the book.

Sutras

- **Thirukural:** woven throughout the book as the essence of each chapter and listed at the beginning of chapters.
  - ◦ Illustrated with close to thirty-five verses from Thirumandhiram.
- **Sivanjnana Potham** outlines the process of Self-Actualization (Chapter 3).

Mantra

- **OM:** Self as States of Awareness (Chapter 6).
- **Si-Va-Ya-Na-Ma**: Five aspects that determine the dynamics of self-actualization (Chapter 2).
- **Sat-Cit-Anandam**: Essence-Realization-Bliss (Chapter 5).

- **OM Tat Sat**: Self (as a state of awareness) directed not toward worldly outcomes but toward Self-Actualization (Chapter 8).

- **Sathyam Sivam Sundharam**: The What, Why, How, and When of our response (Chapter 8).

Visualization

- **Siva, as King of Dance**, performs the **Dance of Bliss** in union with Sakthi (Chapter 2).

- **Siva, as Thatchina Murthy, engages in silent communication** with the Four Saints (Chapter 2).

- **Cin Mudra** – the hand gesture that represents the path to Self-Actualization (Chapter 8).

NEXT CHAPTER

In the next chapter, we will explore four paths toward self-actualization. We will choose various topics discussed throughout this chapter and outline a path for each. Each of us needs to select the path that best suits our current state of awareness and life.

According to Hinduism, one can opt for a single path and make progress toward self-actualization or evolve from one path to another. All of this depends on what works for the individual at different stages of life rather than following a prescribed journey.

What matters is the increasing quality and scale of happiness in our lives.

(9) Q4–Q8: FOUR-FOLD PATH TOWARD SELF-ACTUALIZATION

OVERVIEW

According to Hinduism, each path leads one toward self-actualization, symbolized as the Union with Siva (Ultimate Self). One can also switch from one path to another based on life stages and changes in individual orientations. What is important is which path best fits a given person at a given stage of life.

Four-Fold Path

It is useful to recap the fourfold path described in the "Introduction" chapter:

1. **The Way of Service:** Here, we use every physical and physiological engagement as a steppingstone toward self-actualization. This is an "outside-in" process where we discover who we are in the experience and evolve. [Na-Ma-Si-Va-Ya]

2. **The Way of Worship:** We use our psychological experiences (emotional, intellectual) as a steppingstone toward self-actualization. This is an "inside-out" process where we reform ourselves toward a notion of the Ultimate Self and engage with the world from a reformed state of Self each time. [Si-Va-Ya-Na-Ma]

3. **The Way of Witnessing:** Here, we are primarily witnesses to the unfolding of our life. Just meditating on our life helps us evolve. Worldly engagement and psychological evolution are incidental byproducts. The unfolding of our ultimate nature is the primary phenomenon. [Si-Va-Ya-Si-Va]

4. **The Way of Unity:** This is meditation in action, where we are in continuous union with our ultimate nature and in harmony with life as a whole. [Si-Va-Si-Va]

Features of the Path

We will look at more details of the primary features that differentiate these four paths. Here is the introduction to the features.

Features	
Quality	In Chapter 5, we examined eight qualities. Qualities (1) through (3) are the overall qualities needed to embrace the process of Self-Actualization. Qualities (4) and (5) are designated as the primary focus of the four paths. We will delve into these qualities in more detail, but the following provides a summary: • Qualities Q4 and Q5 are the focus of the Way of Service (Path 1). • Quality Q6 is the focus of the Way of Worship (Path 2). • Quality Q7 is the focus of the Way of Witnessing (Path 3). • Quality Q8 is the primary focus for the Way of Unity (Path 4).
Spiritual State a) Fetters b) Primary Needs c) Self-Awareness	The current spiritual state of the self. It is not about the past or the future but rather the 'here and now.' This is viewed in terms of the primary fetter one is grappling with, one's primary needs (from Maslow's hierarchy of needs), and a state of self-awareness.
State of Awareness (OM) and Self-Actualization	The state of awareness that arises naturally. We previously discussed four states of awareness. Each of us, at different stages of life, has a natural inclination toward one of them, leading us to ask the following: What is the process of Self-Actualization on this Path?

Relationship with the Ultimate Self	For each path, a given model helps us orient ourselves toward our Ultimate Self.
Realm (Physical and Mental)	The spiritual outlook of the environment or realm from which we operate on each path.
Invokable Representation	Mantras (in a different sequence invoking "Si, Va, Ya, Na, Ma") and corresponding visuals help us apply what we are aware of and progress in self-actualization in day-to-day living. We will also explore the visualization of this path based on the Dance of Bliss discussed in Chapter 2.

Four-Fold Path and its Features: Choosing the Path that Fits Best

Now, let's look at each path and how they differ in terms of features.

Each path can lead us toward self-actualization. The most important aspect is to choose a path that fits our nature. Look at the features of each path; each of us can choose the path that best fits our nature. We are in a process of evolution. So, to be most precise, we need to choose the path that best fits us in a given state of evolution. As we evolve, we can continue along the same path or switch to another that best fits our state.

Features	Four-Fold Path			
	The Way of Service (Cariyai)	The Way of Worship (Kiriyai)	The Way of Witnessing (Yoham)	The Way of Unity (Jnanam)
Quality	Transcend dualities of actions and outcomes ('iruvinai oppu')	Transcend a fixed notion of the world and loosen the grip of the first 2 fetters ('mala paripaham')	Become undefinable in worldly terms (i.e., an evolving spirit) and be receptive to meditative intuition (Sakthinipatham)	Unite with the ultimate essence (Verity and Love) in every expression, i.e., to transcend the body-mind experience (Mukthi)

Spiritual State a) Fetters b) Primary Needs c) Self-Awareness	a) Clinging to actions and outcomes (Kanmam)	a) Clinging to a fixed notion of the world – physical & psychological (Mayai)	a) Clinging to the notion of an "atomized" Self (anavam)	a) Fetters unshackled.
	b) Physiological and Security needs	b) Belongingness and Esteem Needs	b) At the threshold of self-actualization	b) Progressing self-actualization
	c) Spiritual Darkness ('irul')	c) Spiritual Murkiness ('marul')	c) Spiritual clarity ('therul')	c) Spiritual blessedness ('arul')
State of Awareness (OM) and Self-Actualization	Physical and Psychological Awareness (A) ("Nanavu")	Psychological awareness (emotions and intellect, memory) (U) ("Kanavu")	Receptive to Revelation/ Intuition (M) ("aRivu")	Wholesome awareness (OM aka AUM) ("seRivu")
	Spiritualize the external engagement	Inner purification	The unfolding of Life as a whole, as a subject of Meditation	Use every situation as a means of union with the Ultimate Self
Relationship with the Ultimate Self	Servant-Lord ("Dasa Margam")	Child-Parent ("Satputra Margam")	Companion-Witness or Friend ("Saha Margam")	Spouse – Union with the Ultimate Self ("San Margam")
Realm (Physical and Mental)	Divine Land ("Salokiyam")	Divine Proximity ("Samipiam")	Divine Likeness ("Sarupiam")	Divine Unity ("Sayujiam")
Invokable Representation	Na-Ma-Si-Va-Ya ("outside-in" approach to life)	Si-Va-Ya-Na-Ma ("inside-out" approach to life)	Si-Va-Ya-Si-Va (all of life unfolds within awareness)	Si-Va-Si-Va ("I" is inseparable from the Ultimate Self)

SUMMARY

In every path, the role of meditation is crucial for mindful living. In the first two paths, meditative awareness serves a subtle, underlying role in elevating the evolving Self beyond the first two fetters. In the third path, meditative awareness moves to the forefront. Meditative awareness integrates into one's being – as a living awareness in the final path. The conscious Self unites with its ultimate nature on every occasion of life. Authentic living is fueled by Love, acting as an ongoing process of Evolution, harmonizing with the Ultimate Nature of Self (Verity and Love).

People are like muddy water.

When muddled in awareness, one cannot find the Ultimate.

Like scooping some water into a mug and letting it settle,

When awareness is clear, the "Self" becomes one with "Siva" (Ultimate Self). [TM-2991]

PATH 1: THE WAY OF SERVICE (CARIYAI)

QUALITY

Q4: The Self transcends beyond the dualities of outcomes.

One goes beyond suffering by moving past the dualities of craving and resentment (outcomes). [TK-04]

Q5: The Self transcends beyond the dualities of deeds.

Those who serve to glorify the Ultimate, unite with it and transcend the darkness-filled dualities of actions. [TK-05]

Qualities (4) and (5) are the focus of the Path of Service, which aims to go beyond actions and outcomes and evolve toward self-actualization. In Tamil, going beyond the dualities of deeds and outcomes is called "iru vinai oppu," as the Self evolves toward the Ultimate.

The Bhagavad Gita defines two key concepts: "Tyagam" and "Sanyasam." "Tyagam" means not clinging to the dualities of outcomes, and "Sanyasam" means not clinging to the dualities of deeds. Clinging in this context means that one identifies with the dualities of outcomes/deeds as oneself ("as I am this") and distorts all future experiences through this lens. To go beyond the outcomes and deeds is a core step in spiritual evolution (or self-actualization). The Gita's advice is to transcend both dualities (i.e., of deeds and outcomes) and anchor to the Ultimate Self as both the goal and refuge.

SPIRITUAL STATE – Fetter, Primary Needs, and Self Awareness

We can only genuinely evolve by starting from our present state. The starting point on this path is addressing the first fetter—Kanmam. Here, we stop clinging to the dualities of deeds and outcomes as independent and ultimate truths. Dualities of deeds and outcomes are based on who we are at a given stage in life. As we evolve, we must let go of the older notions and embrace our new awareness of the truth.

By default, the primary focus in this state is on physiological and safety needs in the hierarchy of needs (Maslow). This state is called "Spiritual Darkness" ('Irul'). In this stage, one mistakes actions and outcomes as the Self and confuses "what one does" with "who one is." Therefore, one has no sense of the real self.

STATE OF AWARENESS AND SELF-ACTUALIZATION

This state is characterized by a natural tendency toward physical and physiological awareness, i.e., external focus ["A" in "OM" as we have seen in Chapter 6]. Self-actualization on this path deals with how a person is using every physical and physiological engagement with the world (i.e., deeds) as a steppingstone to learn from and evolve toward the ultimate. It helps the evolving Self to stop clinging to dualities of actions and outcomes and instead use the body-mind experience as a subject of meditation—to look at the experience of this life, its impact on the self, and see what this experience reveals as a higher truth. By using external engagements only as steppingstones, one realigns his/her anchor on the Ultimate Self. One then looks at worldly engagement in a wider context of self-actualization, i.e., progress toward the Ultimate Self. As we have seen in the Velvi Concept (Chapter 7), the experience of dualities of actions and outcomes is dedicated to offering the fire of evolving awareness. The resulting blessings are the revelation of higher truth, revealing insights into the ultimate nature of ourselves. We then evolve from that experience and engage in the next occasion as a slightly more evolved being. As we use and evolve from every experience of external engagement, we progress toward the Ultimate Self. Every external engagement then becomes a service toward the ultimate in the process of self-actualization.

Thirumanthiram outlines this idea as follows:

> **Actions, thinking of ownership over actions,**
>
> **Shackles Self with it; this line of thinking restricts one's life.**
>
> **To be aware and transcend, to serve with love,**
>
> **Is to sail through the sea of actions and outcomes** (not sink). [TM-2547]

Saint Yoga Swami states, "The ultimate purpose of performing actions is not to perfect outcomes but to perfect yourself." Similar ideas are also outlined in psychology. As Carl Rogers outlined: (1) be open to experience (equanimity) and (2) live existentially (total engagement). Then, once the action is completed and outcomes are experienced, one dedicates both as an offering into the fire of awareness. Awareness consumes it and grows from it. We then engage in the next encounter as a more evolved being. When this process continues, we evolve with each encounter along the path of self-actualization. Yoga means to unite with one's (Ultimate) Self. The Bhagavad Gita defines the word "yoga" in various ways. Here are some that are relevant to this section:

- Yoga is to maintain equanimity. (**samatvaṁ yoga. 2:48**)
- Yoga is action performed to perfection (**yogaḥ karmasu kauśalam 2:50**)
- Disassociation from suffering is Yoga. (**duḥkha saṁyoga viyogaṁ 6:23**)
- Mind is stilled via the practice of Yoga (**cittaṁ niruddhaṁ yogasevayā 6:30**):

Those who seek Divinity here and there move farther away.

Few commit to say, "this is the destined way," and be devoted (to the here and now).

The heart that walks the destined path and finds the lord there.

They will find "That" (Ultimate Self) **as "This"** (Conscious Self) (and live) **in Harmony.** [TM-1503]

To find divinity by serving the moment "here and now," instead of searching for divinity in every other place, is to live fully in each moment (authentic living fueled by love). One can then evolve from that experience through the gained awareness. When you progress along this path, you see the way toward the Ultimate (that) in every arising moment (This) as harmonious progress along self-actualization.

Good and bad things that may happen from a worldly perspective, one way or another, contribute to self-actualization. When good things happen, they provide a sense of ease and boost our confidence. When "bad" things happen, there is an opportunity to evolve – strengthening character and testing faith. Transcending the dualities of worldly actions and outcomes does not mean denying or ignoring them. It means using suffering to evolve and viewing success as encouragement to persevere. Transcendence simply means not using these dualities to define who we are. By letting go of the dualities of actions and outcomes, we serve the Ultimate self.

RELATIONSHIP WITH THE ULTIMATE SELF

In Hinduism, the suitable model for the conscious Self to relate to the Ultimate Self is that of the Servant-Lord ("Dasa Margam"). A servant does their daily chores not because they need them. The actions are performed as a service toward the Lord. Actions and outcomes are dedicated to the Lord. The ultimate goal of the servant is to gain the Master's confidence. In this context, the servant is the Conscious Self, and the Master is the Ultimate Self. Day-to-day actions are dedicated as a service to the Ultimate in the process of Self-Realization.

REALM: Perspective Toward the Living Environment

The Realm of the Living, or a perspective of looking at our surroundings, is that of the "Divine Land." We have explored this concept across various religions – Christianity (Kingdom of Heaven), Buddhism (Pure Land or Sukhavati), and Hinduism (Siva Puram).

The idea is to view your surroundings (the world of actions and outcomes) as an arena for self-actualization. The Lord of that domain is the Ultimate Self because everything done is ultimately dedicated to self-actualization. In that context, we view the world as the Land of the Ultimate, thereby giving it a broader context, and view self-actualization as the overarching goal.

INVOKABLE REPRESENTATION

This path is an outside-in process, using work engagement to evolve our inner selves. The Mantra Sequence is **Na-Ma-Si-Va-Ya**:

- **Worldly Experience (Na):** Engage fully and experience the world, reflecting on each experience's impact on the Self and the truth it reveals about our ultimate nature.

- **Fettered Self (Ma):** Reflect on the notion of a "fettered self" that clings to actions and outcomes and defines itself in their terms. Acknowledge the suffering and falsehood of this notion, understanding that living a life of transient pleasures and pain ultimately leads to suffering. Use this realization to avoid defining ourselves through actions and outcomes.

- **Ultimate Essence (Si):** Reflect on what can be learned about the ultimate nature of the self.

- **Revealing Grace/Actualization Tendency (Va):** Be receptive to the revelations or intuitions that arise from reflecting on the ultimate essence.

- **Evolving Self (Ya):** Embrace new revelations/intuitions resulting from meditation and engage the next moment as a more evolved being. Progressively realign our sense of self-awareness from the dualities of actions and outcomes toward the Ultimate Self, based on evolving awareness.

Hence, this is an outside-in process, starting with an external context and using that as a steppingstone to evolve on the overall journey toward self-actualization. Thirumandhiram describes this as follows:

Divinity is One in this world.

One is the Spirit of this world.

See well this as the good Na-Ma-Si-Va-Ya fruit.

Eat, experience, and absorb its deliciousness. [TM-962]

This mantra advises us to experience the world and use these experiences to evolve along the path of self-actualization. That is, go from the experience of the world (Na), re-examine our (fettered) nature (Ma), use that to meditate on the Ultimate Nature (Si), gain more awareness (Va), and evolve oneself (Ya). Now, let's look at this process visually in the context of the Dance of Bliss we explored in Chapter 2.

Image20: Na-Ma-Si-Va-Ya

PATH 2: THE WAY OF WORSHIP (KIRIYAI)

QUALITY

Q6: The Self transcends beyond the outlook of the world.

To leave the sensual experiences with the senses and to lead a heavenly life by adhering to the discipline of truth. [TK-06]

This quality is about evolving psychological capabilities (emotions, intellect, memory, sense of self) to aid in the process of self-actualization. This is achieved by aligning these capabilities with the sense of truth — the truth about us and the truth about the world, i.e., the notion of the Ultimate Self.

We perceive the external world through bodily senses and then develop cognitive or psychological constructs — an emotional and intellectual overlay of bodily experience. If these constructs become rigid, they can impede our evolution along the path of self-actualization.

To evolve our minds, we must make them receptive to higher awareness (or intuitions) that arise from each experience and evolve with them. This quality is about inner purification to achieve such alignment.

STORY: Son of God — Jesus

Birth

The birth of Jesus was set in a very unusual context. Any child growing up in that context would have difficulty reconciling the contradictory and non-worldly elements regarding Jesus's birth. This includes the notion of the immaculate conception of Mary — where neither Joseph nor any known man was identified as the biological father. Imagine if we were advised that God is our father, and our origin is via the immaculate conception and at a time when adultery was punishable by stoning death. Adding further to the drama is the prophecy of the savior, which triggered the king's order to kill all children under the age of two. This is further accompanied by the events that Jesus was born in a manger and visited by the three wise men who were paying their respect.

Let's now, for this book, suspend judgment of the view of the divine origins of Jesus and instead view this as a situation where a human being, by directly engaging with these "not-normal" circumstances, evolved to a state of divinity (as the Son of God).

Childhood

Even as a child, Jesus might have begun to believe that he was a son of God on a deeper, spiritual level. At the age of twelve, when he went missing and everyone was looking for him, Jesus was eventually found in the company of the learned, having a deep discussion on spirituality. When asked why he went missing and how anxious others were, he innocently replied, asking why they did not look for him in the most obvious place: his "father's house."

Adult Life

During his 40 days and nights of fasting and meditating, Jesus committed himself to a spiritual path to lead those who follow him beyond material temptations:

- Turning stones into bread to relieve his hunger.
- Jumping from a pinnacle and relying on angels to break his fall.
- Worshiping the tempter in return for all the kingdoms of the world.

During the phase of the ascent of worldly impact, where he had an ever-growing followership, performed miracles, and was extolled as a savior, he attributed all the glory to his Father in Heaven.

When Jesus was captured and underwent inexplicable physical and mental torture, he still maintained his faith in his Father to the cross.

To be unwavering in faith as a Son of God in both the ascent of worldly impact and also in the most trying circumstances is a testament to Jesus's faith in his Father.

Message

The core of Jesus's message was based on the following two commandments:

- Love the Lord thy God with all thy heart, and with all thy soul, and with all thy mind. This is the first and greatest commandment.

- Thou shalt love thy neighbors as thyself.

To love God is to embrace and accept all aspects of life. To accept the truth of who one is and of life. If one believes in God, one should embrace the truth of who one is and what life is. That is the way of Verity (truth).

If one can embrace the truth about oneself, and if that increases happiness in one's life, one can also help others do the same in their lives so that they too can find higher happiness in their lives. Love for oneself can evolve as love for others.

These ideas drive one to lead an authentic life (**V**erity), evolving with each experience (**E**volution), and being fueled by **L**ove, i.e., VEL.

Culmination

Jesus's culmination was to overcome his last temptation on the cross and find resolution with the same faith he had lived with all his life. The following statements are a testament to Jesus's conscious act of courage and the highest conviction:

- "My God, my God, why have you forsaken me?"

- "It is finished," and he bowed his head.

- "Father, into thy hands I commend my spirit," and having said this, he gave up the ghost.

Jesus was hailed as a savior, performing miracles and being pursued by many followers before he was captured, ridiculed, tortured, and eventually crucified. The final moment on the cross would have been the ultimate test of faith. Anyone in his position would have hoped for some Divine intervention, some miraculous end to this journey. There he was, crucified and facing his final moments. To embrace even the most trying circumstance as his Father's wish and to commend his spirit into the hands of his "Father" was an extraordinary display of courage and conviction, the final step for a person who walked among people in flesh and blood to complete his evolution toward Divinity.

Image21: Jesus on the Cross

Image22: Jesus, the Son of God

SPIRITUAL STATE – Fetter, Primary Needs, and Self Awareness

The starting point for this path is to address the second fetter—Mayai. This path focuses on not clinging to the false notion that the world experienced by the body and mind is an independent and ultimate truth. Our experience depends on who we are, and as we evolve, our notion of the world also evolves. The focus of this path is to evolve our psychological faculties along with our awareness of the truth.

The default needs that people focus on in this path are the Belonging and Esteem needs in Maslow's hierarchy of needs.

This state is called "Spiritual Murkiness" (Marul). One is more evolved in this stage than in the previous stage (Spiritual Targets). However, one mistakes the body-mind experience (or profile) for the Self. Here, one confuses one's "view of the world" at a given point in time with one's Ultimate Self. One, therefore, has a confused sense of Self.

STATE OF AWARENESS AND SELF-ACTUALIZATION

The Way of Worship is suitable for those naturally inclined toward psychological awareness, as we described in Chapter 6. This path is appropriate for individuals driven by evolving relationships and seeking recognition. They feel comfortable when their day begins by enriching their relationships or seeking recognition.

Looking back at the "Velvi" concept of self-discovery described in previous chapters, emotional satisfaction (belonging) and intellectual joy (Legacy) are offered to the growing fire of awareness. What are the blessings, then? The blessings come from moving beyond psychological notions and profiles and sublimating this psychological experience into a process of inner purification through the Way of Worship.

How do we do that? We view each relationship with another being as a means of relating to the ultimate. As manifest beings, we may initially struggle to relate to the ultimate directly. However, we understand how to relate to other humans from birth. Similarly, we may struggle to be recognized in terms of our self-actualization progress, although we know what recognition and legacy mean in the external world. This path utilizes this psychological experience and awareness as a steppingstone toward self-actualization.

Human relationships can be elevated as a means of relating to the Ultimate. The idea of "our Father in Heaven" is a common concept in

Hinduism and Christianity. In the Bhagavad Gita, Krishna (the Ultimate) advises Arjuna, saying, "I am your father, mother, grandfather, Guru," etc. The idea is to use the relationships we have in this world as a steppingstone to relate to the ultimate. Similarly, we spiritualize our legacy needs. Here, the worldly outcomes are incidental. The psychological realm (emotions, intellect) creates opportunities to experience and evolve on our journey toward the actualization of our ultimate nature, i.e., self-actualization.

Kierkegaard states this as "God as Goal and Standard" to intensify and "infinitize" the self.

> **As "Mayai" conceals, the subtle** (Ultimate Self) **remains concealed.**
>
> **As "Mayai" is dispelled, it** (Ultimate Self) **appears.**
>
> **For those who can dispel "Mayai,"**
>
> **They have no body** (fixed form) **nor** (worldly) **intent.** [TM-2548]

As one shifts their anchor points toward the truth of the Ultimate Self ("I" as an evolving process), emotional and intellectual capabilities are trained to serve the evolving awareness as one progresses along the path of self-actualization. Life becomes a worship of the Ultimate Self. Getting to know, relating to it, and recognizing oneself for their proximity to the Ultimate Self are all part of this path.

Thirumandhiram describes the process as follows. In Siththam, the comparison of transforming copper to gold is often used to describe the transformation of the Self from being a fettered Self to evolving toward the ultimate. The transformation agent is meditative intuition.

> **I melt in Love and worship you,**
>
> **The lotus feet** (the path toward the Ultimate) **that turned my embodiment into gold,**

Bless me to dedicate all my expressions to you,

The light within my bones (intrinsic) **that enlightens** (my world)." [TM-1456]

In the Bhagavad Gita, Yoga (toward union with the ultimate) is also defined as the cessation of the distortion of awareness (through emotions and intellect). A similar definition is found in the Yoga Sutra of Patanjali.

RELATIONSHIP WITH THE ULTIMATE SELF

In Hinduism, the suitable model for this path, for the conscious Self to relate to the Ultimate Self, is that of the Child-Parent ("Satputra Margam"). To be gender-neutral, this applies to the Child-Parent model. The child takes after their parents, relates to and loves the agents, and takes pride in carrying forward the legacy that their parents leave behind. The evolution is indirect through a subtle osmotic process. By relating and emulating, the child evolves.

Similarly, on this path, the evolving Self looks at every relationship as a steppingstone to relate to the Ultimate Self. Every recognition serves as a steppingstone to carry forward the legacy of the Ultimate Self. Through this path of devotion, one transforms psychological engagement with the world to progress along the journey of self-actualization.

REALM: Perspective Toward the Living Environment

The realm here is called "Divine Proximity." It involves establishing a more intimate relationship with the Ultimate Self beyond merely living in a Divine Land. It entails getting closer to the Ultimate Self, similar to a child's relationship with their parents. This involves relating more closely from a psychological perspective and not just providing dedicated services, but rather having a sense of worship.

INVOKABLE REPRESENTATION

This process is more of an inside-out process, i.e., evolving one's psychological awareness and taking that to the world, i.e., engaging with the world as an evolving psychological being.

- **Ultimate Essence (Si):** Relate to the Ultimate Self in the same way one would relate to another being.

- **Revealing Grace/Actualization Tendency (Va):** Learn more about the truth of the Ultimate Self, using every psychological experience as a subject of meditation.

- **Evolving Self (Ya):** Embrace the new revelations/intuition and let meditation evolve as a psychological being.

- **Worldly Experience (Na):** Take the refined inner Self to the world and act from within.

- **Ferreted Self (Ma):** Progressively let go of the fettered notion of Self as a fixed psychological profile ("I am This"). Instead, become an evolving psychological being with an evolving awareness of the Ultimate Self.

Here, one starts with questions like, "What is my ultimate nature (Si)?"; "What do I see (intuition) as my truth (Va)?"; "How do I evolve myself in this context (Ya)?" From this vantage point, "How do I experience the world (Na)?" And with this experience, "How do I go beyond my fettered nature (Ma)?"

Through this method, one focuses on transforming one's psychological Self into a spiritual one, like the alchemist transforms copper into gold.

Cheap indulgence in debates about our lord

Focused on the light (awareness), **with a melted heart.**

With enlightened prayers of Si-Va-Ya-Na-Ma

The alchemy to transform the nest into gold (enlightens the living space). [TM-2709]

Image23: Si-Va-Ya-Na-Ma

PATH 3: THE WAY OF WITNESSING (YOHAM)

QUALITY

Q7: The Self as the witness to the expressions of the Ultimate Self (the Divine Dance).

To transcend mental suffering is to identify with the essence of (the Ultimate), which is beyond description in terms of the body-mind experience. [TK-07]

In the first two paths, we explored qualities that help transcend worldly engagement and the mental outlook of the world as a whole. Meditative Intuition is used as a lever to continue uplifting and evolving toward self-actualization.

This quality deals with using meditative awareness as the primary and direct means to elevate our view of the Ultimate Self. It involves uplifting our spiritual outlook on life as a whole.

To witness life as a whole and view it as an unfolding of the Ultimate Self – a Dance of Bliss by the divine dancer – is the essence of this path. The primary focus is not on worldly engagement or psychological outlook (relationships and esteem), but on being a companion or witness to the unfolding of life itself.

STORY: Consummate Mindful Living – Buddha

Birth

Buddha was born to King Śuddhodana and Queen Maya in Lumbini around 500 BC. When his mother was pregnant, an astrologer predicted that Buddha would be spiritually evolved or an emperor. His father wished that Buddha would become an emperor.

Childhood

King Suddhodana took meticulous care to ensure that his son only saw the pleasures of the world. Buddha grew up without knowing any sadness in life. He was not allowed to go out into the real world but instead lived in a fantasy world his father had established for him.

Buddha married, and his wife gave birth to a son.

Adult Life

One day, Buddha took his chariot into the city for the first time. There, he witnessed death, old age, and illness for the first time. He also encountered a monk engaged in meditation. Despite Buddha's father's efforts to shield him from the real world, the truth always has a way of surfacing at some point in one's life.

An effort to shield Buddha from the truth only created a situation where everyday occurrences for most people created an existential crisis for Buddha. Upon encountering the transient nature of worldly life, Buddha set out on a spiritual journey.

He could no longer find meaning in a life that was anchored in transient aspects of life. He gave up his throne, walked away from his family, and became a spiritual seeker. For him, nothing made sense until he could find the anchor points of life. For years, he studied under various spiritual masters.

Upon reflection, this must have been a great shock to Buddha's system to give up a life as a crown prince and search for eternal truth for years in monasteries and jungles. His courage of conviction must have been great for him to stay the course and become spiritually evolved.

Finally, he resolved to meditate on the truth and find his way. In the process, he became enlightened. He found the anchor points of his life, which are now called the Four Noble Truths and the Eightfold Path.

The love in his heart must have also been substantial for him to spend the remaining part of his life (close to forty years) teaching others what he learned.

Message

Buddha spent the rest of his life teaching what he had learned, contributing to a school of thought and religion known as Buddhism. The core of his message is also referred to as the three turns of the wheel of dharma:

- First Turn (Theravada Buddhism) is to take a basic rational approach to spiritual life (self-actualization).

    ◦ The four noble truths outline the transient nature of the body-mind world that leads to suffering (Four Noble Truths), and the way out is to lead a spiritually evolved life (Eight Noble Paths).

- Second Turn (Mahayana Buddhism) introduces the role of Wisdom (the pursuit of truth) and Compassion (Love) as critical pillars in the path of self-actualization.

- Third Turn (Vajrayana Buddhism) emphasizes the "here and now" aspect of life.

These are not three independent strands of Buddhism but three evolutionary strands, with one evolving from the foundation of the other. The first focuses on the path of truth (Verity), the second fuels the process with Love, and the third emphasizes that life is a journey of evolution, not a destination (Evolution). These are the core elements of VEL.

Culmination

Buddha lived and taught his spirituality for 40 years. At the time of his death, when his students inquired as to who would lead them, Buddha answered, "dharma," his teachings. In his time, his teachings were practiced without discrimination based on social status (caste) or gender. Buddhism later spread to the north and south of India and most of Asia, including China, Japan, and Southeast Asia. The pursuit of truth (Verity), evolving with truth (Evolution), and fueled by Love is a core aspect of this journey.

Image 24: Young Buddha as a prince witnessing
sickness, old age, death, and a monk

Image25: Buddha, The Consummate Meditator

SPIRITUAL STATE – Fetter, Primary Needs, and Self Awareness

This path begins with addressing the final fetter—Anavam, which is the atomization of the self. This fetter is formed by the other two fetters—Kanmam (clinging to dualities of actions and outlook) and Mayai (the outlook of the world through body-mind experience). However, when the other two fetters are loosened, the final fetter weakens and becomes ready for the final step to transcend all fetters.

This state is akin to Sooran in the Epic (Chapter 1) after his two brothers have been killed. He stands frozen on his feet, resembling a tree—a symbolic representation of a weakened state.

At this point, the Self no longer views day-to-day external engagement (psychological and safety needs) or psychological overlay (relationships and esteem) as the primary pursuits. The primary need that comes to the forefront is self-actualization.

Self-awareness at this stage is referred to as "Spiritual Clarity" ('Therul'). Through experiential understanding, not just academic knowledge, one realizes that "who I am" is the primary factor in life. What happens to us is incidental. Life is comprised of a series of responses, but how we respond to situations depends on our true nature. Therefore, the primary focus at this stage is direct meditation on our ultimate nature, becoming witnesses of external engagements and psychological overlay as if they unfold on their own. This direct witnessing of life elevates our engagement and psychological overlay, leading to mindful living.

STATE OF AWARENESS AND SELF-ACTUALIZATION

The Way of Witnessing suits those naturally inclined toward meditative awareness—("M" in "OM"), as we described in Chapter 6. This path is for those directly driven to pursue the path of self-actualization. The drive "to be the Self one truly is" comes to the foreground of conscious self-awareness.

Looking back at the "Velivi" concept of self-discovery (described in previous chapters), the past sense of "I" itself is offered into the blazing fire of evolving awareness. What, then, is the blessing? To lift "I" from the "atomized" state ("I am this") and align with that which is eternal and ultimate ("I am that I am").

In Hinduism (and Buddhism), it is believed that the root cause of "anavam" is Ignorance. What sustains that ignorance is craving and resentment toward the manifest (body-mind experience). Ongoing meditation on Self and life addresses the root cause by allowing one to first become experientially aware of the truth of dependence arising. It is what it is because we are who we are. To overcome anger and resentment, one must become aware of one's true nature and align with it. That is how we overcome our ignorance of who we are. With the root cause remediated, a sense of anger and resentment toward the "other" (people, events, etc.) slowly fades away.

Thirumanthiram describes this as follows:

Craving, resentment, and ignorance removed.

I, who was deluded,

(now) **pursue the greatness that resides in OM**

Like the resonant sound of a ringing bell. [TM-2436]

When the anxieties arising from the 'chasing mind' disturbed within the body cease,

(meditative) **awareness arises** (i.e., comes to the foreground of the conscious mind).

As chasing desires ceases, the mind becomes blissful and

motivated to witness the Drama (of the Ultimate Self). [TM-2745]

It is in a blissful state, evolved like a ripe fruit.

The ripened fruit of the authentic self,

the heart is ripe, and for those absorbed in a blissful state,

when the fruit is ripe within (i.e., awareness is receptive), **He appears with clarity.** [TM-1494]

When the senses, emotions, and thoughts are still, the mind becomes receptive to meditative intuition or revelations of truth.

As we saw in Chapter 4, the eminent psychologist Carl Jung discovered in his study of religions that meditation's role (as in Buddhism and Hinduism) expands the realm of the conscious mind into areas that were previously part of the unconscious. He found that the unconscious mind excels in dealing with complex and critical aspects of life. Often, one yields to the direction of the unconscious mind in critical and complex matters. Jung goes on to note that what Eastern religions call a universal mind is identical to what he calls an unconscious mind.

In the first two paths, meditation plays a key role as a pause and reflection step. In this third path, meditation plays an ongoing role. What happens outside and within the mind becomes an unfolding drama. Witnessing becomes a conscious activity. But in witnessing the unfolding, one elevates other faculties – senses, emotions, intellect, and the sense of "I."

As we saw in Chapter 4, Kurt Goldstein (a leading neurologist and psychologist who first coined the term self-actualization) found that the whole organism takes part in every encounter—even with something as simple as seeing. Carl Rogers, another eminent psychologist, calls this an Organismic Response.

RELATIONSHIP WITH THE ULTIMATE SELF

In this context, the Evolving Self relates to the Ultimate Self as a companion (a friend or a witness; "Saha Margam"). Similar to a witness, the Evolving Self meditates on life as a whole, seeing it as a drama unfolding the Ultimate Self. Through this act of witnessing, the entire being (body, mind, and spirit) is elevated.

REALM: Perspective Toward the Living Environment

In this path, the conscious self, as a witness, has no separate reality except the auditorium where the drama of the Ultimate Self takes place. So, the realm is called "Divine Likeness" ("Sarupiam"). Witnesses have no qualities of their own and take on the qualities of what they are witnessing—the Ultimate Self.

INVOKABLE REPRESENTATION

This process is more about witnessing life as a whole, as the unfolding of the Ultimate Self, where "Si-Va" is viewed as the essence. "Si-Va" is also seen as expressions, i.e., the manifest world. It perceives itself as a witness, becoming aware of essence and expression as a continuum of the Ultimate Self.

- **Ultimate Essence (Si):** Witnesses the Ultimate Self as Essences.
- **Revealing Grace/Actualization Tendency (Va):** Witnesses its Revelations as an actualization tendency.
- **Evolving Self (Ya):** Sees itself as a witness.
- **Ultimate Essence (Si):** Sees the unfolding of the world as an expression of the Ultimate Self.
- **Revealing Grace/Actualization Tendency (Va):** Sees the unfolding of life as an "actualization tendency" in action and watches itself as an evolving self.

Thirumanthiram describes this process in the following song. When the mind is still, it no longer actively chases after worldly things. Senses, emotions, and intellect become receptive to meditative intuition. The mind witnesses the whole of life as the unfoldment of the ultimate essence as expression, thereby experiencing true bliss. This is an uncaused happiness, not linked to anything specific in the body-mind experience. It is an inexplicable and uncaused happiness that arises just from witnessing.

Anyone who has practiced meditation would have a taste of the following experience: as we practice, the mind becomes still, and there is a subtle and underlying happiness. In this path, one makes life as a whole a meditation session. As such, there is underlying bliss throughout life.

As the mind stills with Si-Va-Ya-Na-Ma,

Perils (Na-ma) **are dispelled and become subservient** (not masters).

Si-Va-Ya-Si-Va arises (i.e., comes to the foreground) **in awareness.**

As Perils are dispelled, there pervades Bliss. [TM-2718]

Image26: Si-Va-Ya-Si-Va

PATH 4: THE WAY OF UNITY (JNANAM)

QUALITY

Q8: The Self as that which is in union with the Ultimate Self (Verity and Love).

Unless one is in union with that which is a synthesis of Verity and Love (Ultimate Self), one cannot swim across the worldly seas (body-mind). [TK-08]

This quality is the culmination of evolving all other qualities. It is a quality that enables progressive, authentic living (Verity), fueled by love as an ongoing evolutionary process of life. As in Chapter 3, life can be compared to a sea with waves of need (as outlined in Maslow's hierarchy of needs). Without embracing the eight qualities, one cannot sail across the sea of life. One will sink or become fettered, as we have discussed. As the culmination of the eight qualities, this quality becomes a key enabler.

STORY: Living as (one with) God – Krishna

Birth

Krishna was born in the shadow of death. His maternal uncle, Kamson, was the crown prince. At the time of Krishna's mother (Devaki) and father's (Vasudevan) marriage, a voice from the sky announced that Devaki's eighth child would be the one to kill Kamson.

When fear overcomes us, it brings out the best or worst in us— either in the form of evolution or toxic self-preservation. Kamson chose the latter path and imprisoned Devaki and Vasudevan. Each of their seven children was killed as soon as they were born.

On the night of Krishna's birth, something paranormal occurred as if through divine intervention. The prison guards were fast asleep, and Vasudevan was able to switch newborn Krishna with a dead child's body. This way, Krishna would live and be raised by a village chieftain.

Childhood

As Kamson suspected foul play and heard about this new child growing up in a village, he sent powerful assassins to kill the child. The story goes that Krishna killed them and survived the assassination, and he did so as if in a divine play.

What is relevant to this book is not the religious details, but that Krishna faced death at every corner since childhood. Yet, he found a spiritual space within himself to transcend the threat and lead a life of levity, even as a child, rather than being overwhelmed by it.

Here is one episode to illustrate the evolution of Krishna as a child:

The story goes that when his adopted mother was about to punish him for playing in the mud and eating it, she saw the entire universe in his mouth when he opened it for her to see.

This is symbolic. The mother might have thought he was eating mud (clinging to actions and outcomes, i.e., the body-mind experience of the world), but he had already realized oneness with the ultimate. Hence, the whole universe was seen inside his mouth. To be highly spiritualized yet engaged in the world without "consuming it" is the evolution of spirituality.

Adult Life

Krishna's evolution from childhood to adulthood included killing his uncle, releasing his parents, and winning the kingdom.

However, the primary aspect of Krishna's life was how he navigated the righteous path to victory against the unrighteous in a great war (Mahabharata—the Hindu Epic). This is a very nuanced and lengthy story, where a series of missteps from one generation to another pitted the descendants of two brothers against each other, culminating in a great war.

Krishna refused to bear arms and take part in the war. Nevertheless, he did not flee from it. He declared that all his armies would support one side, and without carrying weapons, he would serve as a charioteer on the other side.

Duryodhana, the prince from the unrighteous side, chose the army, while Arjuna, the prince and commander of the righteous side, chose Krishna as a charioteer.

Message

Krishna's message is widely known as the Bhagavad Gita. Arjuna, the greatest warrior of his time, asked Krishna at the final moment of truth before the war began who Arjuna's Charioteer was, to take the chariot to a place where Arjuna could see the army on both sides. Arjuna witnessed his loved ones on both sides of the war. There were highly decorated warriors on both sides. His brothers, sons, and relatives on one side, and his grandfather, his teacher, and another set of relatives on the other. Suddenly, he plunged into an existential crisis, losing his knowledge and understanding of good and bad. He further lost his sense of purpose in what victory means if everyone on both sides could die. Even if he could win the war, being the greatest warrior would not prevent the carnage on both sides.

The Gita was advice from Krishna to Arjuna to elevate Arjuna's frame of reference that hinges on the dualities of outcomes, deeds, and a sense of the world based on the body-mind experience. Instead, Krishna coaches Arjuna to find a frame of reference that is anchored in something more intrinsic and ultimate. Krishna transforms the context of the battlefield into a field of spiritual evolution along the journey toward Arjuna's ultimate nature, i.e., the process of self-actualization.

But the Bhagavad Gita is still used by billions. Hence, it holds a universal message in a metaphorical context.

- **Karma Yoga**: the first part of the Bhagavad Gita focuses on the spiritual foundation of how one engages with the world—actions and their outcomes.

- **Bhakti Yoga**: the second part of the Bhagavad Gita focuses on anchoring one's heart to something more intrinsic and transcendental.
- **Jnana Yoga**: the third part of the Bhagavad Gita focuses on the synthesis of unified life, of living as one with Divinity.

In short, it is a comprehensive work of self-actualization involving engaging with the world, engaging with the heart, and evolving toward one's ultimate nature.

Karma Yoga is the pursuit of authentic living, i.e., Verity (swadharma). Bhakti Yoga is meant to fuel this path of Verity with Love. Jnana Yoga is about recognizing that life is a continuous evolution.

Once again, the core aspects of VEL permeate these teachings.

Culmination

Krishna's message and the culmination of his life is to be one with Divinity, even in the middle of a battlefield. Applying the spirituality of self-actualization to navigate through the greatest war and act as one with Divinity is the culmination.

Whether Krishna was a historical figure or a mythological one is irrelevant. The story of his life illustrates how spirituality and the path to self-actualization can be lived despite war. One of the highlights is also the "why" of his way - Love for the well-being of others (as an extension of self-actualization - on a larger scale). This is often symbolized by the "Radha-Krishna" form, i.e., Krishna with his consort as a lover (of other beings).

Krishna's life is an illustration of evolving along the path of Verity, fueled by Love and doing so by being one with the Ultimate along the way.

Image 27: Krishna Navigating toward a Spiritual Order amidst a Great War

SPIRITUAL STATE – Fetter, Primary Needs, and Self Awareness

In this path, one has already begun the process of self-actualization as a conscious and direct aspect of life. All three fetters have been rendered impotent. The primary need is to actively progress along with self-actualization.

This state is called "Blessedness" ('Arul'). It is referred to across religions. In addition to Hinduism (and Buddhism), it is also mentioned in Christianity. As seen in Chapter 4, Soren Kierkegaard refers to this state as Christian Blessedness—to progress along the path "to be the Self one truly is."

Image28: Krishna as one with the Ultimate, with a benevolent outlook toward the world

STATE OF AWARENESS AND SELF-ACTUALIZATION

In this passage, one is already operating in the fourth state of awareness, as seen in Chapter 6. The self-actualization process is well underway as an embedded part of day-to-day life, living a life of sacred "YES," as outlined by Nietzsche and discussed in Chapter 4. The focus here is to keep progressing with self-actualization and not regress backward.

This process is outlined in Thirumanthiram as follows:

> **In the unity beyond the duality of actions and outcomes, is the blessed Sakthi.**
>
> **She comes as the guru** (revealing intuition) **and removes all fetters.**
>
> **With offered awareness,** (fetters beginning with) **clinging to deeds are removed.**
>
> **All three fetters extinguish, and "I" become "Siva."**
> [TM-1527]

The above song outlines the spiritual evolutionary stages as follows: (1) transcending the dualities of actions and outcomes ('iru vinai oppu'), (2) weakening of fetters ('mala paripaham'), (3) descent of intuition as revealing grace (Sakthinipatham), and (4) Self-Actualization or liberation from suffering ('Mukthi').

The following song outlines a similar notion, highlighting the place of OM as wholesome awareness in the Way of Unity ('San Margam'):

> **I' becomes 'Him' with the removal of fetters.**
>
> **In silent OM (Self), one becomes liberated.**
>
> **In 'Blemish less' awareness, experience bliss.**
>
> **'I' becoming 'Him' is the way of living awareness** (San Margam)." [TM-1481]

RELATIONSHIP WITH THE ULTIMATE SELF

In this path, the Evolving Self relates to the Ultimate Self like a spouse ("San Margam"). They are not separate identities, just as a husband and wife are not separated in the context of a family (not in their individual lives). They act as one, similar on every occasion in life. The evolving Self is in harmony with the Ultimate Self, and together, they act as one.

Upanishads describe this as Harmony (shantham), Sacred or Auspicious (Sivam), and Oneness (Advaita).

REALM: Perspective Toward the Living Environment

As the evolving Self is in union with the Ultimate Self, the realm is called "Divine Union" ('Sayujyam'). The Ultimate Self resides in the Evolving Self, and the Evolving Self exists within the context of the Ultimate Self. They are inseparable and in eternal union.

INVOKABLE REPRESENTATION

This is very similar to the previous path of meditation, except that "Ya," as the evolving Self, does not exist as an independent aspect. It is in the union of "Si-Va." So, the Mantra is "Si-Va-Si-Va."

- **Ultimate Essence (Si):** Relate to the Ultimate Self in the same way one would relate to another being.
- **Revealing Grace/Actualization Tendency (Va):** Learn more about the truth of the Ultimate Self by using every psychological experience as a subject of meditation.
- **Ultimate Essence (Si):** Sees the unfolding of the world as an expression of the Ultimate Self.
- **Revealing Grace/Actualization Tendency (Va):** Sees the unfoldment of life as an "actualization tendency" in action and watches itself as an evolving self.

Thirumanthiram outlines this as follows:

Those burdened with bad actions will not realize "Si-Va Si-Va."

As you realize "Si-Va Si-Va," bad actions cease.

As you realize "Si-Va Si-Va," you become heavenly.

As you realize "Si-Va Si-Va," you take refuge in Siva.
[TM-2716]

Image29: Si-Va-Si-Va

CONCLUSION: JOURNEY OF THE SELF

SIVAPURANAM

This is my translation of the masterpiece "Thiruvasaham" by Saint Manikka Vasahar. This translation aims to offer an experiential perspective on self-actualization rather than attempting to reproduce the traditional interpretation of the song. This is my way of harnessing the saint's eloquence to convey the spiritual journey of a soul along the path of self-actualization.

Understanding key spiritual concepts is a preparatory step. The next step is to practice them in a training context with the aid of evocative representations (mantras, visualizations, etc.). Living life with the heart and mind in harmony is the culmination. Finally, repeating this with each evolution of awareness is a life of self-actualization.

"Thiruvasaham" provides a spiritual journey of a soul in a devotional context where the head and heart are aligned. Due to the nature of the subject, I have chosen not to include an explanation of this song. I have done my best to translate it in a way that makes sense to me. It is up to the reader to let natural encounters and evolution unfold. Good luck.

A task-burdened life, surrounded by fetters,

To sever this suffering and create happiness,

Is the higher path of not clinging to the extremes,

The path offered by our ruler, in honey-soaked sacred words.

Celebrate Na-Ma-Si-Va-Ya; celebrate our Leader's path.

Celebrate the path of the one who lives in my heart,

(He who) never leaves even in the blink of an eye, ruling from the sacred shade.

My precious guru saves me in virtuous ways; He is one. He is many. He is Divine.

Victory to His sovereign ways, which stilled my rushed hectic life.

Victory to His evolving ways, the undertaker of all my arising.

Victory to His blossoming ways, who is distant to those who look "outwards" (for the truth).

Victory to His regal ways to find happiness within when actions are in union.

Victory to His sacred ways, which uplift when thoughts are in union.

Praise the ways of the Lord. Praise the ways of our Father.

Praise the ways of the ruler of my domain. Praise His auspicious ways.

Praise Him, who is the purity of my awareness.

Praise the regal ways of the destroyer of false arisings.

Praise the divine ways that rule over the sacred domain.

Praise the ways that shower endless happiness.

Since the Auspicious One resides in my awareness,

By His grace, I celebrate His ways. For the happiness-filled awareness,

I recite His timeless story to end the previous task-burdened ways.

To show His Grace, He fills the vision.

The one whose beauty is beyond comprehension.

Filled the heaven (various seasons of life), the earth (ground realities), and beyond, as revealing light.

Beyond thought, as boundary-less, the greatest truth,

Yet hassle-burdened, I knew not a single word of praise.

Chasing arising after arising as

A lifeless, animalistic, humanistic, malevolent, and/or benevolent being,

Unceasing across various states of mind, circumstances, and contexts (meaning).

I am now exhausted, chasing after all these arisings.

I saw your path as the only truth and became liberated.

(For me) To evolve, you filled my heart as OM, as truth, my purity, the one who directs.

The High, Deep, Wide, and Subtle.

As heat, as cold, as the Lord of my offerings, and as purity,

Arise when all falsehood is dispelled, shine as truth realization, shining truth.

I am ignorant. Oh, Lord of happiness.

One without origin, measure, or end; Creator, Sustainer, Destroyer of all worlds,

Graciously, guide me to pursue you.

You are distant to those clinging to the manifest. Become intimate when all ephemeral things leave the mind, and you remain there as subtle (unmanifest).

Like freshly drawn milk mixed with sugar,

Evolved awareness is soaked with honey called He,

The great one who ends all arisings.

This can be seen in all colors by those evolved,

Hidden from me, the hassle-burdened.

Lost in the darkness, tied up with the sense of good and bad.

Covered up with senses that create an illusion (relative as independent and ultimate truth).

The five senses deceived me with this false sense of reality.

With a beastly mind, I knew not the way to appreciate and melt in your love,

But even for the one with no merit, out of compassion,

You have come to show your ways.

Better than motherly love, you, the essence of compassion,

Pure awareness, fresh illumination,

The Lord of the Auspicious Domain, the honey-filled ambrosia,

The noble one who ends all attachments.

Compassionate to dispel all falsehood from my heart.

The unceasing flow of the great river of compassion,

Endless nectar and measureless Lord,

Shine in the non-clinging hearts,

Melt me to be fluid, to flow with truth, and to become my soul,

One without happiness or sadness and resident within.

Lover of those with love. One who is in everything yet beyond them all,

The light, the darkness, and the glorious unmanifest,

The most primordial, without beginning or end,

Enchanted me and took over me, my fatherly Lord.

Live as the essence of awareness of the enlightened,

View that cannot be seen, most subtle feeling,

Does not go, does not come, does not merge, the blessed one,

Protects me, the great light that cannot be seen,

The joyous river that is hinged within and beyond, revealing the light, inexpressible feeling.

I am aware of the endless variety of the changing world.

You remain my conviction and clarity with conviction, in my awareness,

You flow as the nectar of those who do not cling to the manifest.

I can no longer bear to be bound by the body of meat.

Those who praised, celebrated, falsehood dispelled, and truth embraced,

To be prevented from falling back into the hassle-ridden life.

The able one unties the knot of deceiving sense-constructed boundaries and

Dances in pitch darkness, on the inner platform and the land around.

Eradicator of suffering-laden life.

Those who praise the inexpressible one and

The one who realized the meaning of this song.

Will enter the Siva Puram (Auspicious Domain),

To be in the inner circle under his rule and

To humbly serve for the welfare of many.

I would like to conclude this book with two songs that experientially summarize the OM-VEL Way elegantly.

OM: TWILIGHT DANCE OF SIVA

This song was written by Saint Karaikal Ammaiyar, who is one of the 63 saints extolled in Hinduism, as practiced by Tamils. The song is a symbolic representation of OM. The story goes that when she was walking through a burial ground at twilight, she saw all kinds of ghosts and beasts—a very threatening sight to anyone. Instead of being terrified, she saw the Dance of Siva even on that occasion and sang this song.

Rejecting the ways of sustaining and augmenting (the self) **with the ashes of the dead,**

In the jungle, where the mini-ghost sleeps (in ignorance) **or struggles with thoughts,**

Without missing the heavenly beings' drumbeat,

The handsome dances, the Twilight Dance with a fire-bearing hand.

[Thiru Alankattu Mooththa Thirupathikam - #19]

This is an experiential view of OM (aka AUM) as a Twilight Dance of Siva.

Rejecting the ways of sustaining and augmenting (the self) **with the ashes of the dead,**

The dead refers to the past. Self-actualization requires us not to cling to the past, whether physical or physiological and to see the Ultimate Self that is behind the manifest. This is "A" of AUM (also known as OM), as we have seen in Chapter 6.

In the jungle, where the mini-ghost sleeps (in ignorance) **or struggles with thoughts,**

The mini ghost is the conscious Self or ego. It operates with four faculties — emotional, intellectual, memory, and a "sense of self." It struggles restlessly as it tries to fit the arising moment into the experience of the mind. It struggles because it is trying to force-fit the arising experience within a pre-conceived notion of "I am This". On the contrary,

Self-actualization requires us to progressively discover who we are, with each experience. This is the "U" of "AUM" (also known as OM), as we have seen in Chapter 6.

Without missing the heavenly beings' drumbeat,

Dancing without missing the heavenly beings' drumbeat is to witness all of life's happenings as being in harmony with the process of self-actualization. There is nothing out of rhythm (of the drumbeat), as every occasion is viewed in the context of self-actualization – as an opportunity to experience, become aware, and evolve toward our ultimate nature, i.e., self-actualization. This is the "M" of AUM (aka OM), as we have seen in Chapter 6.

The handsome dances, the Twilight Dance with a fire-bearing hand.

The final line depicts Siva's dance in the twilight with a fire-bearing hand. Fire symbolizes meditative awareness. Twilight (Sandhya) represents the juncture of day (symbolic of worldly life, i.e., explicit) and night (symbolic of spiritual life, i.e., subtle). Siva dances gracefully at the intersection of worldly and spiritual life, with the path illuminated by awareness, i.e., the process of actualization. The Self has become one with the Dance of Siva. This is the synthesis of the three states of awareness represented by "A," "U," and "M". The fourth state is their synthesis as OM (also known as AUM), as we have seen in Chapter 6.

VEL WAY: THE SONG AND THE DANCE OF SELF-ACTUALIZATION

This song is written by Sanit Manikka Vasahar and describes the VEL Way in an experiential manner (not just as acquired knowledge).

> **I want to sing in praise of you,**
>
> **To sing, to melt, to flow.**
>
> **I want to dance** (as a way of) **celebrating** (you) **on the stage** (you have given me),
>
> (To dance) **in the rhythm of your dance and reach harmony.**
>
> **I want to unite with you, leaving behind this decaying cage,**
>
> **By leaving the falsehood that surrounds me.**
>
> **I want to go beyond** (falsehood), **bless me so that I can transcend** (the transient).
>
> **Oh, the** (ultimate) **truth of the truth seekers** (Ultimate Self)!

[Thiruchathaham – 104]

Let's briefly look at the section of this song in the context of the VEL Way:

> **I want to sing in praise of you,**
>
> **To sing, to melt, to flow.**

This is the "Way of Worship" (Kiriyai of the four-fold path) as inner evolution. It also serves to fuel the journey of Self-Actualization with Love.

> **I want to dance** (as a way of) **celebrating** (you) **on the stage** (you have given me),
>
> (To dance) **in the rhythm of your dance and reach harmony.**

This is the "Way of Service" (Cariyai of the four-fold path), where one engages with the world as per the rhythm of the Ultimate Self.

> **I want to unite with you, leaving behind this decaying cage,**
>
> **By leaving the falsehood that surrounds me.**

This is the "Way of Witnessing" (Yoham of the four-fold path), where one transcends body-mind experiences and witnesses' life as a journey toward self-actualization.

> **I want to go beyond** (falsehood), **bless me so that I can transcend** (the transient).
>
> **Oh, the** (ultimate) **truth of the truth seekers** (Ultimate Self)!

This is the "Way of Unity" (Jnanam of the four-fold path), where one unites with the Ultimate Self in every situation of life. Life is lived as a union of the evolving self, the Ultimate Self, and life as a whole anchored in Verity.

In other words, to progressively lead an authentic life (Verity), every moment should lead toward this evolution fueled by Love along the four-fold path of self-actualization, i.e., the **VEL Way**.

BIBLIOGRAPHY

- *Kantha Puranam* by Kachiyappa-Sivacharyar
- *Light on the Yoga Sutras of Patanjali* by B.K.S. Iyengar
- *Mandukya Upanishad* by S. Chinmayananda
- *Motivation and Personality* by A.H. Maslow
- *Mundakopanishad* by S. Chinmayananda
- *On Becoming a Person* by C. Rogers
- *Psychology and Religion* by C.G. Jung
- *Samyutta Nikaya - Discourses of Buddha*
- *Shambhala, The Sacred Path of the Warrior, Chogyam Trungpa*
- *Sickness Unto Death* by S. Kierkegaard
- *Sivanjana Potham* by Meykandar
- *The Archetypes and the Collective Unconscious* by C.G. Jung
- *The Bhagavad Gita* by S. Chidbhavananda
- The Bible
- *The Complete Works of St. Teresa of Jesus* (ed. E.A. Peers)
- *The Confessions of St. Augustine* (tr. R. Warner)
- *The Organism* by K. Goldstein
- *The Yoga Sutras of Patanjali* by S. Satchidananda
- *Thirukural* by Thiruvalluvar
- *Thirumanthiram* by Thirumular
- *Thiruvasaham* by Manika Vasahar
- *Thirvalnkattu Thiripathiham Kairaikkal Ammaiyar*
- *Thus Spoke Zarathustra* by F. Nietzsche
- *Upanishads*

Milton Keynes UK
Ingram Content Group UK Ltd.
UKHW050735201123
432900UK00012B/383